Advanced Social Work with Children and Families

EDITED BY CHRISTINE COCKER AND LUCILLE ALLAIN

Series Editor: Keith Brown

LearningMatters

First published in 2011 by Learning Matters Ltd

British Library Cataloguing in Publication Data
A CIP record for this book is available from the British Library.

ISBN: 978 1 84445 363 4

This book is also available in the following formats:
Adobe ebook ISBN: 978 1 84445 777 9
EPUB ebook ISBN: 978 1 84445 776 2
Kindle ISBN: 978 0 85725 029 2

Cover and text design by Code 5 Design Associates Ltd
Project management by Swales & Willis Ltd, Exeter, Devon
Typeset by Swales & Willis Ltd, Exeter, Devon
Printed and bound in Great Britain by Short Run Press Ltd, Exeter, Devon

Learning Matters Ltd
20 Cathedral Yard
Exeter EX1 1HB
Tel: 01392 215560
info@learningmatters.co.uk
www.learningmatters.co.uk

Advanced Social Work with Children and Families

Other books in this series

Books in the Mental Health in Practice series

To order, please contact our distributor: BEBC Distribution, Albion Close, Parkstone, Poole, BH12 3LL. Telephone: 0845 230 9000, email: **learningmatters@bebc.co.uk**.

You can also order online at **www.learningmatters.co.uk**.

Contents

Foreword to the Post-Qualifying Social Work Practice series

Social work with children and families has never received so much public attention as in recent years. The complexity of social work in this field, coupled with budget pressures and public expectation, has led us to a place where social workers increasingly find this work very stressful and, at times, overwhelming.

It is, therefore, really encouraging to read and review this text, which has been written by a team of highly experienced childcare social workers. The book is full of case studies, guidance and reflections on good practice to help develop and foster the very best social work practice in this field.

While this book alone will not solve all of the stress and pressure of social work with children and families, I'm sure you will agree that it offers all social work practitioners a valuable insight and reflection on the best ways to practise social work.

I trust you, the reader, will find it of real value in your professional practice.

Professor Keith Brown
Series Editor
Director – Centre for Post-Qualifying Social Work, Bournemouth

About the authors

Lucille Allain is a Principal Lecturer and the Director of Programmes in Social Work at Middlesex University. She is also an independent member of a local authority fostering panel. Lucille has written about looked after children in a previous Learning Matters book: (Cocker, C and Allain, L (2008) *Social Work with Looked After Children* Exeter: Learning Matters), and is interested in research and practice with young people leaving care. She has also published research focused on inter-professional education and practice.

Jane Anderson is the team manager of an adoption service for a London local authority. She qualified as a social worker in 1992 and completed her Masters in 2003, which focused on therapeutic communication with children in care. She has worked as a children's social worker and manager within local authorities. Since 2002 she has specialised in adoption and has worked in both the voluntary and statutory sectors in this field.

Anne Babondock is currently a student at Westminster University studying Travel and Tourism. Anne has experience of teaching social work students at Middlesex University and has helped to deliver 'Total Respect' training in a local authority. Along with other young people, she is currently involved in making a film about the care system.

Nikki Bradley is a social worker, ASW and an Accredited Practice Teacher with more than 25 years' experience in children and families social work. Nikki also teaches on the Middlesex University practice teaching course. Nikki currently works as a Specialist Parenting Manager for a local authority FIP service and was seconded for two days per week to the Department of Education (previously the Department of Children, Schools and Families) between January and July 2010, working with the Families At Risk Team.

Patricia Cartney is a Principal Lecturer in Social Work and Learning and Teaching Strategy Leader for the School of Health and Social Sciences at Middlesex University. She practised as a Children and Families Social Worker before moving initially into training and then higher education. Her research interests focus around learning for professional practice, in particular: how assessment can be used to enhance learning; the impact of technology on student learning; how social workers utilise knowledge in practice; and the emotional components of learning and teaching.

Christine Cocker is a Principal Lecturer in Social Work at Middlesex University. She is also an independent member of a local authority adoption panel. Christine worked as a social worker and manager in the statutory and voluntary sectors for 15 years before joining Middlesex University in 2003. Her research and publications are in the area of social work with looked after children, and lesbian and gay fostering and adoption. Her other recent books are: Cocker,

C and Allain, L (2008) *Social Work with Looked After Children* Exeter: Learning Matters; and Brown, HC and Cocker, C (2011) *Social Work with Lesbians and Gay Men* London, Sage.

Dr Helen Cosis Brown is a Principal Lecturer in Social Work at Middlesex University. She also works as an independent foster carer reviewing officer, and chairs a local authority fostering panel. She previously worked as a social worker and manager before moving into social work education. Her publications have been about social work with lesbians and gay men as well as fostering and adoption, and include Brown, HC (1998) *Sexuality and Social Work: Working with Lesbians and Gay Men,* Basingstoke: Macmillan; Brown, HC and Cocker, C (2011) *Social Work with Lesbians and Gay Men* London, Sage; and Brown, HC (2011) *Foster Care Reviews Good Practice Guide* London, BAAF.

Paul Dugmore is Principal Lecturer in Social Work at Middlesex University and Programme Leader for Post-Qualifying Programmes and joint appointment with a local authority where he is Head of Practice Learning. Paul is responsible for the practice education modules at Middlesex, which is also an area of research interest. He is also an experienced social worker, manager and practice teacher. The second edition of his Learning Matters book about Youth Justice will be published in 2011.

Orland Hinds currently works in computer administration. He is a care leaver who has been helping Middlesex University with various projects for social work students, and in addition he has worked to help raise awareness for young people in care. Orland has lived in England all his life and is looking for a long-term career in IT.

Dr Helen Hingley-Jones worked for a number of years as a senior practitioner social worker and later as a manager in children and families teams, specialising in work with disabled children and their families. She gained a professional doctorate in social work from the Tavistock Centre and the University of East London, on the subject of severely learning disabled young people's adolescent development. She teaches at Middlesex University, where she is Programme Leader for Social Work Qualifying Programmes.

Michelle Lefevre is a Senior Lecturer in Social Work at the University of Sussex with a background in child protection, arts psychotherapy, and expert witness work. Her recent book for the Policy Press, *Communicating with Children and Young People: Making a Difference* complements her 2008 co-edited anthology for BAAF: *Direct Work: Social Work with Children and Young People in Care.* She has been a member of the UKCP Psychotherapy with Children Committee and is currently the deputy editor of the international journal Social Work Education.

Sarah Lewis-Brooke qualified as a social worker in 1989. She has worked as a practitioner and manager in fostering and adoption teams in the statutory and voluntary sectors for 15 years. Sarah is now an independent social worker undertaking assessments for court and for fostering and adoption agencies, and is also a lecturer at Middlesex University with particular responsibility for preparing students for professional practice.

Erina Naluwaga has completed a BA (Hons) in creative advertising and is now working with Fostering Network as head of the creative board, putting together creative workshops and activities for care-experienced young people. Erina is currently producing a theatre production looking at different aspects of the care system. Having spent over 15 years in care, Erina feels that her experience enables her to empower and inspire other young people going through similar situations and feelings to those she went through.

Acknowledgements

Thanks to those who have assisted in the writing of this book: Fiona Alderman; Adi Cooper; Frania Cooper; the social work staff from Barnet Council who participated in the workshop referred to in Chapter 9; PQ students at Middlesex University; the American social workers from a partner local authority, who shared their experiences of adapting to social work in the UK and helped us see things slightly differently as a result; and all our colleagues at Middlesex University, many of whom have contributed chapters for this book. Thanks also to the staff at Learning Matters for their guidance and support.

This book is dedicated to:

CC – For Adi, Frania, Rivka and Shane

LA – For Howard, Hannah and Phoebe

Introduction

This book is written for child and family social workers who are practising in the busy front line of children's services in statutory, voluntary and independent organisations. Our aim in writing this book is to help social workers grapple with the complex dilemmas encountered in everyday practice, whether working with looked after children, children who are subject to child protection procedures, children in need, or children and families subject to court processes, including adoption. This work is not easy or straightforward and social work often requires tenacity and persistence in order to conduct rigorous and comprehensive assessments and to undertake skilled direct work with children and their families when intervening in their lives. This is not to say that there aren't rewards in social work, because there are many, particularly the potential to positively influence and support people to change their lives.

However, over recent years, social work has been scrutinised by the media and a great deal of criticism has been directed at our profession in response to the deaths of Victoria Climbié (2000) and Peter Connelly (2007) and a number of other high-profile events. The work of the Social Work Taskforce, set up during 2008–2009 in response to the damaging public perception of social work following the death of Peter Connelly, has avoided being defensive and inward-looking and has tried to provide leadership by bringing together senior managers, social workers and academics to debate issues and find a common way forward, while acknowledging many of the challenges the profession will face in that process. We welcome the development of a national college of social work, as an independent voice representing the profession of social work, with a focus on high standards in practice and in social work education. For too long there has been a divide between social work practitioners and academics. We welcome an opportunity to redress this balance, and this book is a contribution to this process as it is written by social work academics (many of whom are still practitioners), social work practitioners and service users.

We are interested in exploring within this book how theory and research are used in practice, because social work is an applied discipline and so both are important as they directly affect each other. Good research should shape practice, and practice dilemmas and questions should stimulate research questions.

One of the things that has been missing in social work is a critical analysis of the impact of many of the key policy directives and political priorities and the unintended consequences of these. For example, increasing the performance management requirements for front-line staff has had an impact on the amount of time staff are then able to spend with service users (White et al., 2009). The Coalition Government has commissioned Professor Eileen Munro from the London School of Economics to undertake an independent review of child protection with the aim of improving this area of practice. In his letter to Professor Munro, the Secretary of State, Michael Gove MP, commented:

The reforms led by the previous administration were well intentioned . . . the system of child protection in our country is not working as well as it should. We need fundamentally to review the system . . . I want to strengthen the profession so social workers are in a better position to make well informed judgements, based on up to date evidence, in the best interests of children, free from unnecessary bureaucracy and regulation. I want social workers to be clear about their responsibilities and to be accountable in the way they protect children.

(Gove, 2010)

The Coalition Government will no doubt introduce changes to social work following Munro's review, but the current legal framework which governs child protection is likely to remain intact as previous inquiries undertaken in child protection have found the legal framework to be fit for purpose (Laming, 2003). Therefore it is vital for social workers to understand and be able to use the law in everyday practice. We have commented on some of the legal changes that have been introduced by the previous Labour Government in Chapters 2 and 7. What won't fundamentally change, however, are the challenges in everyday practice in supporting children who are vulnerable and parents who are reluctant to receive help, who may also have entrenched, complex issues of their own, which can then make it difficult for them to meet the needs of their children. It is vital to understand your legal duties and responsibilities in such circumstances and it is here that a comprehensive knowledge of the law, including secondary legislation and guidance, is invaluable.

The aim of this book is to be a companion on your journey through practice as you wrestle with the realities of making the right choices for children and their families, often with limited information, where the stakes are always high. We hope this book will inspire you to undertake post-qualifying (PQ) and other courses at a university, which will help you to develop your practice and give you some much needed thinking and reading time to update yourself with current theory, policy, research and practice. This book is written for people undertaking PQ study, from the consolidation module and specialist level awards, through to higher specialist and advanced awards. It is also written for social work practitioners and colleagues from allied professions wanting to gain knowledge and reflect on their practice in working with children and families. There are a number of reflective exercises contained in each chapter, which will assist the reader in thinking critically about their own practice and practice within their organisation.

Post-qualifying standards

There are a number of generic post-qualifying standards within social work and this book is written in such a way to incorporate all of these standards. Each chapter will directly refer to the relevant specific post-qualifying standards (GSCC, 2009a) and the relevant children and families PQ requirements (GSCC, 2005) that directly apply to that chapter. Currently, most social work practitioners are undertaking PQ training at specialist level; we have therefore listed below the generic requirements for students studying at this level. For students studying at the higher specialist or advanced levels, the generic standards can be found at:

www.gscc.org.uk/Training+and+learning/Continuing+your+training/Post-qualifying +training/New+post-qualifying+framework+documents.htm

Generic specialist level PQ requirements

In order to satisfy approval requirements, specialist programmes must show how they will enable qualified social workers to:

i. *Meet the relevant academic standards associated with social work at this level.*

ii. *Think critically about their own practice in the context of the GSCC codes of practice, national and international codes of professional ethics and the principles of diversity, equality and social inclusion in a wide range of situations, including those associated with inter-agency and inter-professional work.*

iii. *Consolidate and consistently demonstrate in direct work with users of social care services and carers the full range of social work competences across all the units of the* National Occupational Standards for Social Work *and in the context of one area of specialist social work practice.*

iv. *Draw on knowledge and understanding of service users' and carers' issues to actively contribute to strategies and practice which promote service users' and carers' rights and participation in line with the goals of choice, independence and empowerment.*

v. *Use reflection and critical analysis to continuously develop and improve their specialist practice, including their practice in inter-professional and inter-agency contexts, drawing systematically, accurately and appropriately on theories, models and relevant up-to-date research.*

vi. *Extend initial competence so as to develop in-depth competence in the context of one area of specialist practice to agreed national specialist standards, drawing on knowledge and experience of the range of settings and service systems that impact on the lives of service users.*

vii. *Work effectively in a context of risk, uncertainty conflict and contradiction.*

viii. *Teach, mentor, and support social work or other students and/or colleagues and contribute to assessment against national occupational standards.*

ix. *Take responsibility for the effective use of supervision to identify and explore issues, develop and implement plans and improve own practice.*

x. *Effectively manage own work and demonstrate a capacity to plan for and respond to change in organisational, inter-organisational and team contexts.*

xi. *Develop and implement effective ways of working in networks across organisational, sectoral and professional boundaries, demonstrating a well-developed awareness of the relationship between social work and other roles and an ability to overcome barriers to multi-agency and multi-disciplinary communication, thereby promoting inter-professional working and delivering integrated and person centred services.*

(GSCC, 2009, pp16–17)

In addition to these requirements, students must also demonstrate competence in standards for child and family social work. Again, we have listed the specialist level standards,

3

and if you want to see the standards for Higher and Advanced levels, please refer to the GSCC website (see **www.gscc.org.uk**).

PQ requirements for children and families social work

Requirement 4 All programmes at the specialist level must meet the requirements for consolidation of competence in a specialist context. At all levels, programmes of education and training must show that they have integrated the five outcomes for children shared by all members of the children's workforce with the national occupational Specialist standards and requirements for post-qualifying programmes for children and young people, their families and carers standards for social work. In order to be approved, specific evidence must also be provided so that programmes will promote the development of relevant knowledge and skills and assess effective and competent practice in the following areas:

  i. *Working in partnership with children, young people, their families or carers including effective communication, support, advocacy and involvement of children and young people in decision-making.*

 ii. *Application of assessment models and frameworks (including the selective use of the common assessment framework) to assessment of needs, including additional or complex needs associated with:*

   a. *The physical and mental health needs of children and young people (including a knowledge and understanding of how to use the services that exist to meet those needs).*

   b. *The risks associated with and the impact of drug and alcohol misuse on the lives of young people (including a knowledge and understanding of how to use relevant services to address these risks).*

   c. *The needs of children and young people with physical impairments and/ or learning difficulties (including a knowledge and understanding of how to use the services that exist to meet those needs).*

   d. *The needs of young people involved with the youth and family justice systems (including a knowledge and understanding of how to use the services that exist to meet those needs).*

   e. *The needs of children and young people in asylum seeking families and unaccompanied asylum seeking children (including a knowledge and understanding of how to use the services that exist to meet those needs).*

   f. *The needs of children and young people accommodated, looked after and leaving care, (including a knowledge and understanding of how to use the services that exist to meet those needs and the nature of the specific responsibilities of corporate parents, such as those associated with responsibilities for development and educational attainment).*

   g. *The social, psychological and legal issues associated with private fostering arrangements and their implications for child welfare.*

iii. Co-ordinating services in a multi-agency service delivery context, including the knowledge and skills required to ensure professional networks are able to meet complex needs and where appropriate undertake lead professional roles.

iv. Identifying, evaluating and managing risks including those associated with safe-guarding responsibilities, together with the ability to intervene in situations to reduce risks.

v. Presenting professional views (orally and in writing) in formal contexts, including those where outcomes are disputed and where effective responses to challenges and counter-arguments need to be deployed, for example in court.

vi. Applying knowledge and understanding of relevant legal frameworks, including the range of statutory responsibilities.

vii. Promoting positive change in families (including extended and substitute families) together with an ability to realistically evaluate the range and extent of the changes associated with the impact of social work intervention.

viii. Responding positively to the full range of changes that can take place in family (including extended and substitute family) systems and family functioning, includ-ing those associated with the separation and divorce of parents and those associated with the separation of children from birth parents or the reunification of children with birth parents.

ix. Actively working with and empowering those affected by poverty, unemployment, homelessness, racism, homophobia, bullying and other forms of discrimination and disadvantage which impact on the lives of children and young people.

x. Working with parental mental health, drug and alcohol misuse, health, illness, disability and domestic violence and the impact of these issues on children and young people.

(GSCC, 2005b, pp10–13)

Embedded values

Requirement 5 In addition to the general underpinning values associated with the GSCC codes of practice, there are a number of specific user-focused values which need to be firmly embedded in social work practice with children and young people their families and carers.

These are:

* engaging with others to develop trust;
* exploring ways to share control over decision-making with young people and their families;
* respect for others, including respect for difference;
* honesty and openness; and

- *an ability and a willingness to look at the needs of children and young people in a holistic way, setting problems alongside overall interests, talents and abilities and drawing on an awareness and appreciation of the diversity of lifestyles and experiences of children and young people in our society.*

(GSCC, 2005b, pp10–13)

Chapter synopsis

Chapter 1 is aimed at practitioners undertaking the consolidation module. It begins by exploring the concept of 'professional knowledge' and acknowledges the tensions when transferring knowledge from practice to educational settings. It draws on the work of Dreyfus and Dreyfus (1986) to explore the journeys newly qualified social workers embark on as they move from 'novice' to 'expert practitioners'. It starts from the premise that 'knowledges' are located in specific social contexts and that learning is influenced by these contexts. In the workplace, a great deal of 'practice wisdom' exists in the form of 'uncodified knowledge' and is not written down for others to see. Practitioners are encouraged to see post-qualifying learning as an important part of their own professional development and also as a way of contributing to the development of effective practice with children and families within the social work profession.

Chapter 2 considers contemporary policy, legislation and guidance pertaining to child and family social work in England and Wales. The chapter discusses why particular legislation (see **www.opsi.gov.uk** to look at individual Acts) and policies have been introduced, with links made to the impact of inquiry reports and Serious Case Reviews on social work practice. This is followed by a discussion about the development of *Every Child Matters* (DfES, 2003) and other related policy initiatives under New Labour. The impact of the Children Act 2004 on new organisational developments, including integrated IT systems, shared budgets and the re-shaping of organisational boundaries to form children's trusts between education, social services and health is discussed. This is followed by an overview of current policy developments in relation to looked after children, with links made to current legislation including the Children and Young Persons Act 2008.

Chapter 3 follows on from the themes raised in Chapter 2. Contemporary child welfare services continue to grapple with traditional tensions involved in the 'care and control' aspects of the social work role. A critical approach is adopted by considering risk management in the contemporary childcare social work field. The chapter proposes a child and family assessment process which is based on a systemic, relationship-based approach. The theoretical explanation for this will be set out, focusing on the impact of emotions in child protection social work where issues of fear, violence, blame and aggression are found.

Chapter 4 examines a holistic approach to working with families with multiple problems using the Family Intervention Project (FIP) model. The chapter discusses the policy context of FIPs with links made to 'Think Family' in particular. The chapter explores how families who are socially excluded can be helped to make changes through professionals from housing, social work, health and education working collaboratively with parents and children.

Chapter 5 discusses direct work with looked after children and their families and carers, re-positioning it at the heart of effective practice by qualified and experienced social workers (Luckock and Lefevre, 2008). What counts as 'skill' in direct work is a key subject of exploration, and the chapter draws on evidence from research studies on effective practice and on reports by children, their families and carers about what they have found helpful or unwelcome. A tripartite conceptual model of 'knowing', 'being' and 'doing' (Lefevre, 2008) underpins the approach.

Chapter 6 critically explores two key areas of practice in fostering. Firstly, the support and training of foster carers that enables them to make effective interventions in children's lives is discussed. Secondly, the findings of the Wakefield Inquiry (Parrott *et al.*, 2007) as they relate to the assessment and review processes for foster carers are highlighted. Current research evaluations of the effectiveness of foster carer training programmes are also considered, and a case study is included that is relevant to the findings of the Wakefield Inquiry.

Chapter 7 is co-written with a local authority team manager and provides an overview of adoption in England and Wales, outlining the issues for social work practice in relation to the changing use of adoption within child and family social work. A number of practice debates in relation to adoption are also included. The chapter sets out the process of adoption for the child and for the prospective adopter and focuses on the tasks that social workers are required to complete within set timescales. The legal framework is explored, including case law that governs practice.

Chapter 8 examines the role of practice assessors, outlining why a social worker might decide to undertake the role, and identifies the benefits for individual social workers, their agency and the social work profession in supporting and assessing students. It considers what practitioners need to do in order to provide a successful practice learning placement and explores the kind of learning opportunities that are found in a children's setting. The role of inter-professional learning and working is outlined and significant attention is given to the role of assessing a student's competence in practice with appropriate supervision models identified for this particular task. The assessment of practice assessors is also discussed, with a focus on how practice assessors evaluate their practice and complete portfolios as part of their PQ training.

Chapter 9 discusses the views of young people leaving care in relation to how children who are looked after experience public care. This chapter is multi-authored and co-written by young people who are care leavers and by two social work academics. The literature in relation to service user perspectives and the participation of children and young people in social work practice and education is examined. There is an analysis of what makes service user involvement in education and practice meaningful and effective and how evaluative approaches can be used to develop good practice.

We conclude this book by drawing out some of the key themes we have encountered through the process of researching and writing this book, and end with some thoughts about the importance of social work research for practice.

Chapter 1

Consolidating practice with children and families

Patricia Cartney

CHAPTER OBJECTIVES

If you are a registered social worker, this chapter will assist you to evidence post-registration training and learning. It relates to the national post-qualifying framework for social work education and training at the specialist level:

> iii. *Consolidate and consistently demonstrate in direct work with users of social care service and carers the full range of social work competences across all the units of the* National Occupational Standards for Social Work *and in the context of one area of specialist social work practice.*

It will also help you to meet the Children and Families standards for social work, specifically Requirement 3:

> *All students must consolidate their initial competence in a specialist context before they move on to other modules. In the case of social work with children, young people, their families and carers, this module must ensure that competence in relation to the 21 units of competence identified in the* National Occupational Standards for Social Work *is fully integrated with the* Common Core of Skills and Knowledge for the Children's Workforce.

Introduction

This chapter discusses how practising social workers move from the point of being newly qualified to becoming post-qualified workers studying on professional and academic award-bearing programmes. The importance of consolidating your practice experience and evidencing what you have learned is a cornerstone of preparing for your continuing professional development. While the emphasis will be on working with children and families, the process of consolidating and articulating learning has importance across all areas of social work practice.

Studying for post-qualified social work awards is hopefully an anticipated trajectory for many social workers. Newly qualified social workers are encouraged to see continuing professional development (CPD) as underpinning future career development (Keen *et al.*,

2009). This chapter focuses on the processes involved in undertaking post-qualified learning and identifies some of the opportunities and challenges you may face as you embark on this journey. The concept of professional knowledge is explored and the 'messy terrain' travelled when transferring knowledge from practice to academic settings is debated. The challenges involved in transferring 'knowledges' and knowing across contexts are explicitly addressed and particular issues about how you evidence the consolidation of your 'practice wisdom' are explored. Strategies to enhance the articulation of practice knowledge are suggested and the opportunity to name and articulate this knowledge is explored as a key part of professional development and an opportunity to contribute to the development of effective practice with children and families.

Setting the context

The revised post-qualifying framework for social workers in England came into force on 1 September 2007. Three separate levels of award are now offered which correspond to different stages of professional and career development:

- specialist;
- higher specialist;
- advanced.

Specialist awards focus on the knowledge and skills needed for consolidating, extending and deepening initial professional competence. Higher specialist awards focus on the knowledge and skills needed for discharging high levels of responsibility and the need for complex decision making. Advanced awards focus on the advanced knowledge and skills needed for the improvement of services at a strategic level, alongside professional leadership. There are five specialisms running across all of these levels. These are:

- mental health;
- adult social care;
- practice education;
- leadership and management;
- children and young people, their families and carers.

The consolidation of competence in a specialist context begins with the study of the consolidation unit, which provides a structured introduction to the specialist award and underpins future studies. To complete this unit successfully, you need to demonstrate that you have consolidated and extended your initial competence as well as developed confidence in one of the specific areas of practice identified above. Successful candidates are expected to use reflection and critical analysis to demonstrate how their practice has developed and to draw on theories, models and relevant up-to-date research in evidencing their consolidation (GSCC, 2005).

The broader context of continued professional development is currently changing across the social work landscape. The first year of practice for newly qualified social workers (NQSWs) is now increasingly acknowledged as a crucial transition point between leaving university and undertaking the responsibilities of a qualified practitioner. The need for high quality supervision and support for NQSWs during this year is acknowledged. The Social Work Taskforce are currently recommending a new 'licensing' system which will introduce an assessed probationary year in employment for new social work graduates, similar to the probationary year for newly qualified teachers. This aims to ensure that NQSWs are both properly supported in their first year of practice and are properly assessed before they are fully licensed. A revamped framework for CPD, underpinned by a practice-based Master's qualification, is also being recommended, so that all social workers can keep their skills up to date and develop specialist knowledge as they progress in their careers (see **www.dcsf.gov.uk/swtf**).

Evidencing your consolidated and extended practice – how you know what you know

Looking at the current post-qualifying requirements (GSCC, 2005) the evidencing of practice appears clearly in line with professional development and a logical progression as you move from being a newly qualified social worker to a more experienced practitioner. You will probably have worked in a broad range of complex situations and have a wealth of experience of working with service users who have presented with difficult situations where your extended knowledge of practice has been crucial in working successfully with them. Surely all you need to do is provide evidence that your practice has improved as your experience has grown and you have developed greater knowledge and more advanced skills?

In the author's experience of teaching on post-qualifying social work programmes for over 20 years, however, many highly competent and experienced practitioners struggle initially with how to articulate and evidence their deepened knowledge and skills. A particular issue is how they write down and identify their evidence in a way which meets the professional demands and the academic requirements of post-qualifying social work awards. It is worth pausing to consider why this might be so and to explore the complexities some practitioners face when writing about their practice knowledge in an academic context. Identifying this as an area to reflect on at the start of any post-qualifying learning journey allows us to anticipate where there might be challenges in advance and to consider how we can best prepare to deal with this. It also encourages us to plan for the journey ahead and be aware of the terrain through which we will be travelling.

ACTIVITY **1.1**

- *Take a few minutes to think about your own knowledge as a practising social worker. Undertaking this exercise will be a helpful starting point for reflecting on the issues explored in this chapter and will act as an aide-memoire for you.*

- *Jot down a few examples of what you know and how you came to know this.*

Comment

Clearly, there are numerous answers you could give at this point. For most practitioners, however, the examples you gave will result from an interplay between many different factors. You may have included your formal knowledge (knowledge you gained from formal education and training), your practice wisdom (knowledge you have built up from doing your job) and personal knowledge (knowledge you have gained from your own and others' life experiences). Evidencing how you have consolidated and extended your practice involves identifying how your different ways of knowing interact to improve your work as a social worker within your specialist setting.

Understanding professional knowledge

In recent years, a great deal has been written about how professionals come to know what they know. Dreyfus and Dreyfus (1986) developed a model to illustrate how people acquire and master a skill. They identified five steps involved in moving from a novice to an expert.

Step 1: Novice

Novices are taught context-free rules to guide their actions. They lack experience of situations and so are not operating with reference to the full context in which they are acting but are following generally applicable rules. When we learn to drive a car, for example, we are taught where to position our hands on the steering wheel, at what speed to change gear, etc. While such knowledge is initially helpful, to become a skilled driver we need to move beyond this to be able to change our driving in line with traffic conditions on the road we are travelling on. To develop our skills further we need to adapt our general knowledge and apply it to particular situations. This stage might remind you of your very first experiences as a social work practitioner on your first practice placement when you were taught how to conduct 'a social work interview' or undertake 'an assessment' in general terms without reference to particular people or more complex situations. Interestingly, it is rather easy to evidence this type of knowledge. You can write what the rule/procedure is and then say how you acted in relation to this without much difficulty.

Step 2: Advanced beginner

After the novice has accumulated considerable experience of dealing with real situations, the person starts to become aware of 'situational' elements in different circumstances. The advanced beginner practitioner now begins to incorporate knowledge from the specific situation they are in as well as the earlier context-free rules. When driving a car we start to become aware of what is actually happening in our driving alongside general rules. We may find the engine in the car we are driving needs us to go up our gears slightly earlier or later than the general rule suggests. Maybe this stage reminds you of your final practice placement on your qualifying social work programme? You may recall beginning to understand that different service users responded differently to variations in your interview style. You may remember starting to adapt the way you communicated in response to this while still holding on to your general rules about how to interview people. While writing about and evidencing this knowledge is a little more complex than at the novice stage, it is still a fairly straightforward process.

Step 3: Competence

The ability to plan as a way of organising knowledge and guiding action becomes increasingly important at this level of professional development. The competent practitioner is doing more than simply following context-free rules and taking into account situational influences. A range of possibilities is seen and the practitioner engages in decision making to choose their plan of action with a clear goal in mind. Knowledge here is related to seeing sets of facts and patterns emerging in situations. Work here is often organised and efficient although it lacks the speed and flexibility of the proficient practitioner. In our driving scenario, we are less concerned with the general rules around operating the vehicle and we drive more with our destination becoming the main goal as we travel. What we know is still conscious and our competence is dependent on being able to think quickly about what we have learnt and to apply it quickly. Drivers who have recently passed their driving test, for example, tend to be aware of what gear they are driving in most of the time. Maybe this stage of learning reminds you of your increasing competence as a social work practitioner as you worked to complete your first year of practice as a NQSW? At this point you knew what you knew and evidencing this was relatively easy as you constantly checked your learning against the requirements of your programme in terms of Core Competencies or Key Roles, etc. In the current post-qualifying framework you may have been studying awards at Specialist level.

Step 4: Proficiency

For the proficient practitioner 'detached decision making' rarely takes place in the way it does at earlier stages. Knowing what to do may appear to 'just happen' rather than be the result of conscious deliberation across a range of alternatives. The idea here is that the knowledge base of the practitioner contains memories of similar situations that the person has experienced in the past and these are triggered by the new situations they encounter. Knowledge about what worked in the past and what might be expected to happen next is brought to bear on current situations. Situations are not broken down into component parts but are seen holistically. Notions of intuition come into play at this point. Intuition here is about experienced 'know-how' and is based on the accumulation of learning and experience. It is not guesswork or 'mystical attunement' but experience-based ability. The proficient performer understands and organises their task intuitively and also still thinks analytically about what to do next. For our car driver here, this knowledge is demonstrated when the person intuitively knows the oncoming bend will be difficult to drive around. Decisions about whether to brake, to slow down or to come off the accelerator are made as the driver approaches the bend. This is the combination of intuitive experienced-based knowledge and conscious detached decision making about how to apply previous knowledge in the particular new situation.

Maybe you can identify with this stage of learning for yourself as a social work practitioner? If you have been qualified for a number of years and/or you have accumulated a range of practice experiences, you might place yourself at this stage of your professional development. You may have worked with a number of children and families where risk has been present, for example, and you may be aware that you are able to identify worrying situations increasingly quickly and then decide on your subsequent course of action from a range of options. If this is where you locate yourself, you may find explaining why you chose from a particular range of options somewhat easier than explaining how and why you instinctively knew particular situations were ones where high risk was present even if this was not identified by others. In the current post-qualifying framework, you may be studying awards at Higher Specialist level.

Step 5: Expert

For the expert practitioner knowledge and 'know-how' are integrated into their practice in a totally different way from earlier stages of learning. Their knowledge of what to do and why they are doing it comes from their 'mature and practised understanding'. Situations themselves are understood very quickly and the associated decisions about the right course of action to take next are processed quickly and apparently effortlessly. Our car driver here becomes one with their car – they experience themselves as simply driving rather than driving a car. There is no longer any need to remind themselves what gear they are in – they just change gear when they know they need to. The concert pianist knows how to play the next note not because they are applying context-free rules but because they are listening to the sound of their music and choosing whether they play the next note softly or not dependent on the sound of the note played immediately before. Performance is more fluid and spontaneous. If anyone asked the expert driver or concert pianist why they drove around the bend in a particular way or decided to play a particular note in one way instead of another, they may find it takes some time to try to find the words to explain this knowledge to another person. You may be too modest to identify yourself as an expert practitioner – even if you suspect this may be the case. Your experience and expertise may also encourage you to shy away instinctively from words like 'expert' and the images of unquestionable knowledge and power such a term can generate. This model is not suggesting that experts are always right, however, or that highly skilled practitioners need never reflect on their work. Experts are encouraged to reflect on their own intuition and acknowledge that unanticipated circumstances may mean that despite their wealth of experience there will be times they get things wrong. This is not an image of an omnipotent unquestionable professional being portrayed. This is someone whose experience and expertise means they perform at a high level and are highly skilled and knowledgeable in the service they provide.

If you do identify yourself as an expert practitioner you are clearly someone whose practice wisdom is very well developed and your experience will be of immense benefit to the service users you work with, your colleagues and potentially the social work profession as a whole. Under the current post-qualifying framework you may be studying awards at Advanced level.

If you are studying at post-qualified level for the first time, the challenge to you at this point may be to learn how to name your expert knowledge and know-how. This is the issue we will go on to explore further but, before we do, take a few moments to consider the following questions as a way of both reflecting on and analysing your thoughts in preparation for your post-qualified programme.

- *In relation to the Dreyfus and Dreyfus model, where might you identify your own level of practice knowledge at this point in time and why?*

- *In your experience, are these stages fixed or do you sometimes feel like a novice or an expert at different times in different contexts?*

- *What challenges do you anticipate you might face when writing about your experience and knowledge?*

Comment

Being at post-qualified level and thinking about how you might evidence how you have both consolidated and *extended* your practice probably places you in the category of a competent, proficient or an expert practitioner. You are expected to evidence your practice beyond the level of basic competence which is evidenced at an earlier stage in your qualifying training. As we have seen in the model we have explored, such extended competence may make you a better practitioner but may also be more difficult initially to write about as the knowledge you draw on may be less easily quantifiable. You might initially experience feelings of being a competent, proficient or expert practitioner in your own agency but feel more of a beginner when you start to write down your evidence on your post-qualifying programme. If you experience such a feeling it is not unusual, nor insurmountable, and may be to do with the nature of evidencing your professional knowledge within an academic arena. Paradoxically, the closer you get to being an expert practitioner, the more complex it may be to evidence what you know.

Naming your professional knowledge

Debates about the interplay between how social workers use formal knowledge, theories and research, and the place of informal knowledge, on-the-job expertise and practice wisdom seem to have been ongoing throughout the history of our profession (Howe, 1992; Payne, 2005). While the relationship between formal knowledge and social work practice is inextricably knitted together, at times the description of this relationship is also characterised by ambivalence, confusion and misunderstandings (Parton, 2000: Sheppard *et al.*, 2000). Earlier debates often distinguished between 'theories of practice' which incorporated explicit theoretical standpoints and were usually subject to research-based verification, and informal 'practice theories' which drew on the accumulation of practice wisdom and incorporated knowledge generated and used by practitioners which was not usually verified. Later commentators have looked at whether knowledge is seen as a 'product' which is researched and ready for use by practitioners, or a 'process' which is connected to how the knowledge is used and put into practice by practitioners (Sheppard *et al.*, 2000) i.e. is knowledge being continually reinvented as it is put into practice? Debates about the relationship between evidence-based practice and the practice of 'on the ground social work' often run along these lines too.

Such debates have not only taken place within social work, however, but are part of a wider debate about the nature of professional knowledge. The essence of such debates goes back at least as far as Aristotle, who distinguished between 'technical knowledge' and 'practical knowledge'. Terminology changes but the fundamental idea is that professional knowledge incorporates both formal knowledge, for example theories you learn about on your social work and post-qualifying programmes, and informal knowledge, for example personal knowledge that you gained from your experience of doing your job and what you have learnt from service users and colleagues.

Formal knowledge is often written down and publically accessible in a 'codified' form which is available for everyone to read and judge its merit. Informal knowledge is a more private affair, however, and exists in an 'uncodified' form, which is known primarily to the person who possesses it. We are usually not accustomed to writing about or 'codifying' our informal knowledge for others to judge publically. Even when we write court reports and formal assessments as social workers, we give our professional opinion and we back this up with evidence but we are not articulating the full extent of our informal knowledge base in these documents – usually just highlighting the paths we travelled as a result of what we knew.

Another key point here is that for many professionals it is difficult for them easily to tell others what they know as a large part of this knowledge may be unconscious or tacit. Eraut (1994) points out that in research around 'knowledge elicitation', which is expressly devoted to developing methods of finding out what experts know, one of the best established findings is that *people do not know what they know* (Eraut, 1994, p15). Polanyi (1967) introduced the term 'tacit knowledge' to describe knowledge that we have without knowing we have it. He famously stated *we know more than we can say* (Polanyi, 1967, p4). Tacit knowledge comprises a range of conceptual sensory images that we draw on to make sense of situations. New situations trigger our tacit knowledge as we try to work out what is happening and draw on both our formal knowledge and our repertoire of informal knowledge.

Ideas about the use of tacit knowledge fit well with the actions of the proficient and expert practitioner in the Dreyfus model we considered earlier. As professional knowledge becomes more extensive and we have a broader and deeper range of experiences to draw on to guide our practice, our use of informal and tacit knowledge is likely to increase. Potentially, this makes our practice more knowledgeable and more skilled but also means it is more complex to write about as we may increasingly not know what we know.

Within the context of professional social work practice, our use of tacit knowledge requires further exploration. Several commentators have drawn attention to the presence of 'avoidable mistakes' in child protection work, for example, where social workers appear to have formed early initial judgements in their assessment of children and families and have proved resistant to changing these initial perceptions, even in the light of considerable new evidence that should have caused the initial assessment to be revised (Macdonald, 2001; Munro, 1996; Munro, 2002). Psychologists have long suggested that our minds process information into pre-existing frameworks that are composed of memories of previous experiences and past reactions (Bartlett, 1932). These pre-existing frameworks incorporate both our 'formal' and our 'informal' knowledge. The tacit knowledge derived from our years of experience and growing practice wisdom that we possess may be beneficial to our overall practice but must also be open to question and challenge to ensure that we do not mistakenly perceive new situations as being too similar to old ones and thus miss out on seeing vital information.

ACTIVITY **1.3**

- *Can you think of a situation where you have known more than you could say?*

- *In responses to this question, experienced practitioners sometimes recall events where they felt instinctively that 'something was wrong' although on the surface all appeared well.*

CASE STUDY **1.1**

Sally, an experienced practitioner, recalled an event where she visited a family home after an anonymous referral alleging that the child there was being physically abused. When she entered the home the situation did not throw up obvious concerns and the family explained they had recently had a row with a neighbour who they felt had reported unsubstantiated concerns as part of their argument with them. Although the child appeared well cared for and the family appeared to relate well to each other, the social worker had a marked physical reaction during the interview. She described 'having goose-bumps' whenever the father spoke directly to the child. Following subsequent work it emerged that the father had been physically abusing his child over a long period of time. A less experienced social worker may well have recommended closing this case and reacted only to the obvious information available to them. Fortunately the social worker here was able to access information from her accumulated practice wisdom which alerted her to problems. Sally explored how to unpack how she knew what she knew and to think about how she might write about this knowledge in her post-qualifying portfolio. This is the area we will now focus on.

Naming what you know

The work of Schön (1983, 1987) focused on how professionals use knowledge further. In an often quoted passage he suggested:

> *In the varied topography of professional practice, there is a high hard ground where practitioners can make effective use of research-based theory and technique, and there is a swampy lowlands where situations are confusing 'messes' incapable of technical solution.*

(Schön, 1983, p42)

Schön saw the informal 'messy' knowledge used by practitioners in the swampy lowlands as crucial to the most pressing and important work professionals undertake and he stressed the importance of previously devalued sources of knowledge. His work built further on the insights provided by Polanyi as he explored how professionals could raise awareness of their own tacit knowledge. He was interested in looking at how professionals could move from a position of 'knowing-in-action' to having 'knowledge-in-action'.

One of the challenges is for experienced professionals not to simply apply the full extent of their formal and informal knowledge in what they do but to be more aware of why they do what they do; in essence, to name what they know and articulate this to others. Schön saw reflection as a key part of articulating the full extent of professional knowledge. The post-qualifying framework for social work follows this way of thinking as you are asked to use reflection and critical analysis to demonstrate how you have consolidated and extended your initial competence.

Schön wrote about two key processes of reflection. The first, 'reflection-on-action', is about looking back on an experience that has happened and fully reflecting in depth on and examining this experience as a way of transferring an event from experience into knowledge. This type of reflective activity is one way of slowing down our thought processes and may provide a potential way for experienced practitioners to mine for knowledge which has become tacit and hidden from awareness. Future action can benefit from reflection on current practice.

There are many suggestions in the literature about how 'reflection-on-action' can best be supported. Within social work the use of 'critical incident technique' has been used for some time. A critical incident is one which causes us to stop and reflect on what occurred and does not fit our usual frame of reference – one which stops us in our tracks and makes us think again. The framework suggested by Crisp, Green-Lister and Dutton (2004) involves a five-stage process for analysing and reflecting on such incidents:

- provide an account of the incident;
- discuss initial responses to the incident;
- highlight issues and dilemmas raised;
- comment on the subsequent outcomes;
- identify the learning involved.

Although this framework is useful in highlighting the learning that occurred it does not direct practitioners explicitly to exploring *why* they did what they did, although this may be addressed implicitly as the learning is evidenced. In terms of evidencing what you learnt from your experience, this framework may provide a useful initial starting point.

At post-qualifying level, however, it is helpful to go further in this process and look for ways of evidencing deeper reflection and a higher level of critical analysis. Drawing on Mezirow's (1990) work on 'perspective transformation' may be particularly appropriate as a way of deepening your understanding of the complexity of professional practice. He highlights three stages in reflective activity. Firstly, people outline the *content* of what happened at a descriptive level. The next reflective level is to describe the *process* and explore how things happened. The third and deeper level of reflection is to explore the *premise* of the event and reflect fully on why what happened did so in the way it did. When you arrive at the point of exploring *why*, this is clearly a more complex activity than the earlier two levels and may need returning to several times rather than being viewed as a one off event.

The quest to engage in deeper reflection and a higher level of critical analysis can also be seen currently in the broader context of social work practice. For example, in 2009, the Social Care Institute for Excellence (SCIE) produced SCIE Guide 24: *Learning together to safeguard children: developing a multi-agency systems approach for case reviews* (see **www.scie.org.uk**). It suggests that Serious Case Reviews (SCRs) and public inquiries have tended to be repetitive and their recommendations very similar. Once faults in professional practice have been identified (Mezirow's *content* and *process* levels) the SCRs and public inquiries have moved to making recommendations. SCIE argues that using a systems approach enables the interaction between the individual and the wider context to be explored and that this is helpful in the quest to understand not just what happened but crucially *why* it happened (Mezirow's *premise* level). An increasing amount of academic literature is also exploring learning from SCRs and public inquiries from the standpoint of *why* poor practice and wrong judgements were made. The work of Munro (2002) and Parton (2006) are examples of authors who are undertaking a deeper level of critical analysis in this area.

ACTIVITY **1.4**

It would be helpful at this point to return to your response to Activity 1.3, where you identified a situation where you knew more than you could say and explore this a little more fully. Using Mezirow's three stages, reflect on:

- *Content – a description of what happened in your example;*

- *Process – an analysis of how things happened;*

- *Premise – why you think things happened in that way.*

Getting into the habit of thinking about your professional experiences in such a way is helpful when preparing for studying on your post-qualified programme. It provides a model to facilitate critical analysis and reflection on your experience, which is a cornerstone of the post-qualifying framework for social work.

The second reflective process Schön (1983) identified was 'reflection-in-action', a type of 'on-the-job' reflection which happens alongside the professional action taking place rather than at a later point. In essence, this is about reflecting on what you are doing while you are doing it. Here Schön is focusing on practice wisdom as a way of knowing how to respond to complex situations and describes the type of action that would be classified as a hallmark of the expert practitioner in the Dreyfus model. Knott and Scragg (2007) argue that this type of reflection is most relevant to qualified social workers undertaking post-qualifying training.

Capturing the knowledge you display when reflecting in action is clearly a complex process. Your knowledge is displayed in real time in what you do, what you say and how your ongoing reflections feed into this. Schön's concept of 'reflection-in-action' is illustrated by his descriptions of his observations of what experienced practitioners actually did. Schön used examples and metaphors as a way of trying to illustrate knowledge which is so difficult to find words to describe.

For our purposes, it is helpful to note that 'reflection-in-action' is a particularly difficult process to capture and describe. Eraut (2007) used observation of the direct practice of newly qualified nurses, graduate engineers and trainee chartered accountants as a way of opening up a dialogue about what people actually do in practice and what knowledge they use in action. It may be helpful to think about how you could use direct observations of your practice by others, for example your mentor, line manager or colleagues, in this way.

ACTIVITY **1.5**

- *How could you use direct observations of your practice to improve your work?*

- *Are there any particular areas you would want to discuss with your observer?*

Comment

You could use the opportunities offered by a direct observation of your practice to discuss what you did in real time and why. Such conversations may be a helpful way of exploring how you use both your formal and informal knowledge in your practice. Discussing this with an observer may be a way of bringing some of your tacit knowledge into the open and may help you identify more clearly the extent of what you know. Taking forward these discussions in other forums with colleagues at work and on your post-qualifying programme is a key way of helping to identify your professional knowledge – both formal and informal. As an NQSW you may want particular feedback on how you used formal knowledge in your practice, whereas as an experienced practitioner you may want particular feedback on your use of informal knowledge – although a mix of both would be required.

Transferring knowledge across contexts

While practice and education settings have both theories and practices, they have very different cultures and very different discourses (Eraut, 2004). As a social worker on a post-qualifying programme, you are likely to be bilingual in both settings and you now need to find ways of translating and transferring knowledge gained in practice to the education setting and vice versa.

Much of the literature on reflective practice encourages the keeping of reflective journals as a vehicle for further enhancing your reflective learning and analytic processes. Such journals are intended not simply to describe events that happened but to be critically analytical about what happened. They are intended to address key questions such as what did you do, why, what knowledge did you draw on, what went well, what would you do differently and crucially what did you learn?

There are several ways in which using reflective journals can enhance your learning.

- They can slow down the pace of your learning and enable you to see things that may be lost in the speed of the moment.

- They can increase your sense of ownership of your own learning and encourage robust and deep learning.

- They can provide a form of 'cognitive housekeeping' and help you link new knowledge with older knowledge you possess (Moon, 1999).

- They can promote emotional insight as reflection helps the emotional side of learning.

- They provide a space to contemplate complexity and the 'muddy lowlands' of your practice.

- They encourage metacognition and help you identify how you learn.

- Writing can help us make links across our experiences and gives space for new ideas and new thinking (Moon, 2006).

For your purposes, one additional advantage of using reflective journals is that they provide a way of writing about – or codifying – your knowledge in a written format which is most appropriate to the academic requirements for your award. If you are a newly qualified social worker, it is good practice to find ways of noting down your developing professional knowledge. If you are an experienced practitioner, particularly if you have been out of formal education for some time, reflective writing may be a way of helping you to reconnect with academic writing.

Academic writing and critical analysis

Although the processes of reflection and critical analysis are often intertwined in professional practice, it is helpful to consider briefly what some of the differences between the two are. Just to remind ourselves, for your post-qualifying award you are asked to use both reflection and critical analysis to demonstrate how your practice has developed. Evidencing critical analysis is a skill which is closely associated with academic learning (QAA, 2008) and is increasingly emphasised in post-qualifying learning. In essence, critical analysis involves appraising what you read (and write) via a process of careful, logical deconstruction of the arguments put forward. Exploring the key points made, examining the validity of evidence put forward to support these claims and assessing the consistency of the argument and whether it leads to a logical and supportable conclusion are all ways in which we can critically analyse an argument.

Elder (2009) outlines how she uses primary questions to help students to analyse written text. She asks the following questions.

- What is the author's fundamental purpose?

- What is the author's point of view?

- What assumptions is the author making in his or her reasoning?

- What are the implications of these assumptions?

- What information does the author use in reasoning throughout the text?

- What are the most fundamental inferences or conclusions used in the text?

- What are the basic concepts used?

- What is the key question the author is trying to answer?

(Elder, 2009)

There are many variants on the above but all contain a logical exploration of the arguments put forward. In the post-qualifying framework it is significant that you are asked not only to reflect but also to critically analyse. This signals clearly that the reflective processes you undertake to evidence your practice and your learning need to move far beyond description. You are expected to analyse the published works of other people, for example critiquing the literature and research you draw on rather than simply using the arguments of others to support what you are saying. Such critical analysis also applies to what you write yourself as well as how you draw on the writings of others.

Critical analytical writing

Although there are many variations in post-qualified assessment tasks, you are usually expected to write about what you know from your formal and informal knowledge bases, what you did and what you learnt from your experiences that enabled you to develop your practice. We have explored some of the complexities involved in this process and suggested ways you might seek to capture evidence of your learning. The next step is to consider how to represent your learning within an academic context.

As a basic guide Cottrell (2003) identifies critical analytic writing as comprising the following key components as it:

- identifies the significance of what is stated;

- evaluates strengths and weaknesses;

- weighs one piece of information against another;

- makes reasoned judgements;

- argues a case according to the evidence;

- shows why something is relevant or suitable;

- weighs up the importance of component parts;

- gives reasons for selecting each option;

- evaluates the significance of details;

- structures information in order of importance;

- shows the relevance of links between pieces of information;

- draws conclusions.

(Cottrell, 2003, p232)

Putting it all together – and making sense

As a post-qualified candidate you are expected to evidence both the formal and informal knowledge you possess, to reflect on both and subject what you claim to the process of critical analysis described above. You are also expected to account for your learning by drawing explicitly on formal knowledge bases identified in terms of theories, models and relevant up-to-date research. Although how you do this will be personal to you, looking at an example of how this might be done may be helpful in clarifying what is involved here.

Sally revisited

We return to Case Study 1.1 which looked at Sally, the practitioner with 'goosebumps'.

What did she know?

She knew the child in the family she visited was at risk although no obvious signs were present on her first visit to the home.

How did she know this?

- **Informal knowledge**: Initially Sally was unable to say how she knew this. She described her physical response in the interview and knew she had 'sensed' a problem here but could not initially explain what had led to her reaction. Sally may have been operating as an 'expert practitioner' in the way the Dreyfus model identified at this point. Her accumulated experience and practice wisdom joined in the moment and alerted her to a problem. Her knowledge was speedy but predominantly tacit in terms of naming how she knew what she knew.

- **Reflecting**: After reflecting on the interview and returning to the scene in her memory several times, Sally started to recall various cues or particles of awareness in the situation that may have triggered her physical response. She remembered that the child had been a little *too* quiet and had appeared very aware of the adults around her. She specifically recalled how the child had returned her father's looks without moving or blinking when he spoke to her. These cues had reminded Sally of the behaviour of other children with whom she had worked in the past who had been physically abused by their parent. They were cues that had triggered her practice wisdom.

- **Formal knowledge**: Sally reflected further and sought out what formal knowledge she had that was also part of her knowledge base. She recalled her formal teaching around child development and recalled that the child in the interview did not appear as talkative and interested as six-year-olds often are. She recalled being formally taught about 'frozen watchfulness' where the abused child looks watchful but unresponsive and carefully tracks adults with their eyes (see **www.safeguardingchildren.co.uk**). She was able to make links with research in this area that highlighted how sustained abuse can cause this reaction in children. She also made theoretical links between her physical experience of goosebumps being a psychodynamic response to the cold generated by the 'frozen watchfulness' of the child and projected onto her as the worker.

- **Critically analysing**: Sally examined the research and literature she had found around 'frozen watchfulness' and critically analysed this material. She looked at whether the sample size was large enough for authors to generalise their findings, whether the findings were applicable across all cultures and whether the findings of the authors jus-tified their conclusion. She analysed the theoretical literature she drew on, using the framework suggested earlier by Elder. She found that the formal material she knew acted as pointers for concern but were not simply applied in a straightforward manner in her practice. The child was not acting in a 'textbook-like' mode around 'frozen watch-fulness' as she exhibited some responsive and engaged behaviours too at times, for example when she showed Sally her doll. Sally used a combination of pointers from her formal knowledge base and combined this with her practice wisdom to make her professional judgement.

Sally also critically analysed her own account of the situation and questioned whether the connection made in terms of transference from the child resulting in her goosebumps actually happened or whether this was a post-hoc theoretical link she had made to explain her feelings. She explored whether such knowledge could be verified and wondered whether it would be repeated in practice if she experienced a similar situation. In this way Sally showed she was reflecting on and critically analysing her own informal knowledge as well as her formal knowledge.

In the brief example above the practitioner effectively used reflection and critical analysis to demonstrate how her practice had developed and drew on relevant theoretical and research knowledge to evidence her consolidation.

Making a broader contribution

Engaging in post-qualified education has potential benefits beyond your own individual practice. It also enables you to make a broader contribution to the profession and pro-vides an opportunity to contribute to the development of effective practice with children and families. Marsh and Doel (2005) point out that post-qualifying education opens up a huge opportunity for the social work practice community to build up its evidence base 'from the bottom'. Post-qualifying portfolios contain codified practice knowledge about current practice and contemporary issues which can be shared with others. The accumula-tion of formal and informal knowledge in this format offers the profession a key opportunity to reassess its knowledge base and to incorporate the sensitive accumulation of practice wisdom to complement more formal knowledge and evidence-based practice. In this context, Doel, Nelson and Flynn (2008, p564) argue that *post-qualifying education is most definitely part of the solution*.

Chapter summary

This chapter has focused primarily on your individualised professional knowledge and the processes involved in both naming what you know and transferring your knowledge from practice to academic settings and vice versa as you prepare for your post-qualified pro-gramme. The concept of professional knowledge has been 'problematised' and the relationship between formal and informal knowledge has been explored. Suggestions about how you might seek to reflect on and critically analyse what you know have been outlined. Hopefully the debates that have been articulated and the strategies outlined for naming and transferring knowledge will be helpful to you in consolidating your practice with children and families. Looking to the broader arena in which social work is practised, naming such knowledge may be part of a wider contribution to enhancing what we know as a profession overall and ultimately improving the services we offer.

This chapter has provided an underpinning to the book as a whole by focusing on how practising social workers move from being newly qualified to post-qualified workers. The emphasis was on how you can consolidate your practice experience and evidence what you have learnt on your post-qualifying programme. The concept of professional knowledge was explored and the Dreyfus and Dreyfus model of professional skills development was used to highlight the complexity of 'expert' professional knowledge where highly skilled practitioners often know more than they can say. The complex interplay of formal and informal knowledge was explored and the challenges involved in experienced practitioners seeking to name what they know were addressed. The issues arising when knowledge is transferred from practice to academic settings were discussed. Strategies to enhance the articulation of practice knowledge were suggested and frameworks to encourage reflection and critical analysis at post-qualifying level were offered. The chapter concluded by acknowledging the broader contribution post-qualified learning can make to consolidating our overall professional knowledge base and improving the services we offer.

FURTHER READING

Particularly for newly qualified workers:

Keen, S, Gray, I, Parker, J, Galpin, D and Brown, K (2009) *Newly qualified social workers: A handbook for practice.* Exeter: Learning Matters.

This is a useful book aimed at supporting newly qualified workers. It is a practical text focused on guiding new workers in terms of induction, supervision, and lifelong learning in relation to CPD and post-qualifying awards. Key social work skills including report writing, record keeping and teamwork are discussed, alongside explorations of 'managing the personal'.

Knott, C and Scragg, T (2007) *Reflective practice in social work.* Exeter: Learning Matters.

This is a clearly written book which outlines the theory of reflective practice and uses a range of exercises to encourage the development of reflective practice within social work. It is written for social work students but should also be a helpful text for NQSWs.

Moon, J (2004) *A handbook of reflective and experiential learning: Theory and practice.* London: Routledge Falmer.

This is an engaging and useful guide to both the theory and the practical implementation of reflective and experiential learning. It is aimed at people working within education but its practical and creative focus makes it a useful resource for any candidate on a CPD programme where reflection is explored.

Particularly for experienced workers:

Benner, P (2001) *From novice to expert: Excellence and power in clinical nursing practice: commemorative edition.* New Jersey: Prentice Hall.

This is a seminal work in relation to the development of professional knowledge within nursing practice but it also has transferability in relation to how other professionals develop their ways of knowing to become experts rather than novices in their profession.

Eraut, M (1994) *Developing professional knowledge and competence.* London: Routledge Falmer.

This book is an excellent exploration of the complex nature of professional knowledge, focusing on how it is both used and acquired.

For all readers:

Dreyfus, HL and Dreyfus, SE (1986) *Mind over machine: The power of human intuition and expertise in the era of the computer.* Oxford: Blackwell

This is an engaging and interesting book focusing on the acquisition of professional knowledge and the role of informal and tacit knowledge in the development of practice expertise.

Mezirow, J and Associates (1990) *Fostering critical reflection in adulthood: A guide to transformative and emancipatory learning.* San Francisco: Jossey-Bass.

This book focuses on how critical reflection can be fostered in adults and explores in a range of practical ways how experience can be translated into emancipatory learning.

Schön, D (1991) (2nd edition) *The reflective practitioner: How professionals think in action.* Aldershot: Ashgate.

This seminal work explores how experienced practitioners use both formal and informal knowledge in their daily work and encourages the development of reflective practice as a means of bridging the 'theory/practice divide' in professional education.

Chapter 2

Policy and legislative frameworks in contemporary child and family social work

Lucille Allain and Helen Hingley-Jones

CHAPTER OBJECTIVES

If you are a registered social worker, this chapter will assist you to evidence post-registration train-ing and learning. It relates to the national post-qualifying framework for social work education and training at the specialist level:

  vii. Work effectively in a context of risk, uncertainty, conflict and contradiction.

It will also help you to meet the Children and Families standards for social work:

  vi. Applying knowledge and understanding of relevant legal frameworks, including the range of statutory responsibilities.

  ix. Actively working with and empowering those affected by poverty, unemployment, home-lessness, racism, homophobia, bullying and other forms of discrimination and disadvantage which impact on the lives of children and young people.

Introduction

This chapter will explain and analyse current policy and legislative frameworks in child and family social work with links made to social work practice within multi-professional teams and networks. At the centre of child and family social work practice is a requirement that we understand and work within policy and legislative frameworks, primarily the Children Act 1989. As stated by Brayne and Carr (2008) social workers are *a creation of statute* (p4). Our work is mainly concerned with individual rights, protection, safeguarding and supporting change in order to improve outcomes for children and families. In order to fulfil the requirements of our role it is therefore *essential for social workers to know about the law* (Johns, 2009, p7). Although it is true to say that legislation leads to policies which are then implemented in practice, the reverse is also true as practice also influences legis-lation and policy, creating a circular process of events.

This chapter describes these circular processes and critically appraises why particular policies and laws in child and family social work have been introduced, themes which are particularly pertinent at this moment in time, with the Social Work Taskforce considering how to 're-professionalise' social work. As well as exploring long-standing policy developments in child welfare we also consider the impact of the political philosophy of the new Coalition Government and the commitment to 'compassionate Conservatism'. At the time of writing, critical changes to the social work profession were being announced including the abolishment of the General Social Care Council: *the GSCC is to be scrapped as part of a government review of quangos* (Dunning, 2010). This chapter summarises some of the significant policy changes being proposed and considers possible implications for social work practice with children and families.

We examine the legislative and policy framework in terms of safeguarding and family support and briefly summarise key policies and legislation in relation to children who are looked after. This is linked to analysing the issues which led to the implementation of the Children Act 1989, the development of the Green Paper *Every Child Matters* (ECM) (DfES, 2003), then *Every Child Matters: Change for Children* (DfES, 2003) and the subsequent Children Act 2004. This entails an exploration of the trajectory of collaborative practice and inter-professional working in child welfare and how this links with New Labour's modernisation agenda (Parton, 2006a; Frost and Parton, 2009; Garrett, 2009a). This is then brought up to date through examining the current child protection review commissioned by the Education Secretary, Michael Gove, and led by Professor Eileen Munro. This chapter should be read in conjunction with Chapter 3, where the discussion about the critical role child death inquires have had in driving forward changes in relation to child protection and safeguarding is further developed (Parton, 2006a; Frost and Parton, 2009). Chapter 2 also considers how government guidance, including *Working Together* (DCSF, 2006b; 2010a) and the *Framework of Assessment for Children in Need and their Families* (DoH, 2000b), has evolved in response to changing practice contexts, research findings and political priorities.

Following this there is a focus on current policies and legislation in relation to looked after children: the Green Paper, *Care Matters: Transforming the Lives of Children and Young People in Care* (DfES, 2006a) followed by the White Paper, *Care Matters: Time for Change* (DfES, 2007a), before the enactment of new legislation, the Children and Young Persons Act 2008. In order to understand the evolution of the current legislative and policy framework we trace contemporary historical developments in relation to social work practice with looked after children. This involves examining the impact of reports and investigations into the abuse of children in public care. These include the Waterhouse Report, *Lost In Care* (Waterhouse, 2000) and the response to Sir William Utting's reports, *Children in the Public Care* (Utting, 1991) and *People Like Us* (Utting, 1997). These reports were highly significant in raising standards and in the development of more robust safeguarding systems for looked after children. Some also influenced policy developments in the 1990s including the Looked After Children project (DoH, 1995a) and Quality Protects (DoH, 1998a).

Given the breadth and depth of the legislative and policy framework in children's services this chapter cannot examine all areas of law and policy in detail. However, we give signposting information and references to more detailed texts in more specialist areas of law and policy. Specific social work law texts you may wish to access include: Brayne and Carr, 2008; Williams, 2008; Johns, 2009; and Brammer, 2010. To help you reflect on key legislation in children and family social work we have included a summary table below (see **www.opsi.gov.uk** to look at individual Acts).

Table 2.1 Summary of legislation

Children Act 1989	The legislation providing the principle legal framework for social work with children and families.
The Human Rights Act 1998	Provides redress in the courts for individuals and groups who feel their rights have been breached under the European Convention on Human Rights.
Children (Leaving Care) Act 2000	Provides details of local authority duties and responsibilities towards children leaving care.
Race Relations (Amendment) Act 2000	Duty on local authorities to eliminate racial discrimination and promote equal opportunities.
The Special Educational Needs and Disability Act 2001	Details education provision requirements for disabled children and young people.
Adoption and Children Act 2002	Overarching legislative framework for adoption law and special guardianship orders.
Children Act 2004	Introduced following *Every Child Matters* (DfES, 2003). Focuses on a duty for all agencies to co-operate, improved information sharing and provided for the establishment of Local Safeguarding Children Boards (LSCBs) in every authority.
Children and Young Persons Act 2008	Extends duties towards looked after children and young people leaving care. Aims to improve placement stability and support education attainment for children in care.
Equality Act 2010	This Act introduces a number of equality measures with changes proposed to the disability discrimination legislation. The Act was due to be implemented in October 2010 although some of it is now being reviewed following a change of government.

(*Source*: adapted from Brayne and Carr, 2008; Johns, 2009; Brammer, 2010)

Recent history: *Every Child Matters*, prevention and multi-agency working

Social policies focused on children and their families which were developed by New Labour have been extensive in their scope and were informed by concerns about social exclusion and the rapid rises in child poverty throughout the 1980s and early 1990s (CPAG, 2009). Policies were shaped by 'Third Way' thinking (Giddens, 1998) which aimed to amend the neo-liberal policies of the previous Conservative governments which New Labour blamed for dismantling social institutions and communities. The effects of globalisation and Tory policies in the 1970s and 1980s had led to large scale unemployment and the very notion of 'society' was questioned. As Margaret Thatcher stated in a famous interview with *Woman's Own* in 1987: *. . . and who is society? There is no such thing! There are individual men and women and there are families and no government can do anything except through people and people look to themselves first* (available at: **www.margaretthatcher.org**). Thatcher had trumpeted the idea that organised social welfare systems ought to be run down, with the family and individuals, rather than the state, taking responsibility for themselves. It could be argued that the new Coalition Government is revisiting these ideas with the notion of the 'Big Society' where citizens and local communities are encouraged to take on tasks which some say should be provided by government. Political debates have focused on how this approach is favoured by Conservatives as they *have an ideological attachment to the apparent corollary of a big society: a small state* (Freedland, 2010).

Combating the impact of social exclusion on individual children and their families was a key New Labour Government policy goal. In order to tackle these problems the Social Exclusion Unit was created in 1997. Problems of social exclusion were seen to be so complex, cutting across the responsibilities of so many different government departments and agencies, that they were identified as being one of the 'wicked issues' (Clarke and Stewart,1997) that government aimed to address. Clarke and Stewart (1997) make an analogy with mathematicians trying to solve very complex, interrelated problems.

Prevention

Some of the seemingly intractable problems in relation to child and family welfare identified by New Labour were described as inter-generational, leading to poor outcomes for children. Specific social problems identified included: poverty; unemployment; high rates of teenage pregnancy; poor housing; the impact of racism; substance misuse; poor mental health; crime and antisocial behaviour; truancy and social isolation. Accompanying these issues of concern was the existence of increasing numbers of people who were deemed to be part of an underclass. Murray, 1990 (cited by Frost and Parton, 2009) asserted that *the existence of an underclass could be diagnosed by three symptoms: illegitimacy, crime and dropping out from the labour force* (2009, p31). The Labour government's preferred method of tackling these issues was to find *joined-up solutions for joined-up problems* (Buchanan, 2007, p202). Policies were highly interventionist and moralistic in character (Parton, 2006a). There was an onus on 'tough love' or the idea that social rights come with social responsibilities, particularly focusing on parents who were targeted to make changes in their lives to transform the futures of children in the next generation (Lonne *et al.*, 2009). In practice, this has meant professionals using a managerialist approach with targets linked to funding across public sector agencies in health, education and social work. Radical restructuring of organisations and professional working practices happened. Cooper and Lousada (2005) argue that this has resulted in *remorseless uncertainty* (p175) for staff as they are required to continuously negotiate tasks and roles with colleagues working within the professional network.

- *Reflect on issues of poverty and social exclusion and consider what it is like for service users to receive help.*

CASE STUDY **2.1**

Ms Smith is a 34-year-old white woman from an inner-city estate where the majority of adults are out of work. She lost her part-time job in retail a year ago and she and her three children live apart from her ex-husband who has a new family. Her 15-year-old son Paul's school attendance is poor; he regularly comes in late and rarely attends for a whole week. His educational achievement is limited, his Year 11 academic scores suggest that he has made little progress in literacy since joining the school in Year 7, though his maths and science scores are better. Paul is unkempt in dress and often appears hungry, taking any food offered to him. He is socially withdrawn, with few friends. What are the risks facing Paul in light of the Every Child Matters *(DfES, 2003) agenda?*

Comment

You may have identified risks relating to being healthy, staying safe and enjoying and achieving for Paul (and his siblings). There are risks in relation to Paul truanting and not engaging in education and training.

How might social, economic and emotional factors be impacting on Paul and his family?

Social, economic and emotional factors are likely to be having a negative impact on Paul's overall well-being. He may feel a sense of despair and need support to re-engage in education which would create a helpful structure for him and alleviate his mother's concerns about his current behaviour and the impact it will have on his future life chances.

What might professionals do to intervene positively to help Paul?

It is important to think about the family holistically and understand that the family members are an interconnected system; supporting Ms Smith will have an impact on Paul and his siblings. She may welcome counselling/parenting support and intensive support in relation to job seeking. If Ms Smith is supported in her parenting role and is able to consider finding employment this is likely to have a positive impact on the family. It may be that you have identified the need for the completion of a *Common Assessment Framework (CAF)* form which is discussed later in this chapter. The family may need intensive outreach support and a mentor for Paul to help him re-engage with education. The lead professional may wish to make contact with the Connexions service, Education Welfare workers and Adolescent Services which may have leisure activities including sports which may help Paul's fragile self-esteem and his limited peer network.

Awareness of how parents, carers and children view the provision of social welfare and which services they find the most helpful is a vital component of working in partnership. For social workers putting social policy into practice with children and families in the community, it is important to be knowledgeable about the 'construction' policymakers place on society and children's place within it. It is also important for practitioners to be reflective about how it might feel to be on the receiving end of services and the unintended consequences of policies intended to end social exclusion. Sennett (2003), for example, has looked at how it can feel demeaning and hurtful to receive some forms of welfare services as *it lays a heavy burden of gratitude on the recipient, who may have nothing to give back but submission* (Sennett, 2003, p149).

Including service users in service planning is essential if parents are to be enabled to care for their children safely while minimising the damaging effects of stigma. Where this does not happen effectively, parents may feel disenfranchised and damaged by contact with professionals. For example, one survey of parents and carers in a local authority showed a mismatch between what local authorities offer and what children and families actually say they want (Buchanan, 2002, cited in Morris, 2008). Out of a 'wish list' of 24 services, parents who were already receiving services wanted: support with depression (38 per cent); counselling (32 per cent) and an opportunity to meet other parents in the same position (33 per cent). Two-thirds, in their view, were not having their needs met by existing services. More, then, can be done by social workers and their managers to bring the needs and wants of children and their families in line with service provision, even allowing for the need to manage risk.

How government policies have impacted on reducing social exclusion for children from birth to 13 years and their families is examined by Buchanan (2007) in a literature review commissioned by the Office of the Deputy Prime Minister. Although some positive outcomes are identified, it is reported that there is some difficulty in the design of some of the evaluation studies which means *they do not allow us to demonstrate a direct relationship between policy implementation and its effect on the incidence and experience of social exclusion* (Buchanan, 2007, p191). Nevertheless, it is concluded that: non-stigmatising services delivered in community venues are important in engaging families; some parents may need one-to-one support before they can join support or employment projects; increase in early years provision has helped to support families and some parenting programmes delivered within youth justice have had a positive impact in terms of family relationships and improved parenting skills (Buchanan, 2007). The findings from this research can be linked to some of the issues identified in relation to Ms Smith's family.

A key government policy priority has been encouraging families to use preventative services (see Chapter 4). Early intervention programmes which were developed by New Labour include Sure Start and the Children's Fund. The belief was that if children and families received the right sort of support at the right time then they were less likely to 'slip through the net' and need more intensive services and professional support at a later stage. This was also linked with the development of 'safeguarding' children and embracing a wider agenda than the previous one, which was focused primarily on protecting children from abuse; instead the emphasis was to be focused on early prevention. The safeguarding agenda which was first outlined in *Modernising Social Services* (DoH, 1998b) clearly outlined a broader and more supportive focus in working with families. However, not all welcomed the interventionist stance of New Labour policies. Jordan (2006; 2007), for example, viewed the changes as altering the fundamental relationship between the cit-. izen and the state, changes based on *blaming and judgemental social attitudes and residualist policies and service* (Lonne *et al.*, 2009, p59).

Prevention and partnership with parents were already central tenets of the Children Act 1989 with Section 17 giving provision for family support and prevention. The legislation states that the local authority should *promote the upbringing of such children by their families by providing a range and level of services appropriate to those children's needs* (Section 17, Children Act 1989). Implementation is specified within Schedule 2 of the Act where there is detailed information about the responsibilities of local authorities and clear evidence that priority should be given to working in partnership with parents plus preventive practice. In Section 18 of the Children Act 1989, further details are given in relation to requirements for day-care and after-school provision (see Johns, 2009, pp47–49). As stated by Parton (2009), the introduction of the Children Act 1989 meant that:

> The concept of prevention was elevated and broadened from simply the duty to prevent children coming into care, to include a broader power to provide services to promote the care and upbringing of children within their families.

(Parton, 2009, p70)

However, there had been persistent and urgent concerns which were instrumental in shifting policy. The roots of the changing policy direction can be seen in the discourse surrounding the refocusing debates in relation to the risk and prevention continuum in the 1990s with *Child Protection: Messages from Research* (DoH 1995b). The research emphasised the significance of the context within which abusive events occurred and found that parenting and home environments which are low on warmth and high in criticism are particularly damaging to children (DoH, 1995b). It was felt that too many children were not receiving services as children in need and were instead subject to *incident driven* (Platt, 2006, p269) narrowly focused child protection investigations which lacked consideration of the broader needs of children and their families, especially in relation to *borderline cases* (Platt, 2006, p269). Other factors included cost and budget priorities plus anxiety about making mistakes following child deaths where there was a great deal of criticism of social workers (Parton, 2006a). These findings resulted in the publication of revised *Working Together* guidance (DoH, 1999a) which had a broader emphasis on safeguarding and more focus on shared responsibility across agencies for promoting child welfare. This emphasis occurred because there had been insufficient progress in relation to preventive practice and research had shown that local authorities *were concentrating almost exclusively on their narrow child-protection responsibilities and were operating very high thresholds for services* (Parton, 2009, p70), of which more is said in Chapter 3. Therefore, a more wide ranging approach to child welfare was prioritised.

In addition, in order to respond to the need for less intrusive and more holistic assessment tools, the *Framework for the Assessment of Children in Need and their Families* (DoH, 2000) was developed. This assessment model is based on ecological systems theory, developed by Bronfenbrenner (1979). It is a theoretical model which offers a holistic approach to assessment as it focuses on the child's relationship with key individuals and their environment, including school, community groups and broader societal structures and systems. There is a central belief that all of the individuals and systems (structures) interact and intersect with each other creating interdependent relationships. Thus in order to assess children and families the interconnecting systems and relationships and their impact on the child's well-being also have to be assessed. Alongside this, there was a commitment to improving organisational systems to enable more effective information sharing, collaboration and understanding between agencies and professionals as part of the assessment process (DoH, 2000).

Both Chapters 2 and 3 discuss and analyse how Serious Case Reviews and inquiry reports into child deaths have had a major impact on shaping policy, practice and legislation. Issues for practice are discussed in Chapter 3 but the policy ramifications are discussed here in relation to the development of *Every Child Matters* and Children's Trusts. Following the death of Victoria Climbié in 2000, an eight-year-old girl who was abused by her aunt and the aunt's boyfriend and died of hypothermia, there was scathing media reporting about the perceived failures in social work services for children (Garrett, 2009b). The Laming Report (2003) identified how despite numerous visits by social workers and involvement with a range of services including in-patient treatment at hospital, Victoria's death was not prevented. The Laming Report (2003) sought to give impetus for radical and transformational change in children's services and identified significant failings in relation to inter-professional working. Specifically, the failures in service delivery were identified as: poor information sharing across agencies and between professionals; lack of co-ordination of services; poor systems of accountability; lack of strong leadership and insufficient support for front-line staff. However, these concerns are not new and were identified in the public inquiry into the death of Maria Colwell in 1974 and have been identified subsequently in numerous Serious Case Reviews (Reder et al., 1993; Reder and Duncan, 1999; Sinclair and Bullock, 2002; Dent and Cocker 2005; Parton, 2006a).

ACTIVITY 2.2

- *Why do you think that Serious Case Reviews and inquiries into child deaths always seem to come up with similar recommendations?*

- *Why do politicians always talk about 'learning the lessons' and yet still more children die?*

Comment

The repetition of recurring themes in government reports and inquiries into child deaths plus the predictability of proposed outcomes and what action should be taken is critiqued by Cooper *et al.* (2003) and Lonne *et al.* (2009). Cooper *et al.* (2003) argue that government policymakers have erroneously created defensive structures in child protection services, stating that although the aim is to minimise risk, the models that have been created are ineffective as they derive from accountancy and other business models where there is a focus on financial risk management. They propose that using a systemic theoretical framework about how organisations function is the way forward.

> *The apparent inability of government to think in terms of systems instead of structures, and cultures instead of procedures, is extremely damaging and has contributed to the apparent malfunctioning of crucial parts of the system.*
>
> (Cooper *et al.*, 2003, p 12)

Currently, a government-commissioned review of child protection is under way and part of the brief is to look at links between social work teams and other services. The review, led by Professor Eileen Munro, is using a systemic approach and part of the process will involve examining risk management protocols and practice with the aim of seeking to avoid the burgeoning blame culture in child protection services. There will also be a focus on reducing unnecessary bureaucracy and regulation and considering how social workers can be given more freedom to make professional judgements (Garboden, 2010). Issues of trust and the importance of listening to front-line social workers is discussed by Munro (2010) as central to creating improved practice in the complex area of child protection.

Lonne *et al.* (2009) also critique systems and structures within child protection services and how the aftermath of inquiries creates a culture of blame and needing to find a scapegoat. This in turn can create further anxiety for social workers who may be afraid of making mistakes and yet they continue to do a very difficult job (Garrett, 2009b). In Laming's Report (2009) following the death of Peter Connelly in Haringey there is specific reference made to concerns about *over-stretched frontline staff across social care, health and police* (Laming, 2009, p11). It is argued by Lonne *et al.* (2009) that instead of policy-makers and politicians seeking to properly understand the circumstances of a child's death and what role social workers and other agencies have had, a stale debate usually ensues. The action then proposed usually focuses on: *developing or increasing a range of the following: reporting; training; risk assessment and inter-agency collaboration* (Lonne *et al.*, 2009, p8). Following the death of Victoria Climbié and the Laming Report (2003) the New Labour government focused their solution primarily on creating greater inter-agency collaboration through *Every Child Matters* (DfES, 2003) and used the opportunity to press forward for significant structural changes in health and social welfare services and the creation of Children's Trusts. Recently, it has been announced that *a forthcoming Education Bill will mean Local Authorities no longer have to set up Children's Trusts Boards and schools will no longer have to co-operate* (Cooper, 2010). In addition, it has been announced by the Government that 'Contact Point' is to be axed. This was created to allow key professionals to find out who else in the professional network was involved in working with a child they were concerned about. Although significant expenditure has already been incurred, the database will close on the 6 August 2010 (Cooper, 2010). The ramifications of these changes will need to be considered to ensure that progress made in developing multi-agency practice models and sharing information is not lost.

Every Child Matters and the Children Act 2004

The Labour government published the Green Paper, *Every Child Matters* (DfES, 2003) followed by the Children Act 2004, with the implementation of the Act underpinning the policy set out in *Every Child Matters* (Brammer, 2010, p181). Although the Green Paper was presented largely as the government's response to the Laming Report (2003) into the death of Victoria Climbié, it is stated by Parton (2006a; 2009) that this was the rationale. Frost and Parton (2009, p38) outline how there was already a plan to strengthen preventive services which was detailed in the 2002 Spen (HM Treasury, 2002, cited by Frost and Parton, 2009).

By its very name it is evident that *Every Child Matters* focuses not only on children at risk of harm but on all children. To manage this more all encompassing approach, a plethora of new procedures, polices, levels and access points were built into the child welfare system. These changes included: the introduction of the Common Assessment Framework (CAF); the role of the lead professional; the development of Children's Centres; new systems for information sharing and a shared focus for all agencies on the 'five ECM outcomes' relevant to all children. They are: being healthy; staying safe; enjoying and achieving; making a positive contribution and achieving economic well-being (DfES, 2003). The aim was to ensure that children who needed additional support would be offered preventative services at an early stage. This created a new approach to child welfare with the aim of minimising the stigma associated with families needing 'welfare' services.

The drive towards more integrated working and 'the team around the child' (CWDC, 2009) resulted in old structures being dissolved and new ones created in the shape of Children's Trusts. Social services departments were dismantled and child and family social workers merged with education services and adult social work services often merged with housing. Although many welcomed these changes, it can be argued that these new structures created another split with a potentially negative impact on joint working between adults' and children's services. In addition, it created uncertainty about professional identity and where social work fits as a profession in the new world of integrated and networked organisations (Hingley-Jones and Allain, 2008).

Alongside this, there were accompanying changes in relation to information technology systems (Hudson, 2005), managerialist approaches and further rigorous performance management systems. Although many of these changes had already been implemented, ECM brought with it a whole raft of new changes in local authority social work services (Garrett, 2008). For more information about the legislative changes within the Children Act 2004, see Brammer (2010, pp 181–189).

The Common Assessment Framework and *Every Child Matters*

Emerging from *Every Child Matters*, the professional remit in relation to preventative work with children is set very wide. A key part of this is the Common Assessment Framework (CAF) which was developed as part of a new system for identifying vulnerable families at an early stage. The aim is to undertake a holistic assessment and appoint a lead professional to work with the child and family so that it *will avoid children and families having to tell and re-tell their story* (DfES, 2006b, p3). Social workers are not generally involved in completing CAFs but may receive referrals following the completion of a CAF. Laming (2009) identified that the strength of the CAF is that it brings together key professionals.

Paul revisited

If we return to Case Study 2.1, regarding Paul, we can see that he might well be offered an assessment with the aid of the CAF by the educational professionals he is in touch with at school; professionals who might have noticed his poor progress at school, his unkempt appearance and social withdrawal, all of which could be impacting on his ability to achieve the five desirable outcomes. Where on the CAF 'windscreen' would this preventative support be located? (See Figure 2.1.)

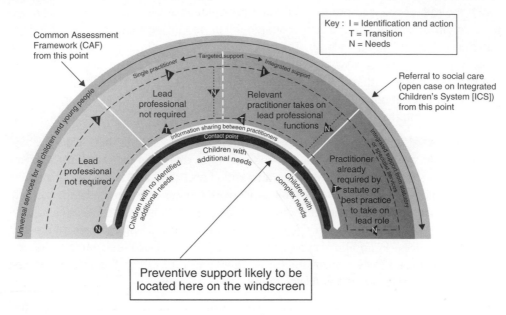

Figure 2.1 'Windscreen model' outlining professional roles and responsibilities

(Children's Workforce Development Council, 2009)

As part of the aim of integrating services for children, any professional working with a child may carry out a CAF and act as the lead professional in co-ordinating work with the child, their family and services.

Health and *Every Child Matters*

Every Child Matters (DfES, 2003) defines 'Being healthy' as children and young people having a healthy start in life, being physically and emotionally healthy, choosing healthy lifestyles, being sexually healthy and choosing not to take illegal drugs. An updated outcomes statement in relation to 'being healthy' (DCSF, 2008a) also includes targets to reduce childhood obesity and improve emotional health and well-being. As part of completing an initial and/or core assessment (DoH, 2000b) the health needs of children are considered. This includes assessing physical and mental health plus parenting capacity in relation to whether children are being given nutritious food, being taken for medical appointments when needed and for older young people having access to advice about sexual health and the use of drugs and alcohol (DoH, 2000b, p19). It may involve assessing children with additional health needs and making referrals to health and medical professionals. If a core assessment is completed and there are concerns about significant harm which may lead to a child protection conference, the core assessment will form the main report to the conference.

In order to improve outcomes for children and families the policy directives issued though ECM have all been underpinned by strategies for improved collaborative working and greater synergy between agencies. Evidence of this collaboration can be seen within the *National Service Framework (NSF) for Children, Young People and Maternity Services* (DoH, 2004) which sets national standards for children's health and social care and was published under the Change for Children, Every Child Matters programme. The values underpinning the NSF and ECM are similar, with recognition that services should be child-centred and meet the needs of families. It is argued by Lindsey (2005) that one of the significant achievements of the NSF is its focus on promoting children's psychological well-being as well as their physical health needs and that *child mental health is everyone's business* (Lindsey, 2005, p227). These issues have been particularly important in relation to findings from research which show that there are higher levels of diagnosed mental health difficulties in the looked after children population (Dimigen *et al.*, 1999; Meltzer *et al.*, 2003). Specific issues in relation to policy developments and the well-being of children who are looked after are discussed later on in this chapter.

Education and *Every Child Matters*

Social workers have close contact with colleagues working in schools and in education services in relation to referrals where there are concerns about safeguarding and promoting the well-being of children (Sayer, 2008). In addition, there are specific issues in relation to education and schools and supporting looked after children which will be discussed later on in this chapter.

In education services, the contribution of schools to the ECM agenda has been central, not only in terms of schools providing additional childcare for working parents but also for some schools to be the location for new child and family welfare services. Underpinning ECM and education has been a commitment to supporting and encouraging parents' involvement in their children's education. The Green Paper identifies parental involvement as an approach which promotes children's resilience (DfES, 2003, 1.13) and in paragraph 1.4 of the Green Paper parents are discussed as partners with education, health and welfare services in supporting their children through education. Schools have always had a central role to play in safeguarding children's welfare and the introduction of the Children Act 2004 strengthened this with the inclusion of a duty to co-operate. However, as mentioned previously this is going to be revoked and schools will no longer have to retain this duty to co-operate (Cooper, 2010).

Information sharing and *Every Child Matters*

Effective inter-professional communication and the importance of information sharing is a theme which, as previously stated, consistently emerges from reviews into child deaths (Reder and Duncan, 2003). It has also been a central part of the *Every Child Matters* agenda (DfES, 2003), which has resulted in the development and implementation of new information and communication technologies (ICT), the prioritising of e-government and the development of shared databases and information sharing between professionals. The overarching aim has been to improve and make more efficient inter-professional information exchange so that concerns about children could be shared at an earlier stage. However, despite the aim being to facilitate working across complex bureaucratic systems, the new technology which was purchased to improve recording and the sharing of information, the Integrated Children's System (ICS) has been identified as having serious limitations (White, 2008; White *et al.* 2009). This national programme providing records of all children where professionals are involved has been contentious throughout its development and implementation (Garrett, 2005a; Garrett, 2005b; White, 2008; White *et al.*, 2009) with issues taken up by the Social Work Taskforce and in Laming (2009).

While we would share the view of Richardson and Asthana (2006) that trust and the development of good relationships between professionals is key, it is also important that technology is developed in consultation with social workers and their managers so that ICT systems can support social work tasks. As White (2008) argues, it is not that new technology is abandoned but that *any system needs to be based on a thorough understanding of the needs of users and their working practices* (White, 2008). Through the voices of practitioners and academics these issues have been acknowledged and commitment has been made to tackle them through the work of the Social Work Taskforce and the review of child protection led by Professor Eileen Munro.

Looked after children – policy and legislative developments

Recent policy developments in relation to looked after children have been shaped by concerns which emerged in the 1990s about the abuse of children in public care (Stein, 2006) and a recognition of the importance of family life and care planning for children who cannot live with their birth families. The Looked After Children project (DoH, 1995a) and the Quality Protects (QP) initiative (DoH, 1998a) were driven largely by the response to Sir William Utting's reports, *Children in the Public Care* (Utting, 1991) and *People Like Us* (1997). Although the Waterhouse Report was not published until 2000, which was after the implementation of QP and the Looked After Children project, the horrifying circumstances of children who were subject to serious physical and sexual abuse in homes in North Wales stretching back to the 1970s had already been widely reported.

These three reports which detailed long-standing and serious abuse of children in public care galvanised professionals and policymakers to consider urgently and safeguard the needs of looked after children. The publication of a response to the Waterhouse Report *Learning the Lessons*, (DoH, 2000c) made a commitment to a programme of new developments which sought to strengthen opportunities and outcomes for looked after children. In addition, there was a focus on developing a better understanding of institutional and systematic abuse and how children can be safeguarded in the care system (Frost *et al.*, 1999).

One of the key areas of policy development has been a focus on the health and educational needs of looked after children and the role of the 'corporate parent' in helping children to succeed. There had been concern that children in public care had not been achieving their full potential in education (SEU, 2003; Harker *et al.*, 2004) and in the Social Exclusion Unit report five main underlying problems were identified and five main reasons why children are not achieving their full potential in education were detailed.

The five main underlying problems identified were:

- capacity – high staff vacancy rates and lack of staff training about the educational needs of children in care;
- management and leadership – lack of commitment and time from senior managers and more junior staff feeling they have limited influence to make changes;
- resources – poorly managed resources;
- systems and structures – lack of collaborative working between key staff and different departments; and
- attitudes – many carers and social workers are positive about children in care, but negative attitudes and low expectations can be commonly found among professionals and wider society.

The five reasons given for lack of progress in relation to education attainment and looked after children were:

- instability in relation to placement moves;
- too much time out of school;
- insufficient help with their education if they get behind;
- carers were not expected, or equipped, to provide sufficient support and encouragement; and
- that children in care need more help with their emotional, mental or physical health and well-being.

(A summary of the key issues from the Social Exclusion Report, 2003, pp3–4)

These issues have been addressed specifically by the White Paper, *Care Matters: Time for Change* (DfES, 2007a) with a focus on meeting the needs of children in care and early years services through to young people who are looked after and are at the stage of attending college and university. Changes have been introduced as part of the Children and Young Persons Act (2008) with a focus on strengthening the role of the corporate parent. Although policy developments in relation to education are significant, there has been a critique regarding the limited analysis of the changing profile of children becoming looked after for short periods and the differences between them and the children looked after for longer periods. In addition it has been argued that more focus is required on analysing the impact of adverse pre-care experiences (Stein, 2006; Cocker and Allain, 2008; Frost and Parton, 2009; Forrester *et al.*, 2009).

- *Think about how the local authority you work for has strengthened the role of the corporate parent.*

- *How might this work in practice?*

You will recall that the corporate parenting task means that the local authority has a collective responsibility to ensure that the practical and emotional needs of looked after children are met on a day-to-day basis. That should result in the local authority ensuring that those delivering care do at least what a good parent would do for their child.

Comment

You may have thought about ensuring that the child who is looked after has access to good educational opportunities and health care as well as ensuring that they live within a loving and nurturing home environment. You may recall that in the *Care Matters* implementation plan it is stated that all local authorities need to develop a Children in Care Council (CIC), although these are still in the process of being established in many local authorities. When they are operational, they will provide an important forum for building communication between looked after children and the professionals who have responsibilities towards them.

The recent White Paper *Care Matters* (DfES, 2007a) states that looked after children have higher rates of substance misuse and teenage pregnancy when compared with children not in care and also a higher prevalence of mental health problems. The issues of higher rates of mental health disorders within the looked after children population was identified in research undertaken by Meltzer *et al.*, (2003) and replicated a study completed in 2000 across all children in England with a sample of 10,000. Briggs (2009) discusses the Child and Adolescent Mental Health Services (CAMHS) agenda and how there are continued attempts to make services more accessible with additional investment in order to improve outcomes for looked after children.

As a social worker for looked after children, you will be responsible for ensuring health and dental checks are completed plus the necessary immunisations. Under the Children Act 1989, local authorities have general duties to safeguard and promote the welfare of children, which includes monitoring children's developmental progress. Within the Children Act (Miscellaneous Amendments) (England) Regulations 2002 the local authority should arrange for an annual assessment of every looked after child. However, young people who are looked after can refuse to consent to a medical examination if they are deemed to be of sufficient age and understanding. In addition, if a child is under five years of age, the health assessment should take place every six months. Reviews for looked after children should be held in accordance with regulatory timescales, which are within four weeks of a child becoming looked after and then three months later, followed by every six months. The Children and Young Persons Act 2008 strengthened the role of Independent Reviewing Officers (IROs) in relation to care planning which requires that children have a named IRO so that the progress of their circumstances can be monitored by an IRO who knows them and their circumstances (Brammer, 2010). This is an important development.

The needs of care leavers have also been prioritised in policy and legislation with the introduction of the Children (Leaving Care) Act 2000. This legislation sought to address previous concerns about the lack of support for vulnerable young people (see Chapter 12, Cocker and Allain, 2008). A key change has been in relation to each young person who is leaving care having a pathway plan which should give information about the young person's health, education and housing needs and how this will help them on their journey to independence. See Brammer (2010, p 304) for a summary of the content of pathway plans and the role of personal advisers.

The *Care Matters* reforms which resulted in the Children and Young Persons Act 2008 marked the government's unequivocal commitment to improving the life chances and well-being of looked after children. The Act has a detailed implementation plan and was closely linked to the content of the White Paper which focused on: corporate parenting; family and parenting support; care placements; education, health and well-being and making the transition to adulthood. There is clear evidence that the needs of looked after children have been a political priority for New Labour (Cocker and Allain 2008; Frost and Parton, 2009) with the developments of *Care Matters* marking a *major landmark in social policy as it relates to children and young people in care* (Frost and Parton, 2009, p95). Given that there is now a Coalition Government, they may choose to focus priorities differently, although the rhetoric of the 'Big Society' theme espoused by them does appear to follow some of the aims of New Labour. Nevertheless, there is still the potential for a return to neoliberal policies under the Coalition Government, perhaps made essential by the economic recession.

Government policy changes and the strategies for cutting costs and bureaucracy in child welfare have begun to emerge. As well as the previously mentioned axing of the GSCC and Contact Point, the role of the Children's Commissioner is also under review. In addition, there are significant changes being proposed for schools with the setting up of 'free schools' and new academies. Some have argued that this may have a detrimental impact on children who are looked after and those with special needs as these schools will not be subject to local authority admissions requirements (Pemberton, 2010). The Coalition Government's social welfare agenda is focused on a philosophical approach which favours helping families to care for their own. The agenda will be shaped by a Childhood and Families Ministerial Taskforce led by the Prime Minister. The Deputy Prime Minister has outlined the vision of the Taskforce: *We are realistic – it is not government's job to create families; our job is to dismantle the barriers that prevent families from giving their children the best start* (Golding, 2010). The likely implications for social work practice is a re-prioritising of services for family support and overall budget restrictions for children's services. On a more positive note, the proposed work of the Child Protection Review led by Professor Eileen Munro looks very promising and we are cautiously optimistic that changes can be introduced which will benefit service users, the profession and local authorities.

Chapter summary

In order to be effective practitioners, Cooper and Dartington (2004) argue that we need to move beyond discourses of competence, performance targets and proceduralism. This involves reflecting on and being aware of the social and psychological needs of children and their parents, as we explore further in Chapter 3. It also requires social workers to understand and be able to locate in time why specific polices and legislation have developed and what the driving forces were. This requires awareness of how our profession is shaped by politics, economics and social problems. This then results in a deepening of our understanding about our professional history and the circular processes involved in shaping policy, legislation and practice.

FURTHER READING

Cooper, A and Lousada, J (2005) *Borderline welfare: Feeling and fear of feeling in modern welfare.* London: Karnac.

This book offers an interesting analysis of current issues with regards to the changes in Britain's welfare system and the development of social policy. It is underpinned by psychoanalytic theoretical ideas and considers the links between rational and scientific approaches and emotional responses.

Frost, N and Parton, N (2009) *Understanding children's social care: Politics, policy and practice.* London: Sage.

This is an excellent book providing a fascinating summary and analysis of key issues in the development of children's social work and associated care services.

Chapter 3

Safeguarding children: the complexities of contemporary practice and the importance of working with emotions

Helen Hingley-Jones and Lucille Allain

CHAPTER OBJECTIVES

If you are a registered social worker, this chapter will assist you to evidence post-registration training and learning. It relates to the national post-qualifying framework for social work education and training at the specialist level:

> v. *Use reflection and critical analysis to continuously develop and improve their specialist practice, including their practice in inter-professional and inter-agency context, drawing systematically, accurately and appropriately on theories, models and relevant up-to-date research.*

It will also help you to meet the Children and Families standards for social work:

> iii. *Co-ordinating services in a multi-agency service delivery context, including the knowledge and skills required to ensure professional networks are able to meet complex needs, and where appropriate, undertake lead professional roles.*

> iv. *Identifying, evaluating and managing risks, including those associated with safeguarding responsibilities, together with the ability to intervene in situations to reduce risks.*

Introduction

This chapter continues to explore the broad theme of safeguarding children's welfare from Chapter 2, but its focus concerns the child protection role that is so central to social work practice with children and their families. In contemporary child welfare, safeguarding involves a wide spectrum of tasks to be carried out in a co-ordinated fashion by the whole range of professionals who are working with children. The aim of safeguarding is to ensure the best possible outcomes for children in meeting their developmental potential, across the five areas identified in *Every Child Matters* (DfES, 2003). For social workers, the central task is the requirement to ensure children are protected from immediate harm and abuse, while assessing need across a broad spectrum so that services can be provided to maximise children's developmental life chances. These are highly technical and complex tasks, which reflect the New Labour and now the Coalition Government view that social welfare should be preventative and interventionist in style. Qualified practitioners, even those who have not worked for long in statutory childcare social work settings, will already be well aware of the kinds of dilemmas and challenges faced in practice in this arena: busy caseloads; burdensome IT systems; the difficulties of working with stressed service users and disturbing incidents of abuse; and the effects on staff morale of recent child death inquiries, to name but a few.

The purpose of this chapter will be to link theory and knowledge with practice realities. Academic learning and research knowledge derived from 'practice-near' sources (Marsh and Fisher, 2008) will be used alongside knowledge of legislation, practice guidance and policy outlined in the previous chapter, to provide space for practitioners to reflect on, and to enhance their capacity to work with, the kinds of phenomena they are grappling with in practice. First, there will be a brief reminder of some historical trends in child protection social work. These show that the dilemma of how to offer support to families and risk management in childcare social work is a continuing theme through time, with which professionals and policymakers are still struggling today. Second, some of the challenges of contemporary practice will be described in the aftermath of recent Serious Case Reviews and inquiries following the deaths of Victoria Climbié (Laming, 2003) and Peter Connelly (Laming, 2009) and in the context of broader concerns about the profession of social work (Social Work Taskforce, 2009). After this, the role of emotion in child protection work will be looked at as a way of focusing on a key element of practice. Literature from psychotherapeutically-informed social work will enable exploration of the topic in a practice-relevant way. Out of these explorations it is then possible to consider contemporary integrated working arrangements in which practitioners are located and what might be needed from these to enhance social workers' capacity to do their safeguarding jobs (Ruch 2007b, Ferguson 2009).

Historical perspectives on safeguarding children in the UK context

One tension in safeguarding policy in the UK, as elsewhere in the world, is between the need to work supportively and preventatively with children and their families and the requirement to investigate and to act on incidents when children have experienced, or are at risk of experiencing, abuse (Lonne *et al.*, 2009; Parton, 2006a; Frost and Parton 2009). The dilemma is not a new one; it relates to the broader social welfare problem of how to balance a family's right to privacy with the children's rights and it has been addressed in different ways over time. Right back at the inception of the National Society for the Prevention of Cruely to Children (NSPCC) in 1884 in England, there was an activist phase which saw the first legislation enabling agencies to intervene when children were experiencing abuse in the family setting: the Prevention of Cruelty to, and Protection of,

Children Act 1889 (Parton, 1985). Lonne *et al.* (2009) explain how in the twentieth century this public, interventionist approach to protecting children dwindled, perhaps fuelled by the ending of the suffrage movement for women which had campaigned on issues to do with domestic life. Secondly, the increasing bureaucratisation of the NSPCC, as it lessened its campaigning role, may also have reduced the organisation's willingness to make children's deaths at the hands of their parents public (Ferguson 1996 and 1997, cited by Lonne *et al.*, 2009).

The Children Act 1948 saw a shift in attitudes away from the tenets of the Poor Law Acts 1601 and 1834, which did not recognise the needs of vulnerable children in the care system for an education or for support in returning to their families. This legislation led to the establishment of local authority children's departments whose task it was to promote the best development of the children they were responsible for (Frost and Parton 2009). This was a phase when supportive, optimistic professional attitudes held sway, with the privacy of family life respected (Parton 2006a, Frost and Parton 2009; Lonne *et al.*, 2009). Through the 1950s and 1960s, the idea that steps should be taken to work preventatively with families, to avoid children having to come into care, began to take hold. The social work professional, skilled in psycho-social intervention skills, took the work on. Meanwhile 'battered baby syndrome', a medical, diagnostic view of child abuse making use of X-ray technology, surfaced in the USA, influencing thinking in the UK. This suggested that physical abuse had often been overlooked in children under three years old and that the medical profession was now in a position to diagnose it, even when hidden from view in the privacy of the family (Kempe *et al.*, 1962).

In the UK, the establishment of the generic family service in the 1970s, following the Seebohm Report (1968) and the Local Authority Social Services Act 1970, was an essentially optimistic phase in UK child welfare provision, which Frost and Parton (2009) show fell open to heavy criticism in the 1970s after the death of Maria Colwell in 1973 and subsequent inquiry (DoH and DHSS, 1974). Maria Colwell died aged seven years at the hands of her stepfather, after being returned to her parents' care, having spent most of her life in the care of her aunt and despite being on a Supervision Order and having visits from social workers. The findings of the inquiry echoed many of the findings of the subsequent 29 child death inquiries over the next ten years (Parton, 2006a) and beyond:

- there was a lack of inter-disciplinary communication;

- front-line practitioners were poorly trained and inexperienced;

- supervision had been inadequate;

- the needs of the children had not taken centre stage, with parents' and family needs taking precedence.

(Parton, 2006a, p32)

The inquiry into the death of Jasmine Beckford in 1984 continued to highlight the shortcomings of professionals involved (London Borough of Brent, 1985; DHSS, 1987). Following this inquiry, the statutory nature of the social work role was opened up for scrutiny, with social workers blamed for following the 'rule of optimism' in hoping that a severely neglected child would be adequately cared for when returned to her parents after a period in care. Criticisms of a similar nature were also made during two subsequent, high-profile child death inquiries: those of Tyra Henry (London Borough of Lambeth, 1987) and Kimberley Carlile (London Borough of Greenwich, 1987; see Parton, 2006a).

Swinging the pendulum in the other direction, highlighting concerns about invasions of family privacy, the Cleveland Inquiry (Secretary of State for Social Services, 1988) found that statutory services in this case had overstepped their role when, on the basis of a medical diagnostic test for child sex abuse, invented by two paediatricians in Middlesbrough, over 100 children were removed from their parents' care (Parton, 2006a).

Out of these developments, the Children Act 1989 can be seen to represent an attempt *to establish a balance between the public authorities and the private family in the care and upbringing of children* (Parton, 2006a, p37). Government-led research and guidance has increased its emphasis over time on the need to place assessments of children at risk of significant harm as part of a continuum of need (DoH 1999a; DfES 2006c). Frost and Parton (2009) show how the first version of *Working Together* (HMSO, 1991) which followed on from the arrival of the Children Act (1989) hardly addressed the requirement to work with children in need under the provisions of Section 17 of the Act. Instead, its focus was on how workers could consider whether or not thresholds had been met to prove that children were at risk of, or actually suffering from, 'significant harm'.

Child Protection: Messages from Research (DoH, 1995) revealed that the Children Act's aims of balancing the supportive, preventative side of welfare provision were being sacrificed in favour of an over-emphasis on risk assessment. Referrals to child welfare teams in local authorities were 'funnelled' (Parton, 2006a, Frost and Parton, 2009; Lonne *et al.* 2009). For example, out of initial referrals to child protection duty services in eight local authorities, one survey which informed *Child Protection: Messages from Research* (DoH, 1995) showed that 26 per cent were filtered out at the first stages after initial checks and no contact with the child or family while, at the investigation stage, 50 per cent were filtered out and just 15 per cent of those left were placed on the child protection register. Some 44 per cent of those investigated led to no further action (Gibbons *et al.*, 1995, cited in Parton 2006a). Analysis of the data showed that many of the families referred came from vulnerable sections of society, with high proportions of children previously known to social services (65 per cent), domestic violence evident in referrals (27 per cent), along with mental health problems (13 per cent) and a high proportion of families reliant on income support (54 per cent) (Gibbons *et al.*, 1995, cited in Parton, 2006a).

Chapter 2 looked at the refocusing debates which emerged in response to this research, with *Working Together to Safeguard Children* (DoH, 1999a) issued in tandem with the *Framework of Assessment for Children in Need and their Families* (DoH, 2000b) which drew on ecological perspectives as a theory base for social work assessment (DoH, 2002c). Subsequent legislation and guidance, mentioned in Chapter 2, has also influenced practice (for example DfES and DoH, 2004b; DfES, 2006c; DCSF, 2010a).

RESEARCH SUMMARY

Themes and concerns in contemporary safeguarding: the role of Local Safeguarding Children Boards and Serious Case Reviews

Every Child Matters *(DfES, 2003)* and subsequently Working Together to Safeguard Children: A Guide to Inter-agency Working to Safeguard and Promote the Welfare of Children *(DfES, 2006c)* saw the introduction of Local Safeguarding Children Boards (LSCBs). Taking over from the non-statutory Area Child Protection Committees, LSCBs now have direct accountability for child protection in their area. The responsibilities of LSCBs are broad:

> . . . firstly, they engage in activities that safeguard all children and aim to identify and prevent maltreatment, or impairment of health or development, and to ensure that children are growing up in circumstances consistent with safe and effective care; secondly, they lead and co-ordinate proactive work that aims to target particular groups; and thirdly, they lead and co-ordinate arrangements for responsive work to protect children who are suffering, or likely to suffer, significant harm.

> (DCSF, 2010a, p12)

LSCB responsibilities include monitoring all child deaths in their area and they identify cases requiring a Serious Case Review (SCR). The purpose of an SCR is to learn lessons from the case; the aim is to improve the practice of individuals and agencies involved towards safeguarding and promoting the welfare of children.

It is without doubt that SCRs into the deaths of children have had and continue to have a profound impact on policies, legislation and practice in child and family social work. As we have already seen, a number of child deaths in the 1980s and the Cleveland Inquiry (Secretary of State for Social Services, 1988) were highly influential in developing the Children Act 1989. The death of Victoria Climbié and the subsequent Laming Report (2003) led to the Children Act 2004 and the formation of Children's Trusts. The death of Peter Connelly in Haringey in 2007 resulted in a further report by Laming (2009) and the creation of a Social Work Taskforce to examine social work education and practice over a number of areas.

A key message from many SCRs and inquiry reports focuses on concerns about inter-professional practice in relation to communication between professionals and agencies and how professionals work together to assess and support children and families (Laming, 2003; DfES and DoH, 2004b). As mentioned previously, this was identified as a key issue in the inquiry report into the death of Maria Colwell, who was killed by her stepfather in 1973, and as one of the issues in child death inquiries throughout the 1980s.

SCRs provide an important means of examining key messages regarding what has happened to children who have been abused and neglected and what role professionals have had. Munro (2008) argues that more could be learnt from inquiries and SCRs if blaming individuals is avoided. Instead she advocates focusing on what could be learnt for future practice. She makes an analogy with the black box found on aircraft which is examined after a tragedy, not so that 'blame' can be apportioned but so that professionals can understand what went wrong. This approach is advocated by Reder *et al.* (1993) who

47

state that it is crucial to understand professional and family systems, including the alliances, conflicts and dilemmas, in order to see the case as a whole. It was hoped that the new integrated children's departments would improve inter-agency collaboration, out-comes and service provision for vulnerable and at-risk children and families. However, structures are only a part of the story as it is people, and how they share information, work inter-professionally and communicate with each other and children and families which are key and some have argued that these features have been overlooked in policy making (Cooper, 2005). More will be said about this later in this chapter.

Referral rates

Another pressure affecting front-line practice is the increased referral rates to statutory childcare services following Laming (2009). Research carried out by Loughborough University, commissioned by the Local Government Association (LGA), indicates that nearly two-thirds of social workers reported an increase in workload in the latter part of 2009 following publication of the report and child protection social workers are now working with an average of 14 cases. Social workers also reported that they were spending three-quarters of their time form filling and only one quarter seeing families (LGA, 2010).

Concern about increased referral rates is borne out by government statistics. Examining the child protection statistics for the year ending 31 March 2009 (DCSF, 2009h) shows that there were an additional 4,900 children who were the subject of a child protection plan (29,200 in 2008 and 34,100 children in 2009). There has also been an increase in overall referral rates to social services with an additional 8,500 referrals in 2009 (538,500 in 2008 and 547,000 in 2009). Initial assessments have also been on an upward trajectory, with 290,300 completed in 2005; 300,200 in 2006; 305,000 in 2007; 319,900 in 2008 and 349,000 in 2009. Clearly, increases in referral rates result in increased caseloads for profes-sionals. In Laming's Report (2009) following the death of Baby Peter there is specific reference made to concerns about *overstretched front-line staff across social care, health and police* (Laming, 2009, p11). Despite this, many social workers and their managers report having to fight very hard for additional resources to meet rising referral rates. Accompanying increasing workloads is a requirement that performance targets continue to be met, often within existing resources. These complex challenges are discussed by Laming (2009) who outlines the inadequacy of some performance indicators (PIs) in the area of child protection and safeguarding and highlights that some of them are having a perverse effect, emphasising process and timescales over other important factors. He states that *there is an urgent need to develop effective indicators for safeguarding chil-dren . . . and secure better outcomes for them* (Laming, 2009, p15).

Interestingly, despite the rise in referrals, there has been an increase in completion of ini-tial assessments within timescales of seven days from 226,300 in 2008 to 250,000 in 2009, and for core assessments from 83,700 completions within timescales (35 days) in 2008 to 94,300 completions within timescales in 2009.

Clearly, child and family social workers are required to carry out their role in the complex world of child protection where anxiety about risks to children and dilemmas about deci-sions are ever present. Overshadowing this is concern about making mistakes which could lead to harm for children and the resultant political and media opprobrium (Garrett, 2009b) which was clearly evident following the death of Baby Peter in the London Borough of Haringey. The report by Laming (2009) which examines issues in relation to practice and organisational factors reported that although there was evidence of progress *. . . there remain significant problems in the day-to-day reality of working across organisational boundaries and cultures* (Laming, 2009, p10). Despite the turbulence and concern about practice following events in Haringey, there have been improvements and new developments. Examples of these include the work of the Social Work Taskforce (see **www.dcsf.gov.uk/swtf**), a return to focusing on relationship-based approaches in social work (Ruch *et al.*, 2010) and a review of how information technology systems are used in childcare social work (White, 2008).

In the face of these pressures of demanding workloads, challenging performance indicators and IT systems, media scrutiny and the ever-present anxiety of working in the child protection field, what kinds of knowledge and skills might help practitioners to stay resilient and focused on the difficult tasks in front of them? The following section will consider the role of emotions and inter-professional communication as vital tools for practice.

The impact of emotions on child protection social work

In recent times, there has been a call to improve the bureaucratic skills associated with social work practice in child protection work, in the hope that this would avert child death tragedies such as those of Victoria Climbié and Peter Connelly, in 2000 and 2007 respectively. Writing about the death of Victoria Climbié and the subsequent child death inquiry (Laming, 2003), Cooper (2005) describes how Victoria died in horrific circumstances, having been severely beaten and maltreated over a significant period of time. This was despite the fact that she had been known to many different professionals, including social workers, housing officers and medics she met during hospital admissions, when she was seen to have non-accidental injuries and a disturbingly servile relationship with her aunt.

Cooper focuses on Laming's comment in the report: *I am convinced that the answer lies in doing relatively straightforward things well* (Laming, 2003, quoted in Cooper, 2005, p4). The Inquiry's concern to get bureaucratic and managerial processes and procedures right fed into the construction of the Children Act 2004 with its emphasis on developing integrated services for children, leading to mergers of education and social services departments and the development of IT systems, geared at integration of children's records. For Cooper however, a focus on administration and bureaucracies of practice is not enough to improve things:

> *Structures, procedures and protocols may be necessary but they are not sufficient conditions of good practice. They are surface instruments capable of guiding us and organising us towards the relevant point of contact with the deeper, more complex and ambiguous realities with which we need to engage in child protection work, but little more.*

(Cooper, 2005, p4)

Echoing Reder and Duncan (2004), Cooper suggests that 'human factors' can get in the way of simplistic, bureaucratic solutions to child protection issues. Munro (2008) too, describes how the technical, analytic view of child protection social work practice, with its emphasis on evidence-based practice and attempts to employ diagnostic testing in relation to risk assessment, is often set in opposition to more traditional, empathic, emotions-led social work practice. Emotionally-aware social work practice implies that social workers need to develop the skill to listen to their 'gut feelings' about the work. In her view, these two approaches should not be seen as oppositional, but should instead be placed on a continuum. To practise effectively in safeguarding, there is a need to be able to work with technical, rational risk assessment processes, with an awareness of how research informs these (for example Cleaver *et al.*, 2010), while social workers also need to be alert to feelings and emotions, or 'human factors', in the work as these too are informative.

REFLECTION POINT

- Before hearing more about what some social work academics think on this issue, what 'human factors' can you think of that may have got in the way of the safeguarding work you could do on a case you know well?

- Were those factors to do with you, your team, your agency, inter-professional issues, wider policy issues or more to do specifically with the child and family you were working with?

Considering 'human factors'

Looking at 'human factors', Ferguson (2005) suggests that by focusing on bureaucracies of practice the mistaken assumption might be reached that the child protection field is a 'rational' place to be, when in fact this is often not the case at all. To illustrate his point, Ferguson looks at research that he and others have carried out on social workers' experience of working with resistant, sometimes hostile service users. Reporting on one survey (Ferguson and O'Reilly, 2002, cited in Ferguson, 2005) he describes how 34 per cent of parents and carers worked with by one childcare social work team were 'involuntary clients'. They did not want a service and did not welcome the involvement of a social worker. Thoburn *et al.* (1995) found in another survey that in 17 per cent of cases worked with by another childcare social work team, there was major resistance to social work intervention. Smith *et al.* (2004) report on social workers' experiences of fear, showing that a significant number of these professionals have experienced violence at the hands of angry or distressed service users, not just in the child protection field.

How thinking about and reflecting on the experience of fear and other emotions can inform assessments of risk

If social workers face real resistance and hostility, and even violence, when trying to engage and to work with families who may be harming children, what is the impact of this on the professionals concerned and therefore the possible consequences for vulnerable children? Listing several possible areas of impact, Ferguson (2005) considers why rational, bureaucratic solutions to child protection problems are not always enough in themselves to ensure good practice in the real world.

First, he discusses the danger of 'Stockholm syndrome': collusion with and empathy for the hostage-taker. Faced with an intimidating service user or parent, but one who the social worker is still expected to work in partnership with, there is a danger of colluding with or placating them. How much easier is it to avoid or downplay difficult, sensitive issues when interviewing and assessing someone who is only just tolerating being with you? Ferguson suggests that, in such circumstances, the professional may become a 'captive' of the abusive or potentially violent service user. Fearful of confronting a service user with their concerns about abusive and harmful behaviour, the professional may be unable to think clearly enough to do their job. There may be real fear of retaliation and of harm coming to the professional or their family.

It is in this kind of situation that there is a danger of the child becoming an 'afterthought'. Reder *et al.* (1993) describe this in terms of the professionals involved mirroring the patterns within a family where paradoxically a child can only be tolerated when they are not seen or thought about. So the professional visits the parent in order 'not to talk about' the child who is the object of concern; to collude in not thinking about the child and in doing nothing to protect them. Tanner (1999) provides an analysis of this kind of dynamic in relation to the death of Rikki Neave in 1997. Rikki Neave was on the Cambridgeshire Child Protection Register when he died; his mother, Ruth Neave, later convicted for child cruelty and neglect, was described during the subsequent child death inquiry to have been experienced by social workers as *aggressive, threatening and hostile* (the Bridge Consultancy, 1997, quoted in Tanner, 1999, p20). The social workers would only visit in pairs. The Bridge Consultancy independent report (1997) found that the question was never asked by professionals: well, if the social workers find the mother frightening, how do the children experience her? The fear that the professionals felt on being with Ruth Neave was valid information, but it was not used to assess the risk to the children. In common with many other child death inquiries, the inquiry found that little attempt was made to uncover the children's views at all during the work, despite the fact that many practical resources were made available to the family, as though this would avert any possible risk.

ACTIVITY **3.1**

Think of a time when you have felt frightened or intimidated on visiting a service user where there were child protection concerns and consider:

- *What helped you to carry out the work?*

- *Did you receive support from a colleague, a manager or agency?*

- *What might have made the task more manageable?*

- *Were you able to assess the child's situation so that you felt they were adequately safeguarded?*

Comment

Perhaps you found this a painful exercise if you have experienced real fear on trying to engage in work with an intimidating family? Next, we are going to reflect a little further on some more uncomfortable feelings which may be aroused by working with 'difficult' families; not to increase your stress, but with a positive intention! We will be going on to explore the idea that feeling unpleasant emotions may actually help to inform and shape social work assessments of need and risk for vulnerable children and their families. Later in this chapter reference will be made to skills and knowledge derived from psychoanalytic ideas, which are worth beginning to master, to assist practitioners in making sense of the dynamics of these uncomfortable encounters. Afterwards, we will consider what supports and structures need to be in place to facilitate social workers making use of these ideas in a manner that should benefit practice.

More 'human factors': fear of contamination

Ferguson (2005) discusses another fear which can arise when carrying out child protection work: a fear of contamination. This may involve a fear of catching an actual infectious disease, as was raised in the case of the Laming Inquiry (2003) into the death of Victoria Climbié, whose scabies infection was used as a justification for professionals not to visit her at home. Fears of contamination may also include psychological factors, for example the fear that we may become like the abuser. In the case of working with those who may be sexually exploiting or abusing children, there may be a fear that the worker will become contaminated by the close contact with those who are sexually transgressive. This can make workers anxious, either that their own children may become victims, or by stirring up unconscious worries they may have about their own sexuality and fears about what they themselves might be capable of. Agass (2005) describes some of the unconscious processes which may be at work in such situations:

> *Encountering such abuse presents special difficulties for the worker, who is likely to feel abusive or abused, and in some degree contaminated . . . by exposure to the client's experience.*

(Agass, 2005, p186)

Upsetting and worrying emotions are potentially aroused by working close to abuse, and those living with it either as perpetrators or victims. It is worth considering further, therefore, what kinds of knowledge, skills, supports and structures are needed to enable social workers to think freely and clearly in practice, enabling full and well considered assessments of need and of risk, the kind of thinking Marion Bower *et al.* (2005) describe as 'thinking under fire'.

Rationality and emotion: some useful theory/practice ideas

There is a long tradition of social workers drawing on psychoanalytic and systemic ideas to provide useful ways of making sense of the emotional and interpersonal dimensions of the social work role (for example, Salzberger-Wittenberg, 1970; Preston-Shoot and Agass, 1990; Sudbery, 2002; Trevithick, 2003; Bower, 2005) and in child protection work specifically (for example, Reder and Duncan, 2003; Agass, 2005; Daniel, 2005; Cooper, 2005). Developing expertise and knowledge of these perspectives takes time, through reading, attending courses, making use of specialist supervision and consultation (Bower, 2005). Some have argued, however, that developing expertise in these areas is necessary if some of the current criticism of social workers is to be countered in relation to failures in child protection work (Ferguson, 2005; Cooper, 2005). This is not simply to advocate a return to the optimistic times of the 1970s in social work, when supportive therapeutic social work was considered enough to contain all forms of distress and child abuse in the families worked with, leaving social workers having *to accept considerable responsibility on the parents' behalf for trying to bring about improvements* (Parton, 2006a, p30). Robust uses of psychotherapeutic knowledge, within well structured agencies, supported by clear child protection policies, can contribute instead to an informed approach, *congruent with the realities of practice* (Bower, 2005, p4).

Piecing together the interplay of psychological, emotional and social factors in a social work child protection assessment is highly complex, yet essential work. Identifying tentative links between social and emotional deprivation in childhood and its possible impact on parenting capabilities in adults is helpful in exploring factors which may become evident to social workers through similar fear inducing experiences described by Ferguson (2005) that were outlined above. An awareness of these patterns of relating may be useful to inform social workers engaging in child protection assessment work.

Learning to make sense of unconscious communications

Attempts to identify risk factors in parents and carers which may impact on children's well-being and development often dwell on specific diagnostic categories, for example where parents experience mental health conditions, have learning disabilities or drug and alcohol problems (Cleaver *et al.*, 2010). While it is clearly vital to assess the impact of these issues on the parenting of dependent children, many other parents are also living their adult lives in the aftermath of difficult early experiences, in part due to social and emotional deprivation that they may have experienced, which may have more subtle, 'sub-clinical' effects on their emotional development, in turn affecting their ability to parent successfully. This area is perhaps harder for social workers to navigate; it requires knowledge of both the theory and research into how social and emotional deprivation may lead to emotional and psychological difficulties in adults as well as the practical, interpersonal skills of knowing how to relate to 'difficult people' in order to assess risk to children in their care.

One attempt to look at the possible impact on parenting capacity of early childhood experiences of severe emotional abuse and deprivation is described by Howe (2005) in relation to borderline personality disorder. He shows that this form of personality disorder seems to be particularly associated with individuals who have experienced the high stress of traumatic physical or emotional abandonment or abuse as children. Describing the impact of post traumatic stress disorder, Allen (2001, cited in Howe, 2005, p167) suggests that *the essence of trauma is feeling terrified and alone*. Sometimes, experiences of deprivation will have occurred from the earliest ages when individuals were totally dependent on their caregivers to attune to their emotional needs and to protect them. Instead of internalising regular, reliable, emotionally responsive attention from their caregiver, the individual has developed a chaotic internal world, where others cannot be relied on, emotions cannot be contained and there is limited potential to form solid relationships with others.

In terms of risk management in child protection work, parents and carers can therefore respond in 'irrational' ways to professionals' attempts to create a positive working alliance; even covertly harming children when they appear to be co-operating. For example, in the case of Peter Connelly who was discussed earlier, his mother appeared at times to have shown professionals a dependent side of her personality; she asked for help and was thought to have a good relationship with professionals such that they were not able to imagine that she was involved in harming and failing to protect Peter. For a combination of reasons, Peter was not then examined properly by a paediatrician who might have helped the professionals to 'see' and take-in the possibility that he was suffering non-accidental injuries (Laming, 2009).

Social workers will often be working with parents who have had their share of chaotic emotional experiences in their early life without showing outward signs of, or having been diagnosed with, a personality disorder. Using psychoanalytic ideas however, an understanding of the unconscious defense mechanism of projection can be helpful in aiding professionals' understanding of how people can carry on functioning despite having significant emotional problems. Caring for needy, dependent children is challenging for any parent, but when the parent has had little containing, reliable and emotionally attuned parenting themselves, neediness in their own child can arouse extremely anxious feelings (Harvey, 2010). In psychoanalytic theory (Bion, 1962) the primitive unconscious defense mechanism of projection is thought to function to help the parent manage their anxiety. When anxious feelings are so overwhelming, they can be unconsciously projected out onto those nearby who are receptive. The feelings can be very hateful and angry or they may be more idealised and loving. Professionals can unconsciously take in either set of feelings, experiencing them as 'projective identification' (Bower, 2005). Clues that this is happening may be that the worker perhaps goes home feeling disturbed and upset, with feelings that they sense they do not 'own'. The social worker might be feeling things that seem alien to them, for example that they feel extremely angry or that they might abuse or harm someone, and this may be a clue in itself as to how the service user was feeling. Alternatively, the worker might feel that they are wonderful and caring, the service user having unconsciously projected warm and loving feelings in such a way as to stop the professional picking up on aggressive feelings, which could be hiding their ability to harm and abuse. It is in the latter case that the social worker can fall into the colluding, rescuing mode of relating, where it is hard to imagine that the parent or carer could harm their child. Either way, professionals need to take their feelings and examine them carefully through developing their own capacity to reflect and through having supervision available to them from someone experienced in helping to untangle and to make sense of such emotions.

CASE STUDY **3.1**

Jane, a white British girl of eight years of age, lives at home with her mother, Wendy, and brother, Jake, aged two. Jane's school has referred her for social work support as there has been deterioration in her physical appearance in the last six weeks and she has become socially withdrawn, wetting herself in class recently when the teacher raised her voice. Wendy does not come into school regularly, expecting Jane to make her own way between school and home. No one picked up the phone when the class teacher phoned home recently. The health visitor has seen Jake occasionally, but she feels that Wendy may be deliberately out when she calls for booked appointments. She has not seen the family in the last three months.

You are the social worker in the local duty team and have been allocated to do an initial assessment with the family. When you phone to book an appointment, a man comes on the phone who coolly, but firmly tells you that there is no need to visit as Jane has flu and 'everything is fine' at home. You ask to speak to Jane, but he refuses, saying she is sleeping. He also refuses to tell you his name or relationship to the family.

REFLECTION POINT

- *As you plan to visit the family, what thoughts and feelings go through your mind about what might be happening to Jane, Wendy and Jake?*

- *How would you prepare yourself practically and emotionally for the visit?*

- *What would you hope to achieve by the end of the visit and beyond?*

Comment

There are many unknowns in this case situation and it will be very important to keep an open mind and remain curious about what might be going on in the home. Carrying out agency checks may reveal concerns for domestic violence or substance misuse, for example, or nothing of that nature. It will be important to speak to the children alone, spending some time interacting with them through play and also creating the space during the visit to observe how they are responding to the adults in the home and to you as a new person in their lives. Making time afterwards to record what both children actually did and said, how the adults reacted to this and also how you felt about this will be important. You will need to ask yourself during and after the visit whether what the adults say in relation to your enquiries about Jane's welfare is coherent, but also does it feel right? Are you picking up on anything communicated non-verbally or do you leave with feelings or emotional responses that need to be further explored in supervision?

55

ACTIVITY 3.2

Ruch (2007b) looks at the kinds of support that may be helpful to social workers who are trying to engage vulnerable children and their families. Read her article and consider the following questions.

- *What opportunities are there within the team where you are based to carry out case discussion such as Ruch suggests?*

- *What could you do to encourage greater space to reflect on your casework?*

Comment

Ruch (2007b) looks at some of the features of social work teams which can enable workers to navigate difficult case work situations. She draws on Daniel (2005), a systemic psychotherapist and social worker, who describes how the social workers she has supervised repeatedly reveal certain characteristics. First, they can be overly certain that particular outcomes will occur; second, they seem to feel overly responsible for outcomes in the casework; third, they can feel undervalued, helpless or hopeless; and fourth, they can fall into blaming and pathologising others involved in a case. It is easy to see, given the emotional as well as practical dimensions of the work that have been outlined in this chapter, how such responses can come about in social workers.

Considering what might work to improve the situation, Ruch's prescription involves the idea that social workers should be supported in developing two kinds of thinking: *it needs to be emotionally informed, thoughtful thinking as well as the more prevalent practical and procedural thinking that dominates practice* (Ruch, 2007b, p375). A case-discussion model is then proposed in which the emotional impact of child protection work is explored regularly in teams. In this way, experiences such as those discussed in this chapter, fear, contamination, rescuing feelings and so on, can be opened up to discover what might be learnt, to help the case move forward. Ruch encourages the notion that social workers should not become too fixed in their views of casework situations. Instead, workers should remain curious about what is going on, coming up with hypotheses to inform the next steps to be taken.

Chapter summary

This chapter started by providing an overview of the history of child protection work in the UK and the continuing struggle to balance prevention and risk management, reflecting the dilemma of how both to respect the family's right to privacy and the need to safeguard children's welfare. After this, current themes in child protection were described, as were difficulties associated with the aftermath of several significant child death inquiries, the rise of managerialism in social work, the burden of expectations that affect individual social workers and the future of the profession of social work itself. A critical approach was then offered to the idea that outcomes for children at risk would be improved by simple changes to bureaucratic structures. Social workers need to identify and to learn to work with the complex emotional issues that are involved in engaging and assessing parents and children who have experienced social and emotional deprivation. Ideas were proposed to help make sense of some of the emotional dimensions of the work, including the need for workers to become reflective about their own felt response to working with parents who may be harming and abusing their children, or who have significant vulnerabilities. These feelings can then be taken to supervision or case discussion, so that social workers can explore and remain curious about the family dynamics they are facing in their practice, enabling hypotheses to be formed and thoughtful action to be taken. This always returns to the idea that children's experiences in families need to be seen in terms of relationships between them, their parents and the professionals who are trying to engage in working with them.

FURTHER READING

Bower, M (ed) (2005) *Psychoanalytic theory for social work practice: Thinking under fire.* London: Routledge.

This is an edited text which provides detailed systemic and psychoanalytic perspectives on the kinds of dilemmas facing front-line social workers. It is a useful source to help you to reflect and to make sense of the complex dynamics of practice.

Harvey, A (2010) Getting a grip on social work. *Journal of Social Work Practice*, 24 (2) 139-153.

This is a case study written by an experienced social worker who is trying to understand the complex dynamics of a case situation she has had to work with. Theory is closely integrated into the practice account, leading to an interesting and informative work. There are other articles, in this and other editions of this journal, which may be of interest.

Lonne, R, Parton, N, Thomson, J and Harries, M (2009) *Reforming child protection.* Abingdon: Routledge.

This is a fascinating account of child protection policy and practice issues, providing both historical and geographical comparisons, to help contemporary UK social work professionals reflect on the contexts in which they work.

Chapter 4

Family Intervention Projects: a holistic approach to working with families with multiple problems

Sarah Lewis-Brooke and Nikki Bradley

CHAPTER OBJECTIVES

If you are a registered social worker, this chapter will assist you to evidence post-registration training and learning. It relates to the national post-qualifying framework for social work education and training at the specialist level:

iv. *Draw on knowledge and understanding of service users' and carers' issues to actively contribute to strategies and practice which promote service users' and carers' rights and participation in line with the goals of choice, independence and empowerment.*

It will also help you to meet the Children and Families standards for social work:

iii. *Co-ordinating services in a multi-agency service delivery context, including the knowledge and skills required to ensure professional networks are able to meet complex needs, and where appropriate, undertake lead professional roles.*

ix. *Actively working with and empowering those affected by poverty, unemployment, homelessness, racism, homophobia, bullying and other forms of discrimination and disadvantage which impact on the lives of children and young people.*

x. *Working with parental mental health, drug and alcohol misuse, health, illness, disability and domestic violence, and the impact of these issues on children and young people.*

Introduction

Over the last ten years, there has been greater focus on parenting support initiatives, accompanied by increased surveillance of parents and how they manage their parenting role (Parton, 2006a). Parenting support was an integral part of Sure Start programmes, the development of Children's Centres and of early years provision, and was at the centre of *Every Child Matters* (DfES, 2003). The policy underpinning the *Every Child Matters* Green Paper

(DfES, 2003) was accompanied by a parenting fund, as it was recognised that parental support was a key determinant in improving children's lives. The fund was to be used to develop new parenting programmes, which would add to universal provision and also provide targeted and specialist support to parents of children where there were additional needs. In addition, there was a focus on using research evidence to develop and evaluate parenting and family support initiatives, with an accompanying concentration on outcomes (Moran, Ghate and van der Merwe, 2004; DoH, 2006; Duncan Smith, 2006; DCSF, 2010b).

In this chapter, we explore the Family Intervention Project (FIP) model, which was introduced in 2006. The model aims to support whole families where there are concerns about antisocial behaviour and entrenched problems requiring multi-agency interventions (DSCF, 2010b). A key feature is direct parental support. This chapter outlines the policy context within which FIPs were created. The *Think Family* document (SETF, 2008a) is discussed in relation to the FIP model of intervention, the research on which it is based, and the results of the early FIP evaluations. A case example is used to illustrate the FIPs' emphasis on holistic planning and intervention, the critical partnership between children and adult services, and a range of universal, targeted and specialist provision showing the depth and length of the intervention undertaken by the FIP service.

The development of Family Intervention Projects

Chapter 2 has already outlined the social policy context, which attempted to tackle poverty and social exclusion, so often seen as an *inseparable dyad* (Levitas *et al.*, 2007, p20). Social exclusion has been defined as:

> . . . a complex and multi-dimensional process. It involves the lack or denial of resources, rights, goods and services, and the inability to participate in the normal relationships and activities, available to the majority of people in a society, whether in economic, social, cultural or political arenas. It affects both the quality of life of individuals and the equity and cohesion of society as a whole.

(Levitas *et al.*, 2007, p9)

The previous Labour Government developed services that sought to tackle social exclusion within the context of family support services (Quinney, 2006). The debates at that time centred on whether policies concerning 'problem families' should focus on 'care or control'. The Labour Government (1997–2010) put itself firmly behind an approach which employed both 'carrot and stick'. Family Intervention Projects were introduced as part of the second stage in tackling antisocial behaviour, offering a range of holistic services including parenting support. Funding for the roll-out of FIPs was announced in the *Respect Action Plan* (RTF, 2006) with funding coming directly from central government. Further initiatives were funded in 2008 and 2009: Child Poverty FIPs (2008), aimed at providing a service to families where parents are unemployed and have significant barriers to work, such as mental health; and Youth Crime FIPs (2009), which targeted families where research has shown that children are at risk of offending. In 2010, there were 32 Child Poverty FIPS and 20 Youth Crime FIPs across England. The rest were the original Antisocial Behaviour FIPs. The newer specialist FIPs were expected to use the same model as the original Antisocial Behaviour FIPs. Throughout England, there are over 100 FIPs located in different services, with some managed within children's social care, others within education and community safety services, and some FIPs have been set up in voluntary sector agencies, or registered housing providers.

Context

The precursor to the national introduction and subsequent roll-out of the FIP initiative by the Labour Government was the publication of evaluations of a residential unit run by Action for Children in Dundee in 2005, where families with multiple problems lived on site for an extended period (Parr, 2009). Multi-agency partners worked closely together to offer a consistent approach based on a sanction and reward model for family members. While moving families out of their communities and into residential units was central to this first project, as the model has developed, few FIPs have seen the need to include the residential component but have worked with families in their local communities.

In addition to this project's evaluation, various government departments were also interested in targeting resources to families facing significant and entrenched disadvantage. The Social Exclusion Task Force (SETF) in their Families at Risk Review (SETF, 2007) reported on data collated by the Department of Works and Pensions' (DWP). The review estimated that, in 2004–05, 140,000 families in Britain had entrenched, multiple problems (two per cent of all families in Britain). Those families were ten times more likely to be involved with the police and eight times more likely to have children who were excluded from school. The Cabinet Office used the findings to justify funding projects that would seek to improve the life chances for the children in families with complex and multiple problems and make significant savings to the public purse (SETF, 2007). The Family at Risk Review (2007) identified that the annual cost of exclusion from school amounted to £46 million per annum and that antisocial behaviour costs £3.4 billion a year. The report also identified that 63 per cent of boys whose fathers have been in prison are eventually convicted themselves and that children from the five per cent most disadvantaged families are 50 times more likely to experience multiple disadvantages at the age of 30 than children of families with no identified problems. Sixty per cent of children with low literacy rates at the age of 10 years also have parents with low literacy scores and children who experience parental conflict and domestic violence are more likely to go on to experience this as adults (DCSF, 2009b).

The Social Exclusion Task Force also used the research of Fahmy *et al.* (2009) which used the Bristol Social Exclusion Matrix (B-SEM) (Levitas *et al.*, 2007) to consider the depth of social exclusion experienced by working-age adults without children over the age of 25 years in order to look at protective factors. The B-SEM measured people's experience of life against three domains with further sub-domains of potential exclusion:

> *Quality of life (health and well-being, living environment, crime harm and criminalisation); resources (material/economic resources, access to private and public resources, social resources); and participation (economic participation, culture, education, skills, social participation, political and civic participation).*

> (Levitas, *et al.*, 2007, pp117–118)

The research suggested that 2.6 million adults experience multi-dimensional disadvantage at any one point. However Fahmy *et al.* (2009) found that key factors such as finding employment, having a partner, being childless and high self-esteem in adolescence were protective factors in not becoming socially excluded. The Labour Government therefore decided to fund the FIP service, which aimed to reduce the number of families caught in the inter-generational patterns of unemployment, crime and dysfunction.

Family Intervention Projects

The first FIPs were specifically set up to target antisocial behaviour (ASB FIPs) and are a non-statutory service offering voluntary support services to families. Their intervention plans sought to develop the protective factors identified in the research of Levitas *et al.* (2009) to maximise the potential for families to participate in society. The teams comprised of multi-disciplinary workers, who brought expertise to the services offered to the families from: social work; probation; housing; early years; education; youth work; youth justice; adult services, particularly mental health and drug and alcohol services; and domestic violence backgrounds. All workers use the expertise from their discipline to disseminate knowledge to the rest of the team. The approach is not dissimilar to the Common Assessment Framework (CAF) (DCSF, 2006a) model, drawing all relevant agencies together to gather information about the family and to facilitate co-ordinated planning across these agencies. A key worker is chosen, normally the FIP worker from one of the professional groups listed above. The key worker is proactive in planning, monitoring and undertaking a significant amount of direct work with the family.

CASE STUDY 4.1

The Williams family is a white working class extended family. Seven people live in a two-bedroom flat on the fifth floor of an inner-city block of social housing. There are no adult males living in the house. Annie (74), the grandmother, is in poor health, smokes heavily and has severely neglected her own self-care for years. Her daughter, Rose (48), mother of Lydia (26), Carly (14) and Donna (12), is agoraphobic and hasn't left the family home for more than six years. Food is purchased for the family online. Lydia has two children, Jack (7) and Sara (9), who are of dual heritage. Their father, Peter, is in prison serving a seven-year sentence. Both children have poor school attendance, and often arrive late, smelling of urine. Carly and Donna are on the brink of school exclusion for poor attendance and challenging behaviour. They are reported to spend their evenings on the stairwell drinking with local men. Neighbours suspect that they are 'prostituting themselves for drugs'. There are nine cats in the family home and the neighbours complain about the soiled cat litter that is regularly dumped onto the balcony.

The adults are resistant to engaging with services and usually do not answer the door to any visitors, although there has been some social work support in the past. Both education and housing services are concerned about the children and the housing officer has observed that the house is in a poor state with the beds and carpets soaked in cats' urine and excrement. As a result of this the housing provider has initiated eviction proceedings and made a referral to the Local Authority Children and Families Social Work Department due to safeguarding concerns.

The family were referred to the FIP initially by the housing provider. The FIP worker visited the day of the referral with the housing officer. Following this visit the family was discussed by the Social Inclusion Panel, a multi-agency forum, which is a critical part of the FIP process. In addition, an initial assessment was undertaken by a child and family social worker, given the safeguarding concerns about the children's welfare.

> **REFLECTION POINT**
>
> - *If you were the social worker from Children's Services who had been trying to work with this family, what would be your most pressing concern?*
>
> - *If you lived next door to the family, what would concern you most?*
>
> - *If you were Carly, what would you say about your home life?*
>
> - *If you were the housing officer, what would be your most pressing concern?*
>
> - *If you were Rose, what might be your biggest worry?*

Comment

The perceptions of the different people affected by such a complex set of circumstances will vary and will depend on where they are in the network – whether they are part of the family, part of the neighbourhood or in the professional network. An awareness of each other's concerns is likely to affect how effective the partnership working will be. Consider the following.

- The family feel overwhelmed by their problems and believe there are no solutions.

- The children feel shame and embarrassment and want life to be different.

- The housing officer is primarily concerned with the payment of rent, maintaining a good quality external environment and reducing complaints from the community.

- The social worker is aware of her responsibilities to safeguard and promote the well-being of children under Section 47 and Section 17 of the 1989 Children Act but may also be concerned about how to engage with a family who have resisted professional intervention in the past.

Using the FIP model was an appropriate option here in order to tackle the long-standing and multi-generational problems this family are experiencing.

The FIP model

The development of the FIP model of intervention was driven centrally by the Family Delivery Team (FDT) in the Families at Risk Division (FARD) of the DCSF. Since May 2010, the responsibilities and functions of this team have been transferred to the Department of Education. The FDT provided direct support and guidance to every FIP, and FIP specialists based in the FDT provided a linking role between local areas to ensure that good practice and integrated provision could be shared and evaluated (DCSF, 2010b).

The core components of the FIP model are:

- a dedicated key worker with a low caseload and a persistent and assertive working style who takes the lead in co-ordinating the different agencies and doing the direct work;

- the family has to agree to the intervention and is involved at all stages in identifying and solving their problems;

- whole family assessment ensures the needs of the whole family are met;
- the contract sets out the expected changes in behaviour, the support that will be vided and the sanctions applied if the family does not comply;
- intensive and structured support enables the key worker to focus on their families as long as necessary to achieve change;
- a co-ordinated and integrated response from partner agencies, which agree objectives and share resources to resolve the family's difficulties. The work begins with a multi-agency forum which considers the referral; and
- data is collected by the National Centre for Social Research (NatCen).

(SETF, 2007, p9; DCSF, 2010b; DCSF, 2010d; FDT, 2008)

There is clear guidance concerning the stages of interventions, which overall continue on average for 12–14 months, and is common to each type of FIP, although each intervention is tailored to the individual family's needs. It is important to note that while the intervention offered is of a voluntary nature, the families are made aware of the consequences of not co-operating. The FIPs work with agencies which have statutory powers. An example of this is that a housing provider might put a stay on eviction proceedings, while the family work with the FIP. Options might involve moving families away from the sites of antisocial behaviour into 'dispersed accommodation', where their tenancies are not secure until completion of the FIP tasks. These Family Intervention Tenancies (FITs) were created by the Housing Regeneration Act 2008 (DCSF, 2010b). The process from referral to closure is laid out in the intervention model (DCSF, 2010d), which highlights the need to take a multi-agency perspective, including the perspective of the family. The process is punctuated with regular review meetings.

> Cases should only be closed where there is clear evidence that the agreed outcomes for the family have been achieved. FIP workers should continue to monitor and do follow-up visits for the first 12 months after closure.

(DCSF, 2010d, p1)

CASE STUDY *4.1* (CONT.)

An initial agreement was made with the Williams family. The housing provider made a referral to the Local Authority Children and Families Social Work Department, which then became a partner agency. The social worker was the named key worker, due to the safeguarding concerns. It was agreed that the FIP would start work with the family immediately. Lydia agreed to Section 20 Children Act 1989 accommodation of the two youngest children to allow the FIP worker and the housing provider to secure alternative housing for her and the children. Eviction proceedings were temporarily stayed on the condition that the family had daily contact with the FIP worker and they developed a contract with her to this effect. Annie agreed to an assessment of her needs by Adult Social Care. Rose agreed that the FIP worker could work with her youngest children at school. The housing provider arranged an external clean-up of the balcony. An area of disagreement was that the cats were removed by an animal welfare agency without the agreement of the family, although they had been formally warned about the unsatisfactory living conditions. Annie and Rose refused to work with the FIP worker but Lydia did agree to do so and attended the necessary meetings.

ng questions:

f the children's social worker in this case study? How did it differ
vorker?

...y s right to self-determination balanced with the need to take protective action in relation to child neglect?

Comment

The children's social worker and the FIP worker share a responsibility to safeguard and promote the well-being of children (the Children Acts 1989 and 2004) The children's social worker has a statutory role with duties to investigate whether a child has suffered or is likely to suffer from significant harm (Section 47, the Children Act 1989). It is their role to accommodate children under Section 20 of the Children Act 1989 should this be necessary and should those with parental responsibility agree. The FIP worker may or may not be a qualified social worker but has a non-statutory role. If children have a child protection plan or a children in need plan, the social worker from children's services becomes their key worker and if the FIP remains involved it is as a support service. The roles are set out in *Working Together to Safeguard Children* (DCSF, 2010a, p290) which decrees how individuals and organisations should work together to safeguard and promote the welfare of children.

When dealing with such complex situations one needs to look at the balance between the needs of the individuals within the family and society as a whole and the needs of children to be safeguarded from harm. The Children Act 1989 (Part 1) identifies the needs of children as paramount in any intervention by a statutory agency. Section 47 of the Children Act outlines the duty of the local authority to investigate any situation where children may be at risk of significant harm.

Contracts

The tasks for all the workers and each family member are set out in an explicit contract using plain language. The time frame and the consequences of non-completion and completion are explicitly explained. Many of the tasks are drawn up by the family as it is recognised that the starting point should be working on areas that the family prioritise. Within the contract the other priorities and responsibilities of all the services involved are also recorded. In the case study, the housing provider agreed to clear up the external areas as that was their priority. No one has a mandate to interfere with the inside of the house unless it is assessed as being likely to cause 'significant harm' to the children. In this case, the children's services social worker assessed the two older children as needing a child protection plan. The younger two children were not subjects of a child protection plan, as Lydia agreed to the children being accommodated. Once the family were rehoused they had a children in need plan. These plans worked in parallel with the FIP contract (see Table 4.1).

Table 4.1 Example of part of a contract for the Williams family

Problem that has been identified	Responsible person and role	What needs to be done	By when?	Consequence if this is completed	Consequence if this is not completed
Sara and Jack are often late to school.	Lydia. FIP worker to teach skills in building a routine.	Lydia to ensure that S and J have an evening routine that ensures enough sleep and that they wake up in time to have breakfast and travel to school on time.	Next Team Around the Family (TAF) review in six weeks' time.	Sara and Jack will begin to catch up in their learning. They will become more involved in their school and with friends.	Sara and Jack will continue to fall behind at school which will affect their life chances in the future. Primary school will consider legal action for non-attendance.
Rose is unable to leave her house. She has to rely on internet shopping and other family members to do things for her.	Rose, the FIP worker and the Community Mental Health Team or another similar service.	Rose and the FIP worker to consider Rose's hopes and aspirations for the future and put together a plan that might begin to help her reach those aims.	Next TAF review in six weeks' time.	By building a trusting relationship, Rose and the FIP worker will understand what is important to Rose and how to support her to become more socially active.	Services may misunderstand what is important to Rose and may not be able to offer her the best service. Rose will remain socially isolated.
The family are finding it difficult to manage their money.	Budget coaches for Annie, Rose and Lydia	FIP worker to accompany budget coaches to the family home to complete a check that everyone is claiming full benefits and to give advice about how the family income could be best used.	In four weeks' when the bulk of the home cleaning has taken place.	The family will be confident that they have their full benefit entitlement. The family will gain more ideas about how to avoid debt and how to get the best from their income.	The family may continue in debt and the risk of bailiff action for catalogue debt will increase. The housing provider will have to take action for rent arrears.

- *Take a few moments to consider the key components of the contract. How might you use contracts in your work to improve communication with families and build up the family's efficacy?*

Think Family 2007

The FIP services were included in the *Think Family* initiative in 2007. The *Think Family* approach emanated from the *Families at Risk Review* (SETF, 2007) and the response to the review *Think Family: Improving the Life Chances for Families at Risk* (SETF, 2008a). From April 2009, all local authorities received increased funding to support the introduction of programmes aimed at providing parenting support, such as Family Intervention Projects. (DCSF, 2010b, pp20–22) This source of funding is now being reviewed by the Coalition Government. The funding has been given to local authorities for the year (2010–11) but is no longer ring-fenced to be used solely for the specialist FIPs.

There are four principles underpinning the *Think Family* approach.

> *No wrong door: Any part of the service will be able to advise and if necessary signpost a service user on to other services. Staff will be alert to wider issues within a family and will see any engagement as an opportunity to identify need and direct support to the wider family.*

> *Look at whole family: Both adults and children's services take into account family circumstances and responsibilities. In particular adult services see their clients as parents and ensure that they are fully supported to fulfil their parental responsibilities.*

> *Build on the family: Services start with the family's strengths. Practitioners work in partnership with families, recognising and promoting resilience and supporting them to build up aspirations and capabilities.*

> *Provide support tailored to the need: Tailored and family-centred packages of support are offered to all families at risk.*

(SETF, 2008a, p7)

This initiative builds on the philosophy underpinning the Children Act 2004 of agencies recognising their corporate responsibility and working collaboratively with other agencies in providing services to families. The thinking behind this model is that service users might experience a more 'joined-up' approach to service provision and professionals might work better together as they understand the whole service provision. One of the challenges for this approach is that, in order for this initiative to work well, workers in adult and children's services need to have a good understanding of service provision provided throughout both departments (SETF, 2008a).

Inter-collaborative work

It was the fact that it was all different organisations that led from one another that helped me personally to grow into the person who I am.

(Service user, *Think Family* video, 2008)

A strength of the FIP model is that it accepts that one service cannot solve all the problems identified for families with multiple and entrenched problems. The resulting focus on using the expertises of a range of services has been an important part of the FIP model, but it is not unique to FIP. Social workers are increasingly expected to work collaboratively with partner agencies in the service users' interests (Children Act 2004; Quinney, 2006). Multi-agency working can be challenging as agencies have different functions in relating to the family and different ways of working, and communication between agencies is critical in ensuring that service provision is effective.

- *In the case study about the Williams family, how was effective working between the agencies modelled?*

Comment

The three agencies worked together to gain access to the Williams family flat. No agency, apart from the housing agency had succeeded in gaining access in the past. All of the agencies participated in putting together a supportive plan that acknowledged the family's priorities as well as the priorities of the multi-disciplinary network and individual organisations.

ACTIVITY **4.2**

- *What theories do you think underpin this model?*

Comment

The model is underpinned by a number of theoretical frameworks that can be adapted to suit the application of the model to specific practice contexts. We have highlighted the core tenets of the main theoretical models used within FIP and invite you to investigate one theoretical approach for yourself:

- **Maslow's Hierarchy of Needs:** The model owes much of its approach to an understanding of Maslow's pyramid model of a hierarchy of need (1954) in which a person's potential to function will depend on having their needs met. Maslow ranks human needs in a hierarchy in which physiological survival needs have to be satisfied first before the person can focus on their other needs: safety; love/belonging; esteem; and self-actualisation. Maslow argued that each tier of the pyramid needed to be achieved before the person could move to the next level. Many of the families worked with are operating on a survival level located on the first two levels of Maslow's triangle. This can potentially block their capacity to see the services offered by external agencies as useful or relevant to them. For example, a person who is concerned that they are about to be evicted may not be able to focus on the long-term impact for the children of their non-attendance at school. The FIP contract often works with problems concerned with survival first so that families can relax and begin to work on their other needs – to meet their children's emotional needs, to become useful members of their community and to be respected by others. However, these needs are written into the contract to acknowledge them from the outset with an action plan and time frame.

- **Strengths-based models**: The *Think Family* model stresses the importance of working from a strengths-based assessment, believing as Rogers (1967) did that families are most likely to successfully make changes that they have engaged in, by using their own experiences as a resource base and by their making sense of those experiences. The worker acts as a coach in continually pointing out the achievements of the service user as a motivator to continue through difficult phases (Saleeby, 2009).

- **Social learning theory:** The FIP model uses social learning theory with sanctions and rewards as a way of creating incentives for service users to change engrained patterns of behaviour. The model is optimistic. One of the key ideas expressed by theorists about this model is that, as patterns of behaviour can be learned, they can also be unlearned. For example, a non-attending teenager might be rewarded with a trip out with friends or decorating their bedroom with the young person once they are reintegrated into school. Bandura's (1977) ideas of modelling desired behaviour can be seen to influence the workers' interventions.

- **Task-centred approaches:** The FIP model with its explicit contract can seem very goal-orientated. Goals are useful on several levels. The service users negotiate the goals and some of their priorities are worked on. The worker works on establishing a trusting, supportive relationship that builds up the self-esteem and self-efficacy of the service user. Traits of the task-centred model (Reid and Shyne, 1969) can be seen to be applied: the service user identifies what needs to change, the worker values the contribution of the service user and encourages them to complete their tasks and to reflect on how they have achieved each goal in order to build up the service users' problem-solving skills and their belief in their own efficacy.

ACTIVITY 4.3

- *The FIP and* Think Family *approaches owe much of their development to the work of Bronfenbrenner (1979) and ecological theory. Spend 15 minutes investigating the main principles of this theory and apply the theory to the Williams case study.*

Comment

In the Williams case study, the work concentrated in the first instance on Lydia, who was the member of the family most open to the idea of change and perhaps with the most capacity to achieve change with support. By helping her to move with her children, the family's overcrowding was addressed and the move empowered her to start to make parenting decisions about her children that enabled them to attend school regularly. Lydia saw the benefits of the new more orderly flat, and then influenced her mother and grandmother on the benefits of making changes. Germain and Gitterman (1995) believe that ecological concepts focus on:

> . . . *people's strengths, their innate push toward health; the modification of the environment as needed so that they sustain and promote the well-being and the need to raise the level of the person/environment to make it fit for individuals, families, groups and communities.*

> (Germain and Gitterman, 1995, p817)

Relationship-based social work

There has been a resurgence of interest in relationship-based social work in the last few years (Sudbery, 2002; Howe, 2008; Ruch *et al.*, 2010). This theoretical framework is critical to the success of this model (Parr, 2009), and is discussed further in Chapter 3 of this book. It underpins all of the other approaches adapted in the FIP model. Many of the families in receipt of FIP services have already had countless interventions but what they consistently reported was that they had not felt listened to previously (DCSF, 2010c). This is consistent with the research findings about what service users most value (MacDonald and Sheldon, 1997; Juhilla, 2009). FIP service users often consider the relationship with the worker to be the most important part of the intervention (Parr, 2009; DCSF, 2010c).

> *This is the most I have felt listened to in my life. I can't believe how quickly things have changed since I've been working with the project.*

> (Father, aged 26, DCSF, 2010c, p11)

Many of the families have low self-esteem and lack trust in professionals. To overcome this, the worker builds a trusting relationship over time. The relationship has several key features. The worker models desired behaviour, such as problem-solving skills, diffusing conflict and working collaboratively with professional partner agencies, which can bring resources and help solve problems. The FIP worker builds up the self-esteem of the individuals within the family by facilitating the service user to initiate their own changes and take pride in newly developed skills. The professionals also reinforce boundaries and consequences of actions through using the contract. During the initial stage, the families may become dependent on their FIP worker as they build up their own skills. This is the first step towards independence. It is within the security of the trusting relationship that service users are encouraged to try out new skills, whether this is in seeking employment, getting their children to school or exerting boundaries with their children. As the work progresses, the intention is that the service user recognises their own efficacy and no longer relies on the FIP worker to solve their problems (Parr, 2009).

Tensions: use of authority, tough love or empowerment

Jordan (2000) cautioned the social work profession about the implications of being expected to roll out the previous Labour Government's 'tough love policies', and warned that the creative opportunities for intervention were most likely to be found in sectors of the helping professions who are not qualified social workers. It could be argued that FIPs, working mostly outside social work agencies, have been given the freedom to develop more creative ways of engaging with hitherto hard to reach families. Although this work is of a non-statutory nature, it focuses on achieving inter-generational change for families and can arguably make a contribution to safeguarding children (DCSF, 2010c, p6). The FIP model balances more authoritarian aspects with those of nurturing and empowerment of the service user. This approach is a useful model which could be developed further in statutory social work.

Evaluation of FIPs

In February 2007, the National Centre for Social Research (NatCen) set up a web-based information system to collect comprehensive data on all families referred to FIPs and on the impact of the intervention (see **www.natcen.ac.uk**). The data is completed by FIP workers in England and Wales and is collated bi-annually. The data collated on the 14 October 2009 has been summarised below and compares the most recent data with that collected in the previous year.

Key findings

By 14 October 2009, 2,734 families had been offered and 2,655 had accepted an Antisocial Behaviour (ASB) FIP intervention.

- Of those families offered a FIP intervention, 1,030 (38 per cent) completed the intervention with a formal planned exit.

- 410 families (15 per cent of all those offered the intervention) failed to engage at different stages of the FIP intervention.

The impact of the intervention

Based on the 1,030 families who completed an ASB FIP intervention by mid-October 2009:

- the proportion of families involved in antisocial behaviour (ASB) had decreased from 89 per cent to 32 per cent;

- the percentage of families with four or more ASB problems declined from 45 per cent to five per cent;

- the proportion of families facing one or more housing enforcement actions declined from 50 per cent to 14 per cent;

- families experiencing truancy, exclusion and bad behaviour at school declined from 57 per cent to 24 per cent;

- families in which there were concerns about child protection declined from 24 per cent to 14 per cent;

- families affected by a mental health problem declined from 39 per cent to 29 per cent;

- families in which domestic violence was a concern declined from 23 per cent to nine per cent (a 61 per cent reduction);

- families with drug or substance misuse declined from 33 per cent to 18 per cent (a 70 per cent reduction); and

- families with drinking problems/alcoholism declined from 30 per cent to 14 per cent (a 53 per cent reduction).

Early indications suggest that these outcomes were sustained for the 108 families who have been followed up 9–14 months after they exited from a FIP intervention (NatCen, 2010).

Evaluation

The projects are at an early stage of evaluation and there is a strong need for more robust research studies to be set up, some of which should be longitudinal studies evaluating the sustainability of the intervention. It is, of course, impossible to offer a long-term view of the impact of the FIP interventions at this stage. However, current figures appear to show some positive trends in terms of improved outcomes for some families. However, there are a number of points regarding the evaluation:

- the statistics are collated by the FIP workers who may not have been trained to record accurately and who have a vested interest in the outcomes of the FIPs;

- the evaluation is not independent as it offers information about outcome patterns only;

- the evaluation is not a research study so we cannot know which parts of the FIP inter-vention work best for which families and why, because there are a multitude of different variables that will affect potential outcomes;

- NatCen have used focus groups with service users, who have provided some insight into the interplay of variables in their own circumstances.

Beecham and Sinclair (2007) outline a model to assess the calculations for costings of such services and also offer recommendations for improving the evidence base within children's social care. The DCSF (2009a) devised the *Family Intervention Projects Negative Costing Tool*. This compares the cost of the intervention with the predicted costs had the interven-tion not occurred. FIPs are expected to use the tool to calculate their cost effectiveness (DCSF, 2009c).

Limitations of the FIP model

Although the FIP model has many strengths, there are inherent weaknesses both within the model and within the methodology of the evaluation design. The Labour Government framed its evaluations in terms of costs to individual families, to society and to the public purse. This has changed the discourse about 'problem families' to one of predicting crime prevention (Powell, 2001; Parr, 2009). By measuring outcomes in terms of whether criminal or antisocial behaviour has decreased, the young person is criminalised instead of being seen as deserving help in their own right as a person in need (Parr, 2009). Additionally, effectiveness is dependent on multi-agency collaboration, as enforcement action can only be undertaken by statutory agencies. Where this collaboration is weak or not underpinned by a strong strategic framework, the effectiveness of FIPs can be undermined. The model would appear to need workers and managers who are highly skilled in building supportive problem-solving relationships across and between different agencies. The FIP workers face highly complex situations where families have been unable to function and are asked to work with parents so that the parents can then provide nurturing environments in which their children can grow to be confident of their place in society. The workers step into a world of uncertainty, difficulty, fear and lack of hope. There is no prescription for success and workers need to be emotionally resilient to offer the families a safe base from which to explore the idea that they can make beneficial changes (Parton and O'Bryne, 2000).

However, since 2010, local authorities have faced cuts to the area-based grant, which includes the funding for FIPs. The Coalition Government has removed the ring-fenced status of the *Think Family* grant which ensured the FIPs' funding. Although the Conservative Social Justice Think Tank has highlighted the need to focus on families to change outcomes for children (Duncan Smith, 2006), it is unclear what the effect of cuts will be on services. It may be difficult for local authorities to maintain funding of non-statutory services as they have to balance their reduced budgets, and therefore to avoid moving the money into statutory services and away from FIPs.

ACTIVITY **4.4**

Take a few minutes to reflect on what you have read so far.

- *What are the main features of this model? Why does it work?*
- *What are the differences and similarities between these teams and the one you work in?*

Comment

The most important aspects in making this family-led model work would appear to be the skill and motivation of the worker, their flexibility and ability to be responsive, and their ability to work with social work values of empowerment, respect and value for the uniqueness of the individual (Parr, 2009). If the pivotal point in the intervention is the relationship dynamic, then this model is transferable. The focus of intervention in social care settings would need to move away from assessment and instead involve social workers doing more direct work with smaller caseloads with families, using the skills and knowledge they gain on qualifying and post-qualifying courses. Social workers would need the support of their managers and effective clinical supervision is seen as critical to support this demanding task. Support at a strategic level is also required to foster strong working alliances with partner agencies, such as the police and registered social landlords.

The availability of the worker is seen as crucial in developing relationships with families who have little trust in external services. An expectation that the worker will work antisocial hours is written into the contract of FIP workers (DCSF, 2010c).

Conclusion

In this chapter, we have explored the context which introduced the Family Intervention Projects. The particular model has been examined to consider what makes it effective in working with some families. Early evaluations suggest that this could be an effective model. FIP workers report satisfaction in what they do and this may have implications for retention of workers. FIP is a model that was developed to work with the most socially excluded families who have been traditionally the most difficult to engage. The success of this model would appear to be linked to its ability to be creative in its work with families and to offer intensive and at times long-term intervention to families, using the relationship between worker and service user to build up self-esteem, and to model problem-solving skills and relationship skills. However, it is acknowledged that front-line child and family social workers with high numbers of referrals would have difficulty in adopting this model in its entirety, unless it was supported by a management strategy and funding. The key components of the model, including the quality of the relationship, however, are transferable to any part of social care and the skills and values employed are at the heart of good social work practice (Parr, 2009; Trevithick, 2005).

FURTHER READING

Department for Children, Schools and Families (2009) *Think Family tool kit.* London: HMSO. Available at **www.dcsf.gov.uk**

This is a comprehensive guide, clearly written, with a lot of case examples. It summarises the research evidence which identified the need for a different approach to working with families most at risk of poor outcomes for their children due to entrenched, inter-generational family problems. Practice guidance Note 4 of the *Think Family Tool Kit* (updated in 2010) looks particularly at the FIP model of intervention.

Jordan, B (2000) Conclusion: Tough Love: Social Work Practice in UK Society, in Stepney, P and Ford, D (eds) *Social work models, methods and theories: A framework for practice.* Dorset: Russell House Publishers.

In this chapter, Jordan succinctly and clearly considers the dilemmas of using 'sanction and rewards' approaches. He cautions against social workers using purely 'carrot and stick' interventions.

Parr, S (2009) Family Intervention Projects: A site of social work practice. *British Journal of Social Work* (39), 1256–1273.

Parr's article describes a small-scale study evaluating a FIP and facilitates our thinking on the strengths and deficits of the model.

Social Exclusion Task Force (2008) *Think Family Video.* London: HMSO. Available at: **www.cabinetoffice.gov.uk/social_exclusion_task_force/families_at_risk/think_videos.aspx**

This video succinctly explains the holistic nature of the *Think Family* approach and the main features of the model. It also has examples of feedback from service users and workers on what it is like to use this approach.

Sudbery, J (2002) Key features of therapeutic social work: The use of relationship. *Journal of Social Work Practice* 16(2), 149–162.

Howe, D (2008) *The emotionally intelligent social worker.* Basingstoke: Palgrave Macmillan.

The quality of the relationship that is allowed to develop over time between the highly skilled worker and the service user would appear to be a significant factor in determining good outcomes for the families who have worked with FIPs. Howe's book and Sudbery's article consider the importance of the relationship. Read more about why and how the relationship needs to be employed as a tool in an effective working alliance between worker and service user.

Chapter 5

Skills in direct work with looked after children, their carers and families

Michelle Lefevre

CHAPTER OBJECTIVES

If you are a registered social worker, this chapter will assist you to evidence post-registration train-ing and learning. It relates to the national post-qualifying framework for social work education and training at the specialist level:

iii. Consolidate and consistently demonstrate in direct work with users of social care services and carers the full range of social work competences across all the units of the National Occupational Standards for Social Work and in the context of one area of specialist social work practice at the advanced level.

vii. Work creatively and effectively as a practitioner, researcher, educator or manager and take a leading role in a context of risk, uncertainty, conflict and contradiction or where there are complex challenges and a need to make informed and balanced judgements.

It will also help you to meet the Children and Families standards for social work:

1. Working in partnership with children, young people, their families or carers, including effective:

- *communication;*

- *support;*

- *advocacy; and*

- *involvement of children and young people in decision making.*

Introduction

Effective engagement, communication and direct work play a central role in involving, assessing, supporting and intervening with children and young people who are looked after, and with their families and carers (Department for Education and Skills, 2005a). Social work-ers, though, do not always feel secure in their practice skills. Many do little direct work and seem to have lost confidence in both their abilities and the importance of face-to-face con-tact and more in-depth involvement (Commission for Social Care Inspection, 2005). This is not welcomed by families. What children in care actually want is a *continuous personal relationship* with their social worker, one that enables them to talk about their worries (Le Grand, 2007, p5). Instead, some children say they *'haven't met their social workers enough to get to know them or find them difficult to get hold of'* (Morgan, 2006, p14). Others find social workers unreliable and that what they say cannot be counted on (DfES, 2007a). Parents want to be able to trust and work with practitioners in contested or emotionally charged situations and need to feel respected, involved, and included in planning and decision making about their children's lives. They can end up feeling frightened, marginalised and disempowered where they are given little opportunity for this (Dumbrill, 2006).

Sometimes, these thwarted family expectations arise because practitioners are overwhelmed with the administrative aspects of their role, such as the huge mound of paperwork that results when a child comes into care, or the logistical challenges of managing contact in complex family situations (de Boer and Coady, 2007). Being bombarded with the emotional pain and distress of children and their families and being required to make complex, finely balanced decisions may also evoke defences in practitioners which prevent them from fully engaging with or responding to the experiences of children in care and their families (Ferguson, 2005; Rustin, 2005).

This chapter seeks to support practitioners in thinking further about the challenges and demands inherent in their role and how they might enhance their capabilities in direct work through expanding their knowledge base, use of self, and skills. The fictional practice vignette of the Carroll family, who live in England, will be used to explore approaches to practice.

The direct work role with children, families and carers

CASE STUDY 5.1

Members of the Carroll family:

- *The children: Alana, 13, and Toby, 7;*
- *Their mother: Faith Carroll, aged 31, white English;*
- *Their father: Johnny, 37, black Scottish, lives in Scotland and has minimal contact with the children;*
- *Mother's partner: Dave, 28, white English.*

The relationship between Faith and Dave has been characterised by mutual rows, substance misuse, and Dave's periodic violence towards Faith. Children's services have been concerned for some time about the level of neglect and emotional harm that the children have been experiencing. Dave's violence has now been extended to Toby, who has recently sustained a bruised eye and shattered eardrum. Attempts to resolve concerns and engage the parents separately and together in working towards safer parenting have not ultimately been successful. The initial plan for the Local Authority to apply for an Interim Care Order with an Exclusion Order attached, so that the children could remain at home with their mother, foundered when it became clear that Faith wanted Dave to return and was secreting him into the household. Consequently the children are now about to be placed in foster care under an Interim Care Order by the social worker, Marina.

Comment

With a situation such as this, there is a risk that social workers like Marina may become preoccupied with the more administrative and managerial aspects of their role, such as writing court reports, finding placements and filling in essential paperwork. Where parents are angry about child protection interventions and children are frightened and confused about what is happening, it may be all too tempting sometimes, too, for workers to want to avoid the uncertain, troubling and challenging nature of conversations and interactions with children, young people and their parents. These must be proactively embraced, not only to meet statutory requirements for consultation and provision of information, but to work towards improved outcomes for children and their families. The main purpose of direct work at the initial stage would be for the social worker to: inform the children and their parents about why care proceedings have been instituted and what will happen next; consult with the children and their parents about the move to a foster placement and prepare them for this; prepare the foster carers for the placement; and support everyone in expressing and working through their thoughts, feelings, fears and uncertainties.

Depending on how the situation moves forward, the direct work role could then develop in a range of ways. In a situation such as the Carroll family's, assessments will be taking place so meetings will be required with all family members, singly and together, to learn more about their intentions, concerns, strengths and struggles. Often, intervention overlaps with assessment, providing parents with an opportunity to develop their parenting capacity and have their motivation, potential and achievements appraised in a more dynamic way (Farnfield, 2008). Family work could be used to rebuild the relationship between Johnny and his children and negotiate with the extended family regarding new and creative strategies for safe care of the children. Therapeutic work might be needed to enable the children to come to terms with what has occurred and to support the adults in working through the unresolved care and control conflicts which have prevented them from parenting effectively (Reder and Duncan, 1999). If children are to remain in care in the longer term then life story work could help them to make more sense of complex and unexplained events, promote their self-identity, and enable them to develop a coherent life narrative (Burnell and Vaughan, 2008). Children, birth parents, existing carers and adopters or long-term carers would also need careful preparation for the transition to a permanent placement in order to reduce the risk of later placement disruption and improve emotional and psychological outcomes (Romaine *et al.*, 2007).

Effective direct work through this range of roles and tasks is emotionally and intellectually demanding and will require practitioners to employ a wide range of knowledge, ethical commitments, emotional capacities, personal qualities, skills, and techniques (Lefevre, 2008). Practitioners will need to be aware of the kinds of theoretical perspectives, informed by research evidence, which help practitioners to understand more about children and their families and how particular life issues and social environments affect them. For example, experiences of abuse, trauma, oppression, discrimination and social exclusion all affect family members' readiness and ability to communicate with others. However, 'practical-moral knowledge' is also required, so that practitioners may critically draw on such knowledge to apply it in particular circumstances (Schwandt, 1997). Skills required include proficiency in a range of models, approaches, skills and techniques, such as systemic, psycho-social and cognitive behavioural therapy (CBT) approaches, listening skills, knowing how to do a genogram, or being able to converse with a family member through an interpreter. Core social work ethics and values will drive practitioners' commitment to fundamental principles, such as promoting participation, working in partnership, adhering to child-centred practice, and attending to confidentiality. A considered use of self, such as being able to engage emotionally in a warm, congruent, caring, authoritative and boundaried way, is the main conduit for these other practices. Effective direct work is, then, as much about who the social worker is as a person, as it is about what they do.

RESEARCH SUMMARY

Views on their social workers were sought from children and young people who were getting help of any sort from children's social care services, including those living away from home and care leavers. Thirteen groups of children participated in discussion groups and 502 children completed question cards.

- *Respondents emphasised the importance of their views being sought before any decisions were made and said that the views and feelings of even very young children should not be ignored.*

- *The personal qualities of social workers were important to the young people. They wanted practitioners to be friendly and approachable with a sense of humour so that they were easy to get on with, not 'stuck up' or too formal.*

- *The ethical commitments of social workers were important; young people wanted them to be dependable, trustworthy, able to keep promises and non-judgmental.*

- *Children wanted to matter to their social workers. They wanted to be listened to and for what they said to be important to the practitioner.*

- *Supportiveness was also required, so practitioners need to be good at calming young people down when they are upset and show that they understand.*

(Morgan, 2006)

Skills for informing and consulting with children and young people

By the time that children and young people become looked after, they will already have had a number of conversations with professionals about their situation and experiences. This should have included an opportunity to discuss their views, concerns, hopes, fears and preferences about their current situation and the proposed move into care so that these can be taken into account in decision making and planning. Being enabled to participate and to have an opportunity to reflect on their thoughts and feelings in a supportive environment is important even when such moves take place on an emergency basis.

Sometimes workers worry less about whether they have involved younger, traumatised or more vulnerable children in discussions about sensitive or complex matters, in the belief that they are not sufficiently able to make a useful contribution to decisions and plans (Leeson, 2007). Others may want to 'relieve' children of the 'burden' of distressing conversations about matters which might unsettle them. This can result in children not being kept informed about their situation, or their views being downplayed or even ignored in certain situations (Winter, 2009). This transgresses not only children's clearly stated preference to be involved in matters which concern them, but also all of the policy and legislation over the last decade that explicitly sets out the statutory obligations regarding children's participation. While shortcomings may have arisen solely from a professional concern to work in line with children's capacities and to protect those who are vulnerable, there are times when professionals' over-protectiveness or incorrect presumptions of children's limited competence may be too much to the fore.

Of course, children should not necessarily be faced with complex dilemmas, distressed by too much explicit detail, or overly burdened with decisions and uncertainties that need to be contained and dealt with by the adults. A judgement should always be made about what should be said, in what depth, and in what way, and this will take account of the child's situation, maturity, level of understanding and current emotional and psychological state. However, children's capabilities in these regards are not fixed characteristics, but vary according to the attitude and skills of the practitioner working with them (Thomas and O'Kane, 2000). When children have information and choices presented to them in child-centred ways, for example using forms of language, clear concepts, and modes of communication that make sense to them, then even very young children have been shown to be able to consider alternatives and possible outcomes carefully and responsibly (Clark and Statham, 2005). This is just as true for those with sensory impairments or learning difficulties; it is the worker's attitude and commitment to children's inclusion that counts. Limited expectations can lead to limited results (Stalker and Connors, 2003).

Skills in creative and activity-based work

Returning to Case Study 5.1, Marina would need to consider how best to facilitate the necessary conversations and interactions with all members of the family. For the children, communicating solely through verbal language may not be sufficient. What children think and feel may be difficult for them to convey as they don't yet possess all the words or concepts that they need to recognise, name and communicate their thoughts and feelings in more direct ways. At 13, and without any learning difficulties, Alana might be better able to manage a direct conversation than Toby about why there is a need for her to come into foster care. She will want her views to be listened to and her queries answered clearly and unambiguously (Bourton and McCausland, 2001).

However, age and disability are not the only factors when considering the most suitable communication approach with children and young people. Many children who have been significantly neglected or traumatised, or who have not been able to develop a secure attachment, may reach adolescence still with neither the language to name their experiences nor the conceptual and affective frameworks through which to interpret and process them (Gerhardt, 2004). This makes it particularly difficult for them to reflect on their inner thoughts and feelings and to convey them in a coherent form to someone else

(Schore, 2001). Much will be communicated by more indirect means, such as through their play, body language or relational style.

The vast range of possible modes in which children communicate with the world around them has been termed *the hundred languages of childhood* (Edwards *et al.*, 1993). Practitioners need to use as many of these as possible. For Toby, this might include observing his play and behaviour to see what they 'say' for him, and using drawings, dolls or puppets to provide information and explanations in a more concrete and visual way. Few practitioners have access to a well-stocked playroom, so will need to collect some props that can be kept in the boot of their car or work bag. At the most basic level, this can be just a few crayons and some paper, but can be expanded to include finger puppets, modelling dough, small figures or animals (including families, vulnerable figures and monsters) and worksheets with happy/sad faces to encourage children into dialogue about their feelings. Where workers have laptops or they are visiting households where there is a computer, art programs may be used for creative visual work, for playing music or video clips, or for purpose-designed interactive computer-based tools (Ahmad *et al.*, 2008). Even many standard mobile phones are now equipped to support more creative work.

These play- and activity-based methods might employ either directive or non-directive approaches. Directive work focuses on a specific purpose which then shapes the method and pace; for example, explaining to Toby that the worries about his safety mean he needs to move into foster care. Non-directive work, by contrast, presents children with open-ended time and space so that what they need to express or convey can surface in the child's own way and at their own pace. This can be extremely effective in gaining a deeper understanding of what is significant to a child or young person and enabling them to process complex thoughts and feelings in a metaphorical form, which is often less threatening (Thomas and O'Kane, 2000).

ACTIVITY 5.1

- *Think of one task you might need to carry out with a looked after child or young person that would work best if it was directive in nature and another that might benefit from a more non-directive approach. For each of these, plan how you would set the work up and carry it out. Consider what play-based or creative activities might facilitate the work.*

Professionals may find that establishing a shared understanding with family members with learning difficulties or sensory impairments is more challenging than usual or that they are required to employ techniques that they are not used to. They should beware of seeing these family members as 'the one with the communication problem' and instead, following the social model of disability, locate the skill-gap within themselves. Visual, creative and play-based methods may be as useful with adults as children. Careful observations will also help practitioners to make sense of what family members communicate more indirectly through their behaviour and interactions (Atkins-Burnett and Allen-Meares, 2000). Assistance should be sought from those who know the family member well, to provide guidance, to interpret, or to facilitate where specific communication systems or augmentative technologies such as Makaton, Rebus, Blissymbolics, picture boards or 'touch talkers' are used. By building up their own skills and making additional effort, success becomes more likely (Stalker and Connors, 2003). Extra time will be needed both for planning (to learn as much as possible about how best to communicate) and for meeting with disabled family members (to provide extended lead-ins to any subsequent discussion and to allow time for interpreting).

Not just the basic content but also the emotional dimension of these conversations will need to be understood and responded to by social workers. For children like Alana and Toby, the chaotic and abusive home environment and the proposed move into care are likely to be distressing and frightening and the children may not want or feel able to express this directly. Alana's feelings, for example, may manifest themselves through her body language (such as her facial expressions and bodily movements) and paralanguage (her speed of speaking, tone of voice, and the loudness, pitch and intonation of her speech) (Thompson, in press, 2011). Such non-verbal forms of communication convey significant amounts of adults' as well as children's thoughts, feelings and perceptions. In fact, research by Mehrabian (1971, cited in Dunhill, 2009) found that only seven per cent of communication involved the actual words spoken between individuals. Thirty-eight per cent was transmitted through paralanguage, with the remaining 55 per cent conveyed through body language, behaviour and other non-verbal signs.

Culturally competent and anti-oppressive communication

These examples demonstrate how 'depth' as well as 'surface' content is conveyed in the engagement and interactions between social workers and families (Howe, 1996). In order for children and their families to feel listened to, it is essential that professionals attune to and respond to the thoughts, feelings and intentions beneath their words (known as meta-messages), as well as what is directly said (Thompson, in press, 2011). In order to 'read' this non-verbal content with all of the family members, practitioners will need to be well versed in how differing cultural beliefs, values and norms all help people to make sense of what each other might be communicating.

Bourdieu's concept of 'habitus' is useful, describing the subconscious conventions and customs which enable individuals of shared social, ethnic and cultural groupings to rapidly appraise and interpret social situations and work out the 'right' or acceptable way to respond (Lovell, 2000). Where people differ in terms of class, ethnicity, religion or nationality, their habitus, too, is likely to differ regarding matters such as level of eye contact, dress, the offering of food and drink to visitors, offering to shake hands, and use of first name or surname/family name. Misunderstandings and miscommunications about mood, intentions and values are then much more likely. For example, there is a risk that family members are pathologised for the way in which they respond to strong feelings or difficult events (Hargie and Dickson, 2004). Increasing their knowledge of the range of families' different cultural practices and norms can enhance practitioners' cultural competence (Caple *et al.*, 1995).

It is important, though, that such information is critically scrutinised to ensure it is not applied simplistically or based on assumptions or stereotypes as there are often individual and sub-cultural variations from macro-cultural patterns. Carefully observing the family of origin and learning from them will be crucial, particularly where a child is placed in a setting where they perceive themselves or are perceived by others to look, feel or behave differently. Practitioners should not only be alert to cultural differences in such situations but also how discrimination and oppression might affect the well-being and identity of family members. Black and minority ethnic family members may feel silenced, marginalised or misunderstood by white indigenous workers, particularly when they indicate through their language or practices that they lack understanding of the effects of racism on identity development and emotional and psychological health, or do not understand the history of black people's oppression (Graham, 2007). Workers may demonstrate their commitment to an anti-racist approach through inclusive language and practices, use of interpreters and translated materials where needed, and a reflective consideration of how cultural norms and values might best be understood and responded to.

With black and minority ethnic children, practitioners must consider how to support their development of a positive ethnic, cultural and racial identity, particularly when substitute carers are not able to model this and where dual-heritage children, such as Toby and Alana, are mainly in contact with white family members. While enhanced contact with their father and his family might support a positive black identity for Toby and Alana, this is not necessarily the same as developing a positive dual heritage identity (Goldstein, 2002).

An anti-oppressive approach is also needed with young people, parents or carers who are lesbian, gay, bisexual and transgender (LGBT) as they will only feel safe to identify themselves and discuss issues of relevance to their sexuality and gender identity if they are given a clear impression that they will be accepted rather than judged, rejected, or treated as abnormal by professionals. Practitioners must avoid homophobic, heterosexist and inappropriately gendered language and assumptions pervading their verbal and written communications. For example, if Marina were to ask Johnny whether he is married, this would immediately convey her expectation of his heterosexuality. By asking him if he has a partner and avoiding terminology such as 'she' or 'her', Marina is much more likely to convey a non-judgemental attitude and encourage Johnny's confidence. With LGB young people, such assumptions will be even more powerful, particularly as homophobic bullying in schools is so prevalent; perhaps 30–50 per cent of young LGB people have experienced this (Warwick *et al.*, 2006). Consequently, direct work with young people will need to include provision of information, guidance, support and acceptance if they are to feel safe enough to communicate openly about their relationships and identity and any discriminatory or oppressive social experiences (Freed-Kernis, 2008).

Working through and with relationships

The extent to which children, young people and their parents will feel safe enough to talk in any depth to their social workers will depend on the nature of the relationships formed with them. Where children have come into care following safeguarding concerns, such as with the Carroll family, creating a context for an effective working relationship is particularly challenging. If children have been abused or neglected, are insecurely attached, or have suffered significant losses, trauma or displacement, their experiences are likely to affect their responses to new workers and the degree to which they are able to engage with them and trust them. Practitioners will need to be sensitive to this and neither expect too much too soon nor give up trying when they are met with coolness, rebuff, or 'testing out' behaviours.

Engaging parents in such contested situations is perhaps one of the major challenges for practitioners in contemporary childcare social work (Yatchmenoff, 2005) as they may feel devastated, confused, helpless, angry or misunderstood. Some will exhibit open hostility towards professionals and resist working co-operatively. Others, who are more wary of the consequences, might feign co-operation to try to show they are 'playing the game' but then are less motivated to actively work on any issues of concern (Dumbrill, 2006).

As families are in the less powerful position, professionals must take the leading role in engaging them in a constructive working alliance. This will be promoted through a collaborative approach where children and their parents feel that they are treated with dignity and care, and power is shared as much as possible. This does not mean workers denying the reality of their own authority, but rather committing to principles of partnership (Turnell and Edwards, 1997). This is promoted by workers who are reliable, accountable and committed to promoting families' welfare; are transparent about professional intentions and goals; acknowledge the unequal nature of power between parents and professionals; recognise that parents have their own needs which should be addressed; and work towards mutual trust and respect (DoH, 2001).

Unsurprisingly, where parents experience workers as disrespectful, judgemental, not wanting to listen or understand and seeming not to care about how they are affected in the situation, they are less likely to co-operate and be open and honest about their difficulties (Drake, 1994). Poor interpersonal skills and a patronising, judgemental manner make parents feel inexpert, belittled, hostile and disaffected (Moran *et al.*, 2004). Conversely, parents are more likely to trust and stay engaged with practitioners who are respectful, friendly, caring, warm, empathic, honest, and good listeners (Drake, 1994; Winefield and Barlow, 1995). Improved parental coping and enhanced parenting capacity are more likely to be the result (Lee and Ayon, 2004).

RESEARCH SUMMARY

Forrester et al. *(2008) analysed 24 interviews between social workers and actors role-playing parents to determine what kind of communication skills are used in child protection situations (albeit simulated ones). Practitioners were generally able to give a clear indication of what their concerns were to the 'client' but not all could engage them. The ratio of 'closed' to 'open' questions was generally too high, with low levels of 'reflecting back', leading the interview at times to feel like an interrogation or even abusive. Where empathy was used, this decreased the 'parent's' resistance and increased the amount of information that they disclosed. This led the authors to conclude that empathic social workers may manage complex and potentially fraught social work interviews better than non-empathic workers (p48). Of much concern, though, was the comparatively low level of empathy demonstrated by most social workers. How to support practitioners in being able to combine raising concerns with parents with a more relationship-based approach that will keep parents engaged was identified as a training need.*

An understanding of 'depth' processes in the work is useful in building relationships with family members and carers. These refer to the personal feelings, perceptions, responses and interactional dynamics evoked between professionals and families which may be out of individuals' conscious awareness (Howe, 1996). Psychodynamic theories provide one way of thinking about how earlier experiences may impact on current behaviour. For example, in the earlier case study, Faith might respond to Marina in a way that derives from her earlier experience of a critical and punishing mother. Such negative 'transference' might reflect a relationship template belonging to her childhood which has been projected on to Marina and could have little to do with what Marina actually says or does (Gordon, 2000). Workers should always consider whether a family member's negative response is a real here-and-now reaction to the worker's coldness, unreliability, lateness, hostility, and so on, before they begin to consider the possibility of transference. Marina, in her turn, might develop a 'counter-transference' response, where she feels as if she wants to be punitive and undermining to Faith, when this is not how she would normally behave. Self-awareness is needed so that practitioners are alert to such situations and do not act them out.

Working with family groupings

Often, social workers do not meet with children and young people alone but in the presence of another family member, carer or professional. This might be so a parent can support them through a meeting or as part of an assessment, such as observing contact, or to explore decision making with them together. Practitioners need to keep such situations safe for children so that any painful or antagonistic feelings which are evoked for the parents do not distress or worry the child.

Children and young people are used to being ignored and marginalised when adults come together so, if professionals start speaking to parents, children and young people may end up feeling they are in the way or less important (Triangle, 2009). Workers should share eye contact between children and their parents so that children know they are being included in the discussion. This also stops parents from trying to take over the dialogue. What both the child and the parents or carers have said must be responded to; parents' views and concerns must not dominate. The intellectual level of the vocabulary and concepts used should always be set to that of the child, so that it is simple and clear enough for the child to understand, even if it feels too basic for the adults. The way the room is laid out should also feel inclusive for the child, for example with smaller lower chairs, or cushions on the floor.

Keeping in touch with children, young people and their families

Regular contact with children and young people in care and their families is essential to ensure that they are kept informed about important matters, that there is regular consultation with them about decisions, choices and plans, to monitor their well-being, and to support them through the emotional and practical challenges that they face. This 'keeping in touch' will not only be through face-to-face visits and meetings but also through some of the technologies most familiar to young people and families nowadays: telephone, text messages and e-mail. Phone calls are a useful way for a social worker to check young people in care are okay or share information with families quickly. But families don't want it all to be in the control of the worker. Young people, for example, have stated that they would like to be able to ring or text their social worker themselves at a time of their choosing and to be able to leave a secure message that they know will get to them, as their experience when ringing landlines is that workers are not there and messages do not always get through (Morgan, 2006).

Mobile phones are an ideal way to achieve this sense of continuity and availability with children in care and their families but require careful boundary-setting. One ground rule is that phones should always belong to the organisation rather than being the practitioner's personal property. The phone will then always be switched off for evenings, weekends and holidays so there is no risk of practitioners answering calls at inappropriate times. A voice-mail facility can confirm when the phone will next be checked. These boundaries should be made explicit to families whenever a mobile phone number is given out so that they do not expect universal availability and instant responses. The same rule applies to e-mail addresses.

The content of text messages and e-mails needs to be carefully considered. Content delivered in such written form may seem more curt or brusque than when paralanguage and body language are available to soften it, so the choice of words and syntax is particularly important (Hunt, 2002). This is particularly so for younger children who are even more dependent on non-verbal gestural cues than teenagers (Doherty-Sneddon and Kent, 1996). Textual conversations about difficult or contentious matters are best avoided as the potential for misunderstanding is too strong. Text messaging is probably best reserved for brief uncontentious matters, such as an appointment reminder or a warning that the worker is running late for a visit.

Working with endings

It is especially important for key workers to give sufficient attention to endings with children and young people who are looked after as they are likely to have experienced separation from/loss of significant people, attachment figures and communities of origin. Many of these separations will have been traumatic in nature (perhaps following abuse or when seeking asylum) and may not have been managed well. For example, the distressing and often complex nature of prior losses may not have been acknowledged or supported by the adults or systems involved and could well have been compounded by unexpected or poorly planned placement moves once in care. Looked after children are also likely to have had contact with numerous professionals, many of whom have changed role with short notice. The key worker for a child or young person in care may, then, take on a very significant meaning for them. Rarely is the worker simply a kind of travel guide or tour operator for them, helping them negotiate their way through services, but often much more of a companion and an ally on their journey through placement (Luckock *et al.*, 2008).

When this practitioner comes to leave it is potentially distressing and unsettling for the child and might also evoke those earlier losses and traumas. Some young people in care have described feeling *'bereft, forgotten and confused'* at such times (Bell, 2002, p4). These feelings might be expressed in a whole range of ways, including sadness, disappointment, clinging, frustration, disengagement or anger. Practitioners will need to recognise the often indirect ways in which such feelings are expressed. They will need emotional resilience, too, for the times when they might be dismissed by young people who have been abandoned or let down too many times to connect with or openly acknowledge where their feelings have been engaged. Where workers themselves have difficulties with facing endings, this is likely to be played out in their work with children and young people unless it is carefully guarded against.

McLeod (2008, p123) advises that *the key to negotiating the end of a piece of work is to bear it in mind and bring the child's attention to it from the beginning*. A good principle is to explain how long you are spending with a child or young person on each occasion, how many more times you are to meet, and how often. If an ending is unplanned or unexpected, this needs to be acknowledged and discussed. Where a relationship has been particularly significant or long-term, worker and child will benefit from together finding a way of honouring and clarifying what has occurred over the time of their working relationship (Bannister, 2001).

Many of the issues raised here may be as relevant for ending the work with parents and other family members, too. Some parents may feel very negative about a particular professional's involvement; for example where they blame the worker for 'taking their child'. For others, the potential feelings evoked by an ending could be positive or very complex, depending on the circumstances and the parents' own previous history of attachment, trauma or loss. A considered use of self will again be essential, with the worker facilitating discussion of the emotions involved. Practical issues, too, must be dealt with as parents may well worry that important information may be lost or misunderstood with a change of worker. Achieving as much continuity as possible should help, with clear summaries of involvement, explicit setting-out of future tasks and goals and a handover visit to enable the parent to feel that the 'holding' of their family situation is transferred along with their case file.

ACTIVITY **5.2**

- *In your team, discuss the extent to which your organisational context validates and supports direct work.*

- *Is there a safe and supportive space for practitioners' emotional responses to the work to be discussed and reflected on?*

- *Are there sufficient resources for the work, including time, tools, and an appropriate environment in which to meet families?*

- *What might need to change or be developed individually and collectively so that workers are enabled to practice more effectively?*

Chapter summary

Effective direct work is the key to engaging, involving, assessing and intervening with children and young people who are looked after, and with their families and carers. A social worker who can form constructive, collaborative and emotionally engaged relationships will be better equipped to help families and carers to express their feelings, reflect on difficulties and work towards resolving challenging issues. Communication and interpersonal skills will be central in ensuring that all family members are kept informed about issues that are important to them and that they are consulted about their views, wishes and feelings. High caseloads, administrative burdens from the ICS and inadequacies in workplace supervision and qualifying training have meant that the training, guidance, support, and uninterrupted time with children and their families required for high quality practice have not always been there. However, the profession is now at a turning point; the social work role is being redefined by the Social Work Reform Board and new commitments are being made to raising the standard of qualifying training, enhancing access to continuing professional development (PQ), improving workload-management systems, reducing bureaucracy and providing high quality supervision (Gibb, 2009; Burnham and Balls, 2009). These should provide a renewed commitment to direct work and opportunities for practitioners to develop the knowledge, skills, values and personal qualities required.

FURTHER READING

Dunhill, A, Elliott, B and Shaw, A (eds) (2009) *Effective communication and engagement with children and young people, their families and carers.* Exeter: Learning Matters.

This book contains chapters by a range of experienced professionals across children's services, providing both theoretical perspectives and practice wisdom to guide communication and engagement with families within a wide variety of roles and tasks. Case studies and exercises assist readers in linking theory and practice.

Hall, C and Slembrouck, S (2009) Communication with parents in child welfare: skills, language and interaction. *Child and Family Social Work,* 14(4), 461–470.

This paper provides a useful review of the literature on communication between professionals and parents/carers and assists readers in learning from good practice in other professions such as medicine and counselling.

Lefevre, M (2010) *Communicating with children and young people: Making a difference.* Bristol: The Policy Press.

This book guides practitioners and students on how best to listen to children, support them, keep them informed, and fully involve them in matters which concern them. In particular, it aims to enthuse readers to develop the most powerful resource they have to offer in their direct work with children: themselves.

Luckock, B and Lefevre, M (eds) (2008) *Direct work: Social work with children and young people in care.* London: BAAF.

This anthology redefines 'direct work' as the day-to-day encounters and interventions with children and young people. Different sections of the book focus on understanding the experience and perceptions of children in care, models and methods of communication and direct work, considering the challenges of specific contexts and tasks, and the role of supervision and consultation in promoting effective practice.

McLeod, A (2007) Whose agenda? Issues of power and relationship when listening to looked after young people. *Child and Family Social Work*, 2007, 12(3), p278–286.

This research demonstrates how the practice of listening to marginalised young people is not straightforward and considers why effective dialogue can be so hard to achieve. Practitioners are advised to take the time to develop a trusting, collaborative relationship and develop a willingness to challenge their preconceptions.

Willis, R and Holland, S (2009) Life story work: Reflections on the experience by looked after young people. *Adoption and Fostering,* 33(4), 44–52.

This is a qualitative study of young people's experiences of life story work, enabling practitioners to gain insight on the emotional dimensions of the work for the young people and how it can enable them to learn more about their own histories and identity.

Chapter 6

Foster care: learning from research and inquiries

Helen Cosis Brown

CHAPTER OBJECTIVES

If you are a registered social worker, this chapter will assist you to evidence post-registration train-ing and learning. It relates to the national post-qualifying framework for social work education and training at the specialist level:

v.   Use reflection and critical analysis to continuously develop and improve their specialist practice, including their practice in inter-professional and inter-agency context, drawing systematically, accurately and appropriately on theories, models and relevant up-to-date research;

and at advanced level:

iv.   Demonstrate a fully developed capacity to take responsibility for the use of reflection and critical analysis to continuously develop and improve own performance and the perform-ance of professional and inter-professional groups, teams and networks in the context of professional practice, professional management, professional education or applied profes-sional research; analysing, evaluating and applying relevant and up-to-date research evidence including service user research.

It will also help you to meet the Children and Families standards for social work:

ii(f).   The needs of children and young people accommodated, looked after and leaving care (including a knowledge and understanding of how to use the services that exist to meet those needs and the nature of the specific responsibilities of corporate parents, such as those associated with responsibilities for development and educational attainment).

Introduction

Fostering has been an established resource for caring for children in public care since the 1940s. Its increasing use since the 1970s, with the move away from the use of residential care for children, has meant that we have now reached a position where the majority of looked after children are placed with foster carers. The Labour Government tried to refo-cus minds on the importance of foster care in facilitating the development of looked after children, to enable them to reach their potential. This was best demonstrated by the

Department for Children Schools and Families' (DCSF) emphasis on the importance of fostering, reflected in the 2007 White Paper *Care Matters: Time for Change* (DfES, 2007a).

According to DCSF figures, there were 60,900 looked after children in England on 31 March 2009. Of this number, 73 per cent, or 44,200, were placed in foster care and this was a five per cent increase on the previous year (DCSF, 2009f). Foster care is not only where most looked after children are placed but it is also an intervention in children's lives that is likely to have a significant impact on their emotional, educational and physical development. The quality of foster care is of great importance.

There are a number of key areas related to social work and foster care that are covered in the literature, for example: kinship care (Farmer and Moyers, 2008); the role of fostering panels (Borthwick and Lord, 2007); managing allegations against foster carers (Slade, 2006); matching looked after children and foster carers; facilitating contact with looked after children's families; support to foster carers; working with disrupted placements; and helping foster carers work constructively with children moving on including work related to transitions for children who are being moved to permanent family placements (Sellick *et al.*, 2004; Sinclair, 2005; Wilson *et al.*, 2004; Sinclair *et al.*, 2007). This chapter is aimed at qualified practitioners working in the field and considers two areas that are pertinent to social work and foster care. Firstly, the support and training of foster carers that enables them to make effective interventions in children's lives is discussed. Secondly, the findings of the Wakefield Inquiry (Parrott *et al.*, 2007) as they relate to the assessment and review processes for foster carers are highlighted. Current research evaluations of the effectiveness of foster carer training programmes will be considered and a case study is included that is relevant to the findings of the Wakefield Inquiry. Exercises are also included that are relevant to foster carer training and the findings of the Wakefield Inquiry.

Policy and regulatory frameworks

Foster care is currently regulated under: the Children Act 1989; the Family Placements Guidance and Regulations (DoH, 1991); and the Fostering Services National Minimum Standards and Fostering Services Regulations (DoH, 2002a). At the time of writing, the DoE was engaged in the process of drafting updated guidance related to the Children Act 1989 and the Care Standards Act 2000 pertaining to foster care. The draft National Minimum Standards for Foster Care, issued under Section 23 of the Care Standards Act 2000, were published for consultation in September 2009 (DCSF, 2009e) and new regulation and guidance is due to be in place by spring 2011. The National Foster Care Association UK Joint Working Party on Foster Care's UK National Standards for Foster Care (NFCA, 1999a) and the related Code of Practice on the Recruitment, Assessment, Approval, Training, Management and Support for Foster Carers (NFCA, 1999b) are seen as necessary documents for fostering agencies and local authorities to be mindful of and to work within, even though they are not statutory instruments. Both the white papers, *Every Child Matters* (DfES, 2004) and *Care Matters* (DfES, 2007a), and the Children's Plan (DCSF, 2007) provide the policy framework for looked after children more generally, including children placed in foster care. For example, the five outcomes for children established in *Every Child Matters* (DfES, 2004) that apply to all children are the outcomes foster carers have to aim to achieve for the children they care for: for them to be healthy; stay safe; enjoy and achieve; make a positive contribution; and achieve economic well-being. This chapter does not discuss the detail of the legislative and policy framework for foster care outlined above as it is covered in detail elsewhere (Brammer, 2010; Brayne and Carr, 2008).

In addition to the legislation and policy that provide the framework for foster care, public inquiry reports also offer important guidance through their recommendations. The Wakefield Inquiry is one such inquiry that was wholly relevant to foster care (Parrott *et al.*, 2007) and is an important document for those working in this field of social work practice.

Foster carer training, support and development

The placement of children in foster care can be, at its worst, just a 'holding operation' until a child is placed back home with his or her birth family, placed in kinship care, placed in residential care or placed with a permanent substitute family, through adoption, special guardianship or permanent foster care. In this circumstance, minimalist expectations of foster care can develop which, as a result, deliver minimal beneficial outcomes for children.

The importance of foster care was recognised by the Government within the White Paper *Care Matters* (DfES, 2007a) which emphasised the need to raise the status of foster care through a number of mechanisms including foster carer support and training. This focus on foster care relates to concern about the number of moves looked after children experience once in the care system and the need to improve both the quality of foster care and the stability children in public care experience.

> *A successful, stable placement is central to supporting the needs of children in care. Carers are the centre of a child or young person's experience of corporate parenting and should provide the mainstay of their support.*

> (DfES, 2007a, p8)

Foster care should provide a safe, containing, stimulating and caring experience of family life for a child. It can also be an effective intervention, improving the chances for foster children to fulfil their potential. This understanding of foster care as an intervention was recognised by the Government by its funding of both the Multi-dimensional Treatment Foster Care in England (MTFCE) pilots and the rolling out of the Fostering Changes training programme (DfES, 2007a) both of which are designed to facilitate foster carers' purposeful and effective interventions in children's lives.

Specific foster care developments such as MTFCE and the Fostering Changes training programme run parallel to the requirements established for all foster carers through the Children's Workforce Development Council's Training, Support and Development Standards for Foster Care (CWDC, 2007a) with their accompanying induction and workbook which foster carers have to complete (CWDC, 2007b). For some time, most local authorities and independent fostering agencies (IFAs) have, as part of the assessment process for prospective foster carers, run the Skills to Foster programme (Fostering Network, 2003). The National Minimum Standards for Foster Care Standard 23 places a requirement on fostering services to *ensure that foster carers are trained in the skills required to provide high quality care and meet the needs of each child/young person placed in their care* (DoH, 2002a, p25). It goes on to say that *each carer's annual review includes an appraisal of training and development needs, which is documented in the review report* (2002a, p26). In the new draft National Minimum Standards for Foster Care, this is reiterated in Standard 23.1, which states that fostering agencies must make sure that *staff receive training and development opportunities that equip them with the professional skills required to meet the needs of the children and the purpose of the service* (DCSF, 2009e, p69).

Commenting on the National Minimum Standards for Foster Care's (DoH, 2002a) training requirements, Mehmet writes: *training is a central and intrinsic part of fostering and all agencies must have a clear plan for the training and development of all who work in the service* (Mehmet, 2005, p34). However, this requirement for training did not set specific expectations related to the content, structure or theoretical coherence of such training. Inevitably there has been a degree of variability in both the quantity and the quality of foster carer training (DfES, 2005c). The one uniform package of training developed since the National Minimum Standards for Foster Care (DoH, 2002a) were published has been the Skills to Foster programme (Fostering Network, 2003), usually delivered to prospective foster carers or those who have recently been approved as foster carers. This lack of consistency in the quality of ongoing post-approval training offered to foster carers was recognised in *Care Matters*: *In order for carers to provide the supportive commitment which is essential for children's development, they themselves must be provided with effective training and support* (DfES, 2007a, p50). The consequent Children's Workforce Development Council's Training, Support and Development Standards for Foster Care were a concrete manifestation of this required 'effective training and support'.

At the time of writing, the impact of the new CWDC's Training, Support and Development Standards requirements on the quality of foster care is not known. The DCSF's and the CWDC's intention that *the standards will play a key role in ensuring that providers make available to their carers appropriate opportunities for development, and that they support them in developing the skills and competence covered by the framework* (DfES, 2007a, pp50–51) might not be realised through the mechanism of the completion of a workbook alone. Some agencies are using it in creative and facilitative ways, helping foster carers to reflect on the detail of their fostering practice with a specific child or birth parent. However, an evaluation of its effectiveness in fulfilling the DCSF's and the CWDC's aims will be important. Unfortunately, the booklet that foster carers have to complete is worded in such a way that suggests that through its successful completion foster carers will have met the CWDC standards, rather than it being used for the development of foster carers through an ongoing process. The completed booklet has to be signed off by the foster carer's agency. The wording of the sign-off section is as follows: *I certify that the above named foster carer has successfully met all the outcomes in the CWDC Training, Support and Development Standards for Foster Care* (CWDC, 2007b, p98). This sentence seems to signify that the completion of the booklet and the meeting of the standards is one and the same thing and that it is a time-limited exercise rather than a developmental process.

There is an underlying assumption in both the DoE's and the CWDC's commitment to training and support for foster carers that it is effective. Therefore it will be important that the current CWDC Training, Support and Development Standards for Foster Care induction and workbook completion is evaluated, as at the present time it is consuming considerable resources of foster carers, supervising social workers and fostering agencies. Both the DCSF's and the CWDC's emphasis on the importance of training for foster carers is based, presumably, on the assumption that training is effective in improving the quality of foster care. However, is this assumption grounded in evidence?

ACTIVITY 6.1

- *As part of your ongoing supervision of a foster carer, try integrating one area of a standard into a supervision session to help you and your foster carer reflect on their ongoing work or on their last placement.*

Comment

An example of this may be that, as the supervising social worker, you might have been working with a single male foster carer who has just helped a five-year-old boy move on to his adoptive family. The nature of this child's circumstances meant that there was an unusual level of confidentiality needed in this piece of work, which prevented the foster carer discussing the case at all with any of his usual support network. Together you could use Standard 1, Understand the principles and values essential for fostering children and young people, and the related Area 4, Confidentiality and sharing information, to reflect on his experience. Discuss what he did well and how he and the agency might do things differently in the future.

What the research tells us about the effectiveness of training for foster carers

Regarding the question of whether or not training for foster carers is effective in improving the quality of foster care, the 'jury remains out'. What is clear from the research evidence is that specific training that has a theoretical base, is well structured, coherent, builds on foster carers' experience and is linked to particular interventions, seems to be more effective than 'general' one-off training events (Pallett *et al.*, 2005). The problem is that most foster carers receive 'general' training on particular topics rather than a coherent training programme. The one coherent training programme that they are likely to receive will be that which is delivered at the time of their approval as a foster carer: the Skills to Foster programme (Fostering Network, 2003).

The Social Care Institute for Excellence's review of the research literature on foster care (Wilson *et al.*, 2004) and Pithouse *et al.* (2002) found little evidence that training of foster carers improved the quality of foster care. There are a number of studies that suggest that foster carers value training (Minnis *et al.*, 1999; Minnis *et al.*, 2001; Ogilvie *et al.*, 2006; Triseliotis *et al.*, 2000). However, enjoying training does not necessarily correlate with improving the quality of care and effective intervention with children. In the study by Ogilvie *et al.*, 68 per cent of the foster carers who attended training rated it as very good or good (2006). However, in the study by Triseliotis *et al.* of the delivery of foster care in 32 Scottish authorities, it was found that both carers and mangers perceived a lack of coherence in the training that foster carers received: *Like many carers, managers referred to continued training being 'periodic'; as having 'no cohesion'; 'erratic'; 'no pattern'; 'variable' or 'irregular'* (2000, p73). Reviewing the research on the effectiveness of training for foster carers, Sellick at al. conclude: *There are few studies of effectiveness of training carers. Research is needed which differentiates between types of training and evaluates content, process and outcomes of the programmes* (2004, p 56). Wilson *et al.* confirm this position, arguing that there is a *lack of evidence that specific forms of training can, on their own, improve outcomes* (2004, p67).

Talbot and Wheal (2005) also argue that there has been little research into the effectiveness of training and its evaluation. One study conducted in Scotland using a randomised control trail concluded that training had been well received by foster carers but that it did not have a significant impact on the emotional well-being of the foster children (Minnis *et al.*, 2001). However, Ogilvie *et al.* (2006) cite a number of studies that indicate that training has been shown to have a beneficial effect in relation to lower rates of placement breakdown, more openness to working with birth families and positive impacts on retention of foster carers. However, they also note that evaluations that look at the impact of training for foster carers have shown limited effects *on children and carers . . . Thus the case for seeing training as a means of improving child outcomes remains unproven* (2006, p14). It would seem then that the assumption that training per se is a good thing has little or no evidence base. The current position is best summed up by Sinclair when he writes: *in general the studies provide plenty of evidence that carers appreciate training . . . Despite this praise the studies provided little evidence that current training has much effect on outcomes* (2005, p119).

Supervising social workers, in line with the expectations set down by the National Minimum Standards for Foster Care (DoH, 2002a), place considerable importance on working with the foster carers to encourage them to attend training. Training expectations are also usually set out in foster carers' annual review paperwork. I have also observed, as an independent reviewing officer for foster carers, that occasionally difficulties that are encountered in a foster carer's practice are not worked with directly by their supervising social worker but rather the foster carer is sent to training as if that in itself will improve the quality of their work. The evidence from the research detailed above calls such practice into question.

That is not, however, to say that there are no positive evaluations of the training of foster carers and the impact that training can have on their care of foster children. These positive examples are linked to specific training programmes or specific foster care initiatives. Two such current examples in the UK are the Fostering Changes training programme and the MTFCE projects.

The Fostering Changes programme

Fostering Changes is a foster carer training programme that was set up by the National Specialist Adoption and Fostering Team at the Maudsley Hospital in London in 1999. The programme focuses on behaviour management and the formation of positive and productive relationships between foster carers and their foster children. This training programme has been developed into a training manual, which a number of agencies now use (Pallett *et al.*, 2005). Two publications summarise the programme's content, structure, process and effectiveness (Pallett *et al.*, 2002; Warman *et al.*, 2006). The theoretical underpinnings of this ten-week programme are cognitive behavioural theory and social learning theory. The programme has a clear structure and underlying values and principles that the programme team believes enhance the learning of participants. For example, importance is placed on valuing foster carers and their experience. Recognising that foster carers' attendance at training can sometimes be a problem, the team visits foster carers at home before the programme starts. The purpose of this is to engage the foster carers and to gather information about their experiences. The rate of retention of foster carers throughout the ten-week programme is high (Pallett *et al.*, 2002, p41). The team also believes that the foster carers should have fun while attending. Their evaluation of the programme in 2002 suggests *this training brings about improvements in the emotions and behaviour of the children in their care, and a better quality of relationship and interactions with them. It also has a beneficial effect on carers' sense of confidence and self-efficacy* (2002, p47). Their 2006 paper confirmed continuing effectiveness and acknowledged that it might be the approach of the programme as much as the content that contributed to its success. The approach is one of active learning and collaborative participation with peers. Learning in this context is a process in which participants are encouraged to play an active role, both inside and outside the 'classroom' (Warman *et al.*, 2006, p27). The strengths of this programme are linked to its collaborative model of learning, which is underpinned by a specific theoretical base. Because the programme runs for ten weeks, it gives participants the opportunity to learn over time within a safe and comfortable learning environment. These factors might be as important as the content of what is delivered and contribute to its success in improving outcomes for both foster carers and their foster children.

Having developed a training manual for this programme, the Maudsley team is keen, as is the DCSF (DfES, 2007a), that this evaluated and effective training programme is rolled out to more local authorities and IFAs. In the meantime, there are particular aspects of this training that can be incorporated into the practice of supervising social workers and social workers responsible for a foster child. One of the strengths of the programme is that the foster carer is required to keep a diary about their own and their foster child's behaviour and their relationship with their foster child so that they can consider, with guidance, what they have done well and what they might need to change.

> . . . the Fostering Changes model does focus on the foster carers' relationship with the children they look after as the medium for bringing about change. The ways that carers relate to children in their care are recognised as having immense significance. How they talk to children, the language they use, their ability to listen, the ways that they respond to appropriate as well as inappropriate behaviour, are all seen to affect the child and the tenor of the relationship. This training therefore encourages carers to act 'differently' and enables them to provide new and subtly different experiences for the children in their care, which can improve how children think and feel about themselves, their immediate relationships and the world around them.

(Warman *et al.*, 2006, p20)

There are many benefits to foster carers and their foster children of being part of the Fostering Changes training programme, not only because of the expertise of those running the sessions and the content but also from the experience of learning from peer foster carers.

Multi-dimensional Treatment Foster Care in England (MTFCE)

The MTFCE is also an evidence-based programme, which was originally developed and evaluated at the Oregon Social Learning Center in the United States of America (USA). Roberts *et al.* (2005) offer a good description of the programme and how it is being implemented in the UK. The government is currently funding pilot projects in England as part of the *Care Matters* (DfES, 2007a) commitment to improving the quality of foster care. The programme is based on social learning theory and aims to improve outcomes for troubled children in public care who might otherwise be in custody or residential provision. Each child and foster family has a multi-professional team working with them, involving health, education and social services. The programme is prescribed and fidelity to the model is considered important as a factor contributing to success: *Evidence from a number of trials concludes that treatment fidelity is a major determinant of outcome and that a high level of fidelity and model adherence is associated with positive outcomes* (National Implementation Team, 2008, p5). There are a number of such projects being funded in England and training of the foster carers involved in the projects is an important aspect in the achievement of the successful outcomes for the foster children involved. As well as the Maudsley Hospital in London implementation team's annual reports and evaluation, there is an independent evaluation being conducted by the Universities of York and Manchester, which was due for completion in 2010.

Foster carers who are recruited to be part of the MTFCE projects undertake the Skills to Foster training programme as would most foster carers in the UK. These foster carers then undertake additional training about the MTFCE model.

> *This provides the basic information needed to understand the principles and practice of operating the programme in the foster carer's home . . . Since last year, foster carers from the English project have also contributed to the training, and their videos were thoroughly enjoyed by the prospective new carers. The two-day training course includes a number of case examples, practice exercises and role plays, information about how attachment theory relates to the behavioural programme and examples of dealing with specific behavioural problems in the English legal and cultural context.*
>
> (National Implementation Team, 2008, p14)

At the time the 2008 annual report was written, 268 foster carers had been trained in this model in England. Like the Fostering Changes training programme, the MTFCE training of foster carers is based on a clear theoretical position and helps foster carers to develop specific skills. It is a coherent programme delivered by a specialist training team. The results of the independent evaluation of the programme and the training will not be known until after 2010 but the USA evaluations of MTFCE and the training component of the programme are very promising.

KEEP (Keeping Foster Parents Trained and Supported) is a training programme originally developed in the USA that evolved from the MTFCE programme. The KEEP programme aims to roll out aspects of the MTFCE programme to 'ordinary' foster carers and placements. The USA study (Price *et al.*, 2009) found that the training and support that these foster carers received did beneficially impact on foster children's well-being.

These successful foster carer training interventions (Fostering Change, MTFCE and KEEP) all have the same factors in common: a coherent theoretical base; a clear structure; that they are delivered by dedicated facilitators and an underpinning philosophy of collaborative learning. If we are to improve the quality of foster carer training to make sure that it has beneficial impacts on the quality of foster care, then we need to take heed of the findings of studies of where foster carer training has been effective.

ACTIVITY 6.2

In your team, identify what training your foster carers are undertaking this year. Conduct an audit of this training using the messages from this section of the chapter regarding effective training. Try to identify the following:

- *What is the theoretical base of the training?*

- *How current is the content?*

- *What principles underpin the training?*

- *What skills will foster carers develop as a result of undertaking the training?*

- *How is the training structured and how do you measure the effectiveness of what is delivered?*

- *How might you improve the quality and coherence of the training you offer?*

- *What can you learn from effective training programmes that have been evaluated (as described above) that could be incorporated into what you offer?*

Comment

Having considered the seven questions above, think about how you might improve the quality of the training you offer by incorporating the key factors for effective foster care training programmes identified above: a coherent theoretical base; a clear structure; that they are delivered by dedicated facilitators and that they have an underpinning philosophy of collaborative learning.

The Wakefield Inquiry

The first part of this chapter has focused on the effectiveness of foster carer training, which the DCSF and the CWDC have placed considerable emphasis on as a mechanism to improve the quality of foster care. However, training is only one aspect of what con-tributes to good quality foster care. In the words of one foster child: *'I think a foster carer's personality is what makes a good foster carer. I am not interested in what qualifi-cations my foster carer has. I am only interested in their kindness, understanding and commitment to me'* (DfES, 2007b). Research has established that foster carers' personal attributes make a difference to the quality of foster care that they offer: *Researchers con-sistently argue that the 'success' of foster care depends on the quality of carers, especially those who have developed a style of parenting which is effective for children who have experienced unsettled and difficult early lives* (Warman et al., 2006, p18). Some of the skills and qualities that foster carers need to enable them to be effective can be developed through training. However, there are some personal attributes that foster carers also need to be effective in their role. The foster child quoted above described these attributes as 'personality', and 'kindness, understanding and commitment' and applicants need to have these qualities to be approved as foster carers. The assessment of prospective foster carers is fundamentally an assessment of their potential to care for children in public care and whether or not they have the necessary qualities to undertake this task competently. The foster care review process, however, looks at the quality of the work that the foster carer has actually done with a specific child or children since their approval or since their last review. In other words, assessment is the consideration of a prospective foster carer's potential and the review is an evaluation of how that potential has been realised. During the assessment process hypothetical questions are addressed about how the prospective carer might deal with a particular situation or behaviour, whereas the review looks at what the foster carer actually did. The Wakefield Inquiry (Parrott *et al.*, 2007) acts as a case example of where the assessment and review process went very wrong. Social work-ers and agencies can learn from this inquiry, both as a case study but also from its recommendations.

In June 2006, two gay male foster carers approved by Wakefield Council were given prison sentences for the sexual abuse of boys they had fostered. Consequently, an independent inquiry was set up to consider the circumstances of the case and to make recommenda-tions. Amongst other topics, the inquiry report addressed the assessment, supervision and review of the carers. Both Parrott *et al.* (2007) and the judge who sentenced the carers at their trial were clear that the carers' homosexuality had no bearing on the case. In sen-tencing, Judge Sally Cahill QC said: *'I stress that this case is not, of course, about homosexuality; what it is about is a breach of trust'*. In summing up, she said that: *'the fact that they are homosexual does not of course make them either more likely or less likely to have committed these offences'* (Parrott *et al.*, 2007, p3). However, the inquiry report does note that the fear of being accused of being homophobic did seem to have impacted on the degree of rigour and scrutiny that was applied by the social workers to the assessment of these carers:

> *. . . alongside anxieties on their part about being or being seen as prejudiced against gay people. The fear of being discriminatory led them to fail to discriminate between the appropriate and the abusive. Discrimination based on prejudice is not acceptable, especially not in social work or any public service. Discrimination founded on a profes-sional judgement on a presenting issue, based on knowledge, assessed evidence and interpretation, is at the heart of good social work practice. These anxieties about dis-*

crimination have deep roots, we argue – in social work training, professional identity and organisational cultures . . .

(Parrott *et al.*, 2007, p164).

Cocker and Brown comment:

This report was a sharp reminder for social workers that alongside the need to make sure that both practice and service delivery should never negatively discriminate against people on the grounds of gender, sexuality, age, race, religion and disability (as indeed is required by law in the UK under the Equality Act 2006) social workers also have a professional duty not to lose sight of the need to analyse and synthesise material to form professional judgements. Discrimination in its correct non-prejudicial form is an essential ingredient in this analysis and synthesis in social work practice.

(Cocker and Brown, 2010, p22)

Fear of being negatively discriminatory can lead to a failure to address key areas in an assessment and needs to be held in mind by social workers and be explicitly addressed in supervision.

The Inquiry report noted that the assessment process of the carers *failed to cover important psycho-social features of them as individuals and of their relationship with each other* (Parrott *et al.*, 2007, p4). This psycho-social assessment should have looked in detail at: each of their childhoods; their relationship with their parents, siblings and wider family, school and community; how their own parents' parenting and their family life impacted on their development; and on their sense of themselves. It should also have addressed how their individual histories as children, the losses they experienced, their adolescences and experiences as adults impacted on how they saw themselves in the present and what impact their histories might have on how they would care for looked after children. The carers' motivation to foster should have been fully explored as should the quality and detail of their relationship with one another and with previous partners. The inquiry report noted that neither gender nor sex and sexuality, nor their experiences as gay men (for example, how they had managed discrimination) had been explored during their assessment. There was also no evidence of their or their assessor's thinking about how their sexuality might impact on them as foster carers. For example, if a birth parent was hostile to them because they were gay, how would they manage this in the interests of their foster child? The assessment lacked sufficient hypothetical questioning and the inquiry team concluded that this lack of an appropriately intrusive, rigorous, analytical, psycho-social assessment was partially due to the assessor's worries about accusations of homophobia.

The Inquiry report identified a number of patterns, one being a bullying dynamic that developed between the foster carers and others, including birth family members of foster children and towards the foster children's social workers. Additionally, the report noted that the fostering team seemed unable to take on board negative information about these carers – they were unable to 'think the unthinkable'. One of the children's social workers described to the inquiry her experience of this:

CSW1 said she felt the fostering service workers were not prepared to listen to their concerns and said in interview, 'I think that one of the problems was that the family

99

*placement team were very clear that we've got these carers and they are unique . . .
they were a gay foster couple . . . we need to do everything to support them, to help
them remain foster carers really and that was very clearly coming across even though
we were sort of saying, although not stating specifically that we felt the boys were
being abused but were saying that we've got numerous concerns about these carers
that need dealing with and . . . whatever we were saying I felt was not really being listened to one hundred per cent because ultimately they wanted these foster carers to
remain foster carers'.*

(Parrott *et al.*, 2007, p74)

The Inquiry report also identified deficits in the foster care review process that meant that
there was a failure to identify patterns that were emerging. These deficits included: poor
preparation for the first annual review for the foster carers; inadequate chairing of the
review; mistakes in the administration form for the review; and a descriptive report from
their supervising social worker that lacked a sufficient level of analysis. Fundamentally,
there was a lack of in-depth exploration and probing during the review itself about: the
foster carers' experience of fostering to date; how they had managed difficulties they had
encountered; how difficulties that had emerged had been managed; the quality of the
working relationship between the foster carers, foster children's birth family members and
other professionals, and how safeguarding matters had been addressed and concluded.

The Wakefield Inquiry provides a detailed case study of social work with foster carers and
with looked after children. As social work practitioners, it is important that we learn from
its findings and its recommendations.

CASE STUDY 6.1

*June and Gavin are a white English couple both in their fifties. They were approved as
foster carers by Rosspond local authority eight months ago to care for up to three children between the ages of five and 12 years of age. Their first annual review is now being
prepared. In their Form F assessment report, there were a number of potential risk factors
that were identified as well as strengths. The strengths included both June and Gavin
having grown up in loving families. Sadly, June's mother died when she was 12 and from
then on she helped her Dad care for her two younger brothers until she went to university
where she met her first husband. Although she described her first marriage as 'happy
enough' she never felt her husband was sufficiently involved with the care of their son
Peter. She divorced her first husband when Peter was ten and felt she did an 'excellent
job' bringing Peter up on her own. Peter retained an independent relationship with his
Dad which June was happy to facilitate. Peter is now in his third year at university and
comes home in the holidays. Gavin's family background was in his words 'stable and
happy'. He had three relationships since he qualified as a physiotherapist when he was
21, none of which lasted for more than a year. When June and Gavin met three years ago,
when they were working in the same hospital, they felt they were well matched and
quickly started living together. Both enjoyed their work, Gavin as a physiotherapist and
June as a children's nurse. However, they felt something was missing and both wanted
the opportunity to parent together so applied to become foster carers as they believed
themselves to be too old to adopt.*

Four months after their approval they had two white Irish sisters placed with them: Daisy (5) and Cindy (7). Between their approval as foster carers and the girls being placed with them they had moved house and got married. Daisy and Cindy had experienced neglect and emotional abuse and were subject to a care order. They had already had two placements in less than seven months, both of which had broken down. They were emotionally troubled and found basic routines difficult to establish and manage. Daisy had regular tantrums and both children were fearful of travelling in a car. Both Gavin and June had to be present to get them into the car when they went to school or to contact. For the first two months of the placement Cindy could only sleep on the floor and would eat her meals sitting on the floor. Both children suffered from enuresis. Daisy was doing well at school but Cindy was described as disruptive, aggressive, and with a short attention span and was unable to read or write. The local authority was undertaking an assessment to see if their grandfather was able to care for them and as a result they went four times per week, after school, to a contact centre to meet with him. They had no contact with either of their parents. June or Gavin took the girls to contact and June in particular established a good relationship with their grandfather.

During the three months Daisy and Cindy were placed with June and Gavin the foster carers' relationship began to deteriorate. June felt that she would cope better on her own and that Gavin made things more difficult with the girls. June felt that he was unclear with the girls and gave them mixed messages, for example one day agreeing that Cindy could eat on the floor and the next getting cross when she insisted that she did the same again. Eventually, Gavin and June gave notice to the local authority that they wanted Cindy and Daisy to move as they felt they couldn't manage. This meant that the girls had to be moved on to yet another foster placement before the assessment of their grandfather's capacity to care for them had been completed.

- *What 'risk factors', alluded to above, do you think might have been identified in their original Form F assessment report?*

- *If you were the supervising social worker for Gavin and June, what evidence about their foster care would you want to gather for the review?*

- *What areas would you want to make sure that the chair of the review explored in the review meeting?*

Comment

The risk factors identified in their Form F assessment would have included June's loss of her mother in childhood and her consequent development of self-reliance. June had to cope as a child, after the loss of her mother, and indeed did this so well that she helped her father care for her two younger siblings. However, this ability, which might have been helpful as a child, meant that as an adult she found sharing responsibilities hard. This was evidenced in her relationship with her first husband and the care of their son. June's self-reliance was also evident in her experience of caring for Daisy and Cindy. In addition, Gavin had three relationships before he met June, none of which lasted longer than a year. The Form F assessment should have explored the reasons for this and any related risks for his future role as a foster carer. Lastly, both Gavin and June wanted to parent together. However, they had no joint experience of this prior to fostering and their fantasy of parenting was likely to have been quite different from the realities of fostering Daisy and Cindy.

As the supervising social worker preparing your report for Gavin and June's review, you would reflect on the implications of their marriage and house move that took place between their approval as foster carers and Daisy and Cindy being placed with them. In addition, the report would need to record the events of the placement, the content of your supervision sessions with June and Gavin and your observations of their direct care of and relationship with Daisy and Cindy. In addition to Gavin and June's own self-evaluative report and reports recording the views of the children, you would need to collate third-party evidence about the quality of their foster care from the contact centre, the school and Cindy and Daisy's social worker.

The chair of the review meeting would need to consider: the implications of June and Gavin's change of circumstances (their marriage and house move) on their fostering, the quality of their direct care of Daisy and Cindy, the events of the placement, the quality of their working relationships with all of the professionals involved with Daisy and Cindy's care plan, how they had worked together as a couple to manage the challenges that the children presented, the quality of their relationship with the agency and their supervising social worker, what use they had made of supervision and training, the quality of their support and facilitation of Daisy and Cindy's educational achievements, how effective their support network was, what led them to give notice to the local authority that they wanted Daisy and Cindy to be moved, the quality of their own relationship and how they see their future. In the review meeting, a key question would be whether or not Gavin and June are emotionally and practically able to foster as a united couple. It would be the responsibility of the chair of the review to make a recommendation to the agency's fostering panel, in their report of the review meeting, as to whether or not June and Gavin should continue to be approved as foster carers and if their terms of approval were still appropriate.

ACTIVITY 6.4

- *Read the Wakefield Inquiry report (Parrott* et al., *2007) and consider how the recommendations and findings are relevant to your fostering agency.*

Comment

Having read the report, you could use this exercise within your agency to consider the following:

- Identify how you prepare for foster carer reviews. For example, what documents are collated for reviews? Do you seek triangulation of evidence about the quality of the foster carer's work? Do you get written reports from the supervising social worker, the foster carer, the foster child's school or health visitor and their birth parent as well as gathering the views of the foster child and the foster child's social worker?

- How do you make sure that matters that were identified in the carers' assessment report by the fostering panel and in previous reviews are addressed explicitly within the annual review? How could you improve your review paperwork and processes within your fostering agency?

Chapter summary

This chapter has considered two areas relevant to social work and foster care: firstly, the effective training of foster carers that will impact on the quality of their foster care and the well-being of foster children; and secondly, the findings of the Wakefield Inquiry that are relevant to both foster carers' assessments and reviews.

The chapter drew out some key areas that arose from the Wakefield Inquiry relevant to the assessment and review of foster carers: firstly, social workers' and agencies' fears of being accused of being negatively discriminatory; secondly, the importance of a psycho-social approach to the assessment and review process; and thirdly, the identification of patterns that emerge in assessments and reviews. The chapter also identified key aspects of foster carer training that makes it effective. These were: a coherent theoretical base; a clear structure; that it is delivered by dedicated facilitators; and that it has an underpinning philosophy of collaborative learning. Research covered in the chapter identified social learning theory as an effective tool in enabling foster carers to work effectively with foster children. This chapter argues for the importance of practitioners to be flexible in their use of theoretical frameworks; to work within a psycho-social theoretical framework at the same time as utilising social learning theory where it is proven to be effective.

Care Matters (2007a) identified the need to increase stability for looked after children as well as improving their ability to fulfil their potential to meet the *Every Child Matters* (DfES, 2004) five outcomes. For these commitments to be met, all of the recommendations of the Wakefield Inquiry need to be noted to improve foster care assessment and review practice. Foster carers require structured, theoretically coherent, regular, collaborative training that helps them develop to enable them to meet the emotional, educational and developmental needs of foster children at the same time as giving them a positive experience of family life.

FURTHER READING

Pallett, C, Blackeby, K, Yule, W, Weissman, R and Scott, S (2005) *Fostering changes: How to improve relationships and manage difficult behaviour: A training programme for foster carers.* London: BAAF.

This text is the handbook covering the Fostering Changes programme.

Parrott, B, MacIver, A and Thoburn, J (2007) *Independent inquiry into the circumstances of child sexual abuse by two foster carers in Wakefield.* Wakefield: Wakefield County Council.

This text is the report of the independent inquiry into the circumstances of child sexual abuse by two foster carers in Wakefield.

Roberts, R, Scott, S and Jones, H (2005) Treatment foster care in England in A. Wheal (ed) *The RHP companion to foster care.* Lyme Regis: Russell House Publishing.

This chapter is a useful summary of what is involved in multi-dimensional treatment foster care. It also reviews the research about MTFCE's effectiveness up until 2005.

Sinclair, I (2005) *Fostering now: Messages from research.* London: Jessica Kingsley.

This book summarises a number of research studies on fostering, foster carers and foster children.

Wilson, K, Sinclair, I, Taylor, C, Pithouse, A and Sellick, C (2004) *Fostering success: An exploration of the research literature in foster care.* London: SCIE.

This book is a review of research about foster care and offers an accessible and useful summary.

Chapter 7
Adoption

Christine Cocker and Jane Anderson

CHAPTER OBJECTIVES

If you are a registered social worker, this chapter will assist you to evidence post-registration training and learning. It relates to the national post-qualifying framework for social work education and training at the specialist level:

v. Use reflection and critical analysis to continuously develop and improve their specialist practice, including their practice in inter-professional and inter-agency context, drawing systematically, accurately and appropriately on theories, models and relevant up-to-date research.

and at higher specialist level:

iii. Demonstrate a substantially enhanced level of competence in a defined area of professional practice, professional management, professional education or applied professional research to the agreed national standards for higher specialist work in this area.

It will also help you to meet the Children and Families standards for social work:

ii(f). The needs of children and young people accommodated, looked after and leaving care (including a knowledge and understanding of how to use the services that exist to meet those needs and the nature of the specific responsibilities of corporate parents, such as those associated with responsibilities for development and educational attainment).

viii. Responding positively to the full range of changes that can take place in family (including extended and substitute family) systems and family functioning, including those associated with the separation and divorce of parents and those associated with the separation of children from birth parents or the reunification of children with birth parents.

Introduction

In 1999, the 'Prime Minister's Review of Adoption' (Performance and Innovation Unit, 2000) spearheaded the modernisation of adoption services, culminating in the passing of the Adoption and Children Act 2002, which provided the legal framework for this transformation in England and Wales. This has heightened the profile of adoption and permanency work nationally, with increased Government pressure to raise the number of children adopted from care and the speed of the process. Many of the initiatives contained within this Act, such as the introduction of an adoption register, an emphasis on adoption support services, special guardianship, the assessment and matching processes for adopters and children being adopted, and contact, has led to different kinds of conversations and debates about adoption as an option for permanence for looked after children in twenty-first century Britain.

This chapter provides a critical overview of a number of these practice debates. The overarching policy document *Every Child Matters* (DfES, 2004a) and the Green and White Papers *Care Matters* (DfES, 2006a; DfES, 2007a) are commendable, with an emphasis on children requiring permanency at the earliest opportunity, as well as incorporating the five ECM outcomes for all children (staying safe; being healthy; enjoying and achieving; making a positive contribution; and achieving economic well-being). The history and policy context of adoption in the UK has been documented and discussed elsewhere (DoH, 2000a; PIU, 2000; Rushton, 2003; Cocker and Allain, 2008; Simmonds, 2009). Garrett (2003; 2009a), Parton (2006a) and Frost and Parton (2009) offer critical perspectives on the previous Labour Government's move to modernise public care more broadly. In practice, policy priorities aren't always met within a performance framework that focuses on service outputs rather than outcomes. The needs of the child must remain paramount throughout, and current debates should reflect this and acknowledge the complexities of practice, which determine successful outcomes.

Since the 'Prime Minister's Review of Adoption', there has been ongoing Government interest in increasing the number of children adopted from care, where adoption is seen as in the 'best interest' of the children concerned. An Adoption and Permanence Taskforce was set up in 2000, and a White Paper *Adoption: A New Approach* was published (DoH, 2000a). The National Adoption Register was also launched in 2001. The voluntary sector organisation Norwood initially oversaw the establishment and development of the Register. In 2004, the British Association for Adoption and Fostering (BAAF) took over this role, and continues to manage the Register.

Over the last decade, numbers of children adopted from care steadily rose from 2,700 in 2000 to 3,300 in 2009, peaking at 3,800 children in both 2004 and 2005. The average age of children at the time of their adoption has reduced from four years and four months in 2000 to three years and nine months in 2009 (DCSF, 2009f). This number fell short of the Government target (DoH, 2000a) of a 40 per cent increase by 2005–06. The increase achieved was 34 per cent, reflecting a significant number of additional children adopted during this period.

Table 7.1 Children looked after adopted during the year ending 31 March

Year	2000	2001	2002	2003	2004	2005	2006	2007	2008	2009
Numbers	2,700	3,100	3,400	3,500	3,800	3,800	3,700	3,300	3,200	3,300
% LAC	5	5	6	6	6	6	6	5.5	5	5
Average age	4.4	4.3	4.5	4.4	4.5	4.2	4.1	4.2	3.11	3.9

(Compiled from DoH/DfEE/DfES/DCSF figures)

Adoption also occurs for a number of other children, including babies who are relinquished at birth, step-parent adoptions and children who are adopted from overseas, but this chapter does not address the specific practice issues associated with these kinds of adoptions. The chapter explores the very difficult decisions made in adoption, and this requires workers to keep the child in mind constantly while balancing many other responsibilities. Research summaries and case studies are provided throughout to assist social workers in thinking critically about their practice in this area.

A summary of the Adoption and Children Act 2002 and relevant case law

Although a detailed examination of the Adoption and Children Act 2002 is beyond the scope of this chapter, a general overview of the most commonly used parts of the Act is provided. The Adoption and Children Act 2002 reformed the Adoption Act 1976 and brought domestic and inter-country adoption in line with many of the principles contained in the Children Act 1989, such as: the paramountcy principle for the child in respect of all decisions regarding adoption; the no-delay principle, or avoidance of undue delay in planning for permanence and adoption; and the no-order principle, where an order will not be made unless it is best for the child. A welfare checklist, similar but not identical to the one contained in the Children Act 1989, was also included (see Cocker and Allain, 2008, p16–17). There is no presumption of contact; however, the Court is obliged to consider arrangements for contact, including at the adoption application stage (Section 46(6)) via a Section 8 order (Children Act 1989), and may also make an order for contact (Section 26) when the adoption order is granted.

The Adoption and Children Act 2002 comprises three parts. Part 1 is the most significant section as it sets out the legal framework for adoption. Part 2 details the amendments to the Children Act 1989, and sets out special guardianship and step-parent adoptions. Part 3 contains a series of miscellaneous provisions designed to improve and regulate adoption, including information about adoption panels.

There are a number of key orders used in adoption:

- **Placement Orders:** Adoption agencies must obtain authorisation from the Courts to place a child via an application for a placement order (Section 22). In order for a child who is looked after by a local authority to be placed for adoption, the placing agency must be satisfied that the child ought to be placed for adoption (Section 18). This can only be done where consent has been given by the birth parent(s) for adoption (Section 19) or where the Court has made a Placement Order (Section 21). The Court cannot make a Placement Order unless the child is subject to a Care Order (Section 31 of the Children Act 1989), or the child has no guardian and the Court is satisfied that the parent or guardian has consented to the adoption, or that the parent or guardian's consent should be dispensed with.

- **Adoption Orders:** Provision for adoption orders (Sections 46 to 51); and adoption order applications (Annexe A) – if the child was placed for adoption by an adoption agency, before an adoption application can be made, the child must live with the adopters for a minimum of ten weeks (Section 42). If the applicants are local authority foster parents, the child must have lived with them for a year prior to the application, irrespective of whether the local authority agrees with the application or not. In step-parent adoptions, the child must have lived with the applicant for six months before the application.

The Act also makes provision for disclosure of information prior to and following a person's adoption (Sections 54, 56 to 65 and 98). The Act includes special guardianship (Section 115), designed to enable permanency for children and young people for whom adoption is not suitable. The Act also regulates: inter-country adoptions (see also the Children and Adoption Act 2006 at **www.baaf.org.uk/info/lpp/law/childrenadoptbill. shtml**); the way in which children can be advertised, and the way in which payments are made in association with adoption. Additionally, the regulation of adoption agencies and support services was improved and extended and the Act also provides the legal basis for the Adoption Register (see Brammer, 2010; Brayne and Carr, 2010).

The Adoption and Children Act 2002 strengthened the support services that must be available from adoption agencies for three years after a child has been adopted. If the child moves out of the area of the placing authority, then the placing authority has a duty to provide a service for three years, after which any services may then be provided through the local authority where the child now lives. Any existing financial arrangements continue to be held by the placing authority. All local authorities must provide as a minimum the following adoption services:

- counselling, advice and information;
- financial support;
- support groups for adoptive families;
- assistance with contact arrangements between adopted children and their birth relatives;
- therapeutic services for adopted children;
- help to ensure the continuance of adoptive relationships;
- an adoption support services advisor and adoption support plans for adoptive families;
- an assessment of the needs of adopted children and their families for adoption support services.

Additionally, the Adoption Agencies National Minimum Standards (DoH, 2003) recognise the specific skills required for social workers and managers undertaking work in this area and set out the qualifications, level of experience and the supervisory support necessary (Standards 14, 19, 20, 21, 24, 25 and 26).

The Adoption and Children Act 2002 broadened out who can adopt, so that now adopters can be single, married/entered into a civil partnership, or cohabiting. Adoption agencies have also developed guidance and policies on maximum ages of applicants, especially in relation to babies requiring adoption placements, but not if the baby has special needs.

In addition to the Adoption and Children Act 2002 and the associated Statutory Guidance (DfES, 2005b), the actions of the adoption service are governed by the Adoption Agencies Regulations 2005, the Adoption Agencies National Minimum Standards for adoption

(DoH, 2003), and the Adoption Support Agencies National Minimum Standards (England) (2005, **see www.dcsf.gov.uk**).

Case law

Case law is an important process in determining how the law is interpreted by the Courts, and depending on the seniority of the Court this then sets precedence for how decisions will be made in similar cases in other Courts. However, it is always important to obtain legal advice from an agency solicitor because, although case law is influential, each case is unique and decisions will be made according to the facts of that case alone. The development of case law is also continuous, and it is important to keep up to date with changes. The significant case law to date in relation to adoption includes the following:

1. Court of Appeal Guidance concerning information being given to adoption panels:

   a. Re: B (2008) EWCA Civ 835: the Court also issued guidance in this area (**www.lawreports.co.uk/WLRD/2008/CACiv/jul1.4.htm**)

2. Secret births – where the mother has given birth to a child in secret:

   a. Re: L (2007) EWHC 1771 (Fam): informing an unmarried father about a child being placed for adoption (**www.familylwweek.co.uk/site.aspx?i=ed864**)

   b Re: C (a child) and XYZ County Council and EC (2007) EWCA Civ 1206: adoption without notification to the family, re Hampshire County Council disclosing the existence and identity of a child to the extended maternal family and birth father. (**www.familylawweek.co.uk/site.aspx?i=ed1147**)

3. Post-adoption contact:

   a. Re: P (a child) 2008 EWCA Civ 535. Para 141–154 sets out the evolving approach to post-adoption contact with a move toward a more 'open' approach (**www.familylawweek.co.uk/site.aspx?i=ed1222**)

4. A judicial review case concerning how agencies should approach decision-making processes for adopters they are minded not to approve:

   a. Re: (ex parte AT and S) v LB Newham (2008) EWHC 2640 (Admin) (**www.familylawweek.co.uk/site.aspx?i=ed27882**)

5. A case that involved poor practice by the local authority:

   a. Re: C v East Sussex County Council [2008] EWCA Civ 439; [2008] WLR (D) 136 (**www.lawreports.co.uk/WLRD/2008/CACiv/may0.3.htm**)

6. A case about an application to set aside adoption orders where wrong findings were made regarding non-accidental injuries to children who were then adopted. This case illustrates the finality of adoption proceedings:

   a. Re: W (children) sub-nom Webster v Norfolk CC and others [2009] EWCA Civ 59 (**www.familylawweek.co.uk/site.aspx?i=ed32412**)

7. A case that involved the placement of children overseas:

    a. Re: Haringey v MA and others [2008] EWHC 1722
       (**www.familylawweek.co.uk/site.aspx?i=ed25020**)

An overview of the work of adoption services

The implementation of the Adoption and Children Act 2002 created the means to improve and extend the regulation of adoption and adoption support services. Since December 2005, a local authority adoption service has had a clear brief detailing the services they must provide and their duties and responsibilities. These include:

- creating permanency for looked after children if they cannot return to the care of their parents;

- being responsible for the creation and maintenance of an Adoption and Permanency Panel;

- preparing, family finding and placing looked after children for adoption where they cannot return to any member of their extended family;

- assessing prospective adopters for both domestic and inter-country adoptions;

- completing court reports for step-parent adoptions and non-agency adoptions;

- providing support services for those affected by adoption such as birth relative counselling and tracing birth family for adult adoptees;

- enabling communication to be maintained, when appropriate, between a child and their birth relatives via the exchange of letters or meeting face to face once a child has been adopted or placed with their special guardian.

An adoption service works closely with the child's social worker, the child's foster carers, the adopters and their link workers, and the birth family of the child, and liaises closely with the Adoption Panel. The core of the work however focuses on preparing children for adoption, finding families for them, supporting the adoptive placements, assessing adults as prospective adopters and providing counselling for adult adoptees who are seeking information about their birth families.

One of the pressures for some local authorities is that within a local authority area there are often an insufficient number of adopters who have come forward to be assessed compared to the number of children who need to be placed. There might not be a good 'match' between those families who are approved as adopters and the children requiring adoption. For example, Selwyn and Wijedasa state that *minority ethnic children are less likely to be found an adoptive family than white children: 18 per cent adopted compared to 23 per cent in the looked after population* (Selwyn and Wijedasa, 2009, p368). For many children there is also a need to live with adoptive families who live some distance from their birth families. To minimise the delay for a child in finding an adoptive family and reduce a child's length of stay in care, local authority adoption services now work much more closely with other adoption agencies. Most local authorities belong to a local consortium of adoption agencies (including voluntary sector and local authorities) where each agency will distribute the details of recently approved families to encourage quicker matching between families approved for adoption and the children who are waiting to be adopted. The National Adoption Register and adoption exchange events also assist in this process by identifying available families. This does result in children being placed with families who have been approved by other agencies in other parts of the country. This is made possible through inter-agency agreements. However, there are implications for the long-term support of adoptive families, as the placing authority remains responsible for post-adoption support for three years after a child's placement. Maintaining sibling contact when siblings are not placed together and are geographically some distance from each other is also another challenge.

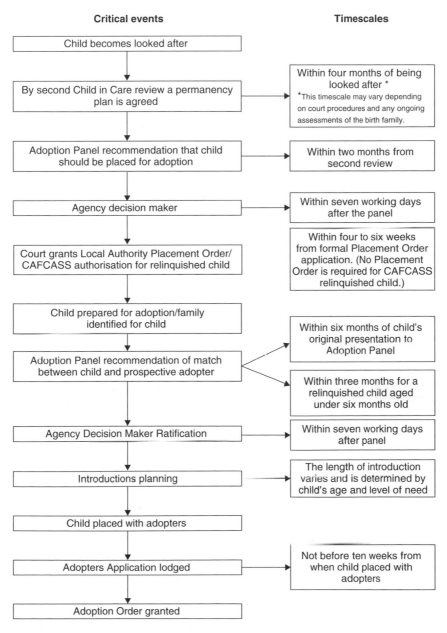

Figure 7.1 Adoption process for looked after child

The adoption process for looked after children

Although there are many aspects of each child's journey through the adoption process that are unique to that child, there are a number of critical events and associated timescales that are prescribed. Figure 7.1 outlines the key stages that children who are adopted from public care will go through. One of the time factors that cannot be predetermined in this process is the length of time a child may be involved in care proceedings.

In preparing children for adoption, adoption social workers will often need to undertake direct work with the child. This is in addition and is complementary to any life story work that has been undertaken by either the child's social worker or foster carer. Practice has shown that, the better the child is prepared for adoption, the less traumatic it will be for the child to make the transition to their adoptive family (Fahlberg, 1994). It is essential that the worker is cognisant of the child's level of learning ability and their attachment style, and that they interact with the child in a way the child can understand. With very young children this can be done through play, and this requires skill and patience as the worker must go at the pace of the child. Workers also need to be able to tolerate difficult feelings and to contain the child's sense of loss and anxiety.

Social workers in an adoption service are working with children and adults whose emotions may be very raw due to the experiences they have had. Skills in reflection and reflexivity are crucial for adoption social workers, in terms of having an awareness of the impact of working in this area on everyone involved, including themselves (Ironside, 2008). For many front-line staff, adoption is seen as the end of the story for those children who have been removed from traumatic environments, but it is also the beginning of a new chapter for these children as they embark on a journey with their new family. If social workers think that adoption is the end point, there is a risk that they will disengage from the process too early. Importantly, the local authority's responsibilities towards the child continue even after the adoption order has been obtained, in terms of post-adoption support and contact, and plans should be made and supported accordingly.

CASE STUDY 7.1

You are the adoption worker in a case that involves family-finding for four children: Ben (18 months); Brandon (3); Bradley (4) and Briony (6). All of the children have the same mother, Joanna, who is white British. Ben's father is Barry, who is mixed African Caribbean/white; Brandon and Bradley's father is Tariq, who is Pakistani/white Irish, and Briony's father is Jack, who is white British. Prior to admission into care, the children were living with their mother, who has a serious drug addiction problem. She is also a sex worker. The children were found home alone, after Bradley was spotted by police wandering down a busy road at 3 a.m. looking for his mother. The children are currently in two separate foster placements, with Ben and Briony placed together, and Brandon and Bradley in another placement. They see each other twice a week. Briony is quite 'mothering' toward her younger siblings and struggles to be a child in her own right. This manifests in her being very controlling of her younger siblings in the contact sessions, and within the foster placement. You have already had discussions with the children's social

CASE STUDY **7.1** (CONT.)

worker about whether the children should be placed together or in a combination of placements. The social worker has commissioned an external organisation to assess the best options for the children, and this organisation has recommended that Ben and Briony are both placed in separate placements, and Brandon and Bradley are placed together. The feedback that you have received from the foster carers suggests that the relationships between all four children are significant. Both sets of foster carers are of the view that the children should remain together if at all possible.

ACTIVITY **7.1**

- *In terms of decision making about placements, how do you determine the best outcome for all four children?*

- *When you are thinking about matching these children to an adoptive family, what factors take precedence, and why?*

- *How do these change according to who is considering the information (for example the children's social worker, the adoption worker, a specialist agency, the foster carers, the birth parents, the prospective adopters, the children)?*

- *What are the needs of each child? How do they differ from their other siblings?*

- *If the children can't all be placed together, what are the options for continued contact between the siblings?*

Comment

These decisions are among the most difficult you will ever have to make as a social worker, and there are no easy answers in terms of what the 'correct' decision is in such circumstances. See Hollows and Nelson (2006) which examines professional judgements and decision making in relation to siblings. Every decision you make will have intended and unintended consequences and it is important that you identify and acknowledge these consequences and think them through when making your decision. You should always clearly record your rationale for your decision making, including: the reasons for decisions; the people involved in making the decisions; the information that you had available to you at the time of making the decision; and the plans you put in place to support the decisions. So, for example, when decisions have to be made about splitting siblings, some of the details you would consider would be:

- documenting decision-making processes, including who made the decisions and when, and clearly explaining the evidence on which decisions were based. This should include information from any expert assessments undertaken, and recommendations made by Adoption Panels;

- documenting efforts to find a placement for siblings together;

- documenting the thinking behind this decision, in terms of the needs of individual children;

- documenting the arrangements for continued direct and indirect contact between children post-adoption.

Matching a child with adopters is also a complex process, due to a range of needs the child may have and then determining which of these needs takes precedence in these circumstances. In addition, for the staff involved, there is an element of having to project into the future to ascertain what problems may lie ahead for the adoption placement and whether the adopters have an understanding about what some of these issues may be. The adoption social worker works closely with a number of other key people, including the child's social worker, the adopters and the foster carers. These working partnerships are critical within the process of matching.

What does an agency look for in a prospective adopter?

For most local authorities, the assessment of prospective adopters is prioritised to reflect the needs of the children who are within their care who need to be adopted. This is particularly true of inner-city local authorities where the child in care population is ethnically and culturally very diverse. The adoption service looks for a wide variety of adopters who can provide 'parenting plus'; that is, find adults who can parent children who have additional needs due to their experiences prior to coming into care and who can then adapt their parenting style to suit that child. They also need to feel comfortable parenting somebody else's child.

The assessment

The complexity of adopted children's needs necessitates thorough assessments of adopters through preparation groups and an individual assessment. This is to ensure that adopters develop a solid understanding of the triangular dynamic created by adoption: the adopters, the child and the child's birth family. Additionally, the agency needs to have confidence in the resilience of the adopters to parent children who have experienced significant loss and/or trauma and to enable the child to maintain links with their birth family.

A good working relationship between the assessing social worker and the adopters is critical as prospective adopters are being asked to reflect on their own histories and share detailed information about themselves. The assessing social worker in turn needs to analyse this information to determine how able an adopter would be to parent and what type of child would 'fit', i.e. that the attachment style held by the adults complements the attachment style of the child. What is becoming increasingly apparent is that not only are the needs of the children who are to be adopted increasingly more complex but also many prospective adopters' lives are equally complex.

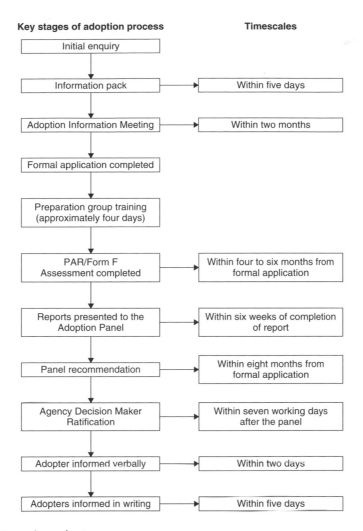

Key stages of adoption process   **Timescales**

Key stages of adoption process	Timescales
Initial enquiry	
Information pack	Within five days
Adoption Information Meeting	Within two months
Formal application completed	
Preparation group training (approximately four days)	
PAR/Form F Assessment completed	Within four to six months from formal application
Reports presented to the Adoption Panel	Within six weeks of completion of report
Panel recommendation	Within eight months from formal application
Agency Decision Maker Ratification	Within seven working days after the panel
Adopter informed verbally	Within two days
Adopters informed in writing	Within five days

Figure 7.2 Assessing adopters

ACTIVITY 7.2

When assessing prospective adopters, one of the areas that is not often commented on in detail in the Prospective Adopter's Report (PAR)/Form F is intimacy within the adopter's relationship. You have been asked to plan and facilitate a discussion in your team meeting about this issue. You will need to include opportunities for people to discuss how they deal with this area currently (or not) and to reflect on the importance of this subject area being discussed with adopters.

* *Provide an outline for this session.*

* *Construct an exercise that will enable participants to articulate the importance of this information for the assessment.*

* *Help participants to identify good practice strategies (including effective practice tools), as well as to acknowledge some of the blocks within current practice.*

Comment

There are many ways in which social workers can, and do, ask prospective applicants about their relationship. In order to do this, social workers have to be clear about the reasons why this information is important for the assessment, as asking someone about the intimate details of their relationship may appear intrusive unless the rationale is clearly and sensitively explained. Social workers need to be sensitive to cultural differences in how this subject is discussed. Some of the questions that social workers may ask applicants include the following:

- What do you do for each other and how has this changed over time?
- What do you do when you have really upset your partner?
- Does your sexual relationship mirror how you are with each other?
- How was sex discussed in your family of origin?
- Depending on the issues and reasons for pursuing adoption, a discussion could be held about the journey a couple has gone through to get to the point of applying to adopt, including (where relevant) any experiences of miscarriage, IVF and/or other treatment, exploring the effect that these experiences have had on the couple's relationship.
- Explore issues of sexual intimacy in the individual sessions with couples – how has this developed over time?
- Are the partners equally happy with how intimacy is acted out? For a single carer, how is this part of their life acknowledged?
- For couples, is there an equal access to intimacy? Is it balanced or is there resentment of any sort?
- How is humour used?

It can be useful for the assessing social worker to talk to the couple together about this, to see how they do talk about it with each other, and to observe the body language between the couple. Intimacy within relationships is outlined as an area for discussion in the PAR/Form F notes. The prospective adopters should have a copy of the assessment format before the assessment starts but in addition the applicants should be given advance warning before this area is discussed. With single adopters, this is also an important issue. Social workers will need to address sexual intimacy and dating and discuss with the applicant how they would manage this when a child is placed. Some single adopters have found it difficult to talk about sexual intimacy if they have had few relationships as there is a stigma attached to having no sex in adult life. With regard to assessing a lesbian or gay couple, social workers should also ask the same questions about sexual intimacy and relationships as they would a heterosexual couple, as it is the quality of the relationship that is crucial to investigate. For further information, including details of the SPRIINT model for assessing intimacy in relationships, see Cocker and Brown (2010).

The introductions

Once a family has been found and matched with the child, the period of introductions, that is the transition from the foster home to the adoptive home, is determined by the amount of time the child needs to engage in the process of beginning to transfer their attachment from one adult to another. This is usually a very intensive period and can be exhausting for all involved. Two sets of strangers have to work closely together for the child to see that the adults are working together to effect the child moving to a new home. The psychological 'permission' given by the foster carer in these circumstances is a necessary but complicated part of enabling the child to move to the adoption placement. It is a period of excitement and nervousness for the child and adopter and a time of sadness for the foster carer and the child as they say farewell to their time of living together. Foster carers will require support over this period from their link worker. It is also a time where the various social workers involved should ensure that the move is the right one for the child, and to provide support to the child and all of the adults involved. The adoption social worker is the one who co-ordinates this process and liaises with all of the parties.

Support for the new placement

The early days of the new placement also need to be well supported as for many adoptive families it is the first time they have parented a child over a sustained period. As most of the children moving into adoptive placements are not babies, they come with established personalities and an experience of the world. The adoption social worker may continue to undertake transition work with the child once they are with their new family to create continuity for the child, helping to consolidate the relationship between the child and the adult.

Post-adoption support

Since 2005, adoption agencies have been required to provide a range of post-adoption services for all those affected by adoption, which can be the birth family, adopted child or adoptive family. These services may be provided by the agency or another service. Placement support should always be discussed at the Adoption Panel. The adoption agency has a duty to provide advice and can also give financial assistance where there is a need. The placing authority is responsible for funding post-adoption support for three years after the child is placed with the adopters, after which the responsibility for funding new services rests with the local authority where the child and family are resident. If additional financial support is provided because of the specific needs of the child that were identified before or at the point of the adoption placement, then the placing local authority will continue to fund these services, but the services will usually be subject to an annual assessment/review.

In addition, two other areas of post-adoption work that adoption agencies are closely involved in are providing counselling/support for adopted adults who are returning to read their files and/or search for their birth family members, and overseeing contact arrangements.

The Adoption and Children Act 2002 required that local authorities offered a much broader range of post-adoption support services. In addition to offering counselling and advice to those affected by adoption, local authorities are now required to make provision for:

- intermediary services for adopted adults – they can be given identifying information of their birth parents without the parents' consent;

- intermediary services to birth families – anyone in the family who was adopted and relatives wanting to trace. The local authority can undertake tracing; however, if the adopted adult does not want any contact then no identifying information can be given to the birth family;

- access to birth records for those living within the local authority or who were adopted through that local authority;

- Schedule 2 birth-recorded counselling.

Counselling is a requirement for those born before 1975 and a recommendation for those born after. While some local authorities undertake this work themselves, many also contract out to other registered adoption support agencies such as Barnardo's and AAA-NORCAP, thereby offering both options to those seeking assistance. The external provider can be seen as a more neutral partner, which can work particularly well for birth parents seeking counselling support during the time of their child being adopted.

The service is also responsible for maintaining and managing a letterbox service, which is a means of maintaining contact between the adopted child and their birth family. Both the adoptive family and the birth family are supported in maintaining this link. Face-to-face meetings between the adopted child and their birth relatives may also be managed and supervised via this service where this is required. The agreements that are drawn up for contact reflect the needs of the particular child. These are not legally binding unless the Court has imposed a defined Contact Order, which is rare. Under the Adoption and Children Act 2002, there is no presumption of contact but the Courts want to see clear evidence of plans for direct or indirect contact, as does the Adoption Panel agreeing the decision for adoption and the match between child and prospective adopters. However, adoption social workers work closely with prospective adopters to ensure they understand the value of such contact arrangements for the child.

Although adoptions are much more open than previously, the information given to the birth family about the adopted family is limited and a degree of confidentiality is maintained. With the advent of 'Facebook' and other social networking sites, this confidentiality has the potential to be compromised in that it is becoming significantly easier to trace people (Fursland, 2010). Potentially, this has far reaching ramifications, both positive and negative, for all those affected by adoption; however, it is too early to identify the breadth of challenges this will bring for adoption. Depending on the age of the children, the fear is that it could cause significant undermining of adoptive placements, through increased indirect contact that is not supervised, but careful and sensitive management of this will reduce any perceived and associated risks, as with many other issues requiring ongoing responsive oversight by the adults concerned.

Step-parent adoptions

These form half of the total number of adoptions that occur in the UK each year. Under the Act, adoption agencies are also responsible for processing applications for step-parent and inter-country adoptions. Applicants must live within the local authority they apply to. Those applying for step-parent adoption are generally families not previously known to the local authority. These adoptions can be relatively complex pieces of work due to the nature of the relationships between the resident birth parent, the applicant, the non-resident biological parent and the child(ren) involved. For children conceived via donor insemination through a clinic, verification of this is required by the Court.

Inter-country adoptions

Inter-country adoption is when prospective adopters in the UK wish to adopt a child from abroad. These are also very complex assessments as they not only need to consider the adopters' capacity to adopt but also their ability to consider the trans-cultural and trans-racial issues that are frequently a part of such an application. For each country that is agreeable to inter-country adoption, there are different rules and systems of referral, some of which are determined by whether they comply with the Hague Convention (see Brammer, 2010). Unlike domestic adoption, where prospective adopters receive a service for free, inter-country applicants have to pay a substantial sum both for the assessment and for the legal processes involved in being matched with a child, therefore those families applying need to have a substantial disposable income in order to proceed. A number of enquiries do come from potential applicants who wish to adopt family members. Although the trans-racial aspect does not apply in these cases, issues relating to changing the family relationship do need to be considered carefully, for example a birth mother becoming an aunt. The rationale for separating children from their families in their country of origin should also be scrutinised.

Adoption panels

All adoption agencies have been required to have adoption panels since the Adoption Agencies Regulations 1983 came into force in 1984. The principal regulations that currently govern the work of panels are the Adoption Agencies Regulations 2005. Each aspect of the agencies adoption work as highlighted above must be considered by the panel and the panel's recommendation must be taken into account by the agency when making its decision. In addition, they must also consider whether a Placement Order application can be made as such an application cannot be lodged in Court until this has happened. The panel's key role is *to provide an independent scrutiny of the proposals presented and to determine whether all the issues have been appropriately clarified; and whether the proposal is sound* (Lord and Cullen, 2006, p1). Brammer (2010) highlights the three principal issues over which panels can make recommendations:

1. whether adoption is in the best interests of the child;

2. the suitability of prospective adoptive parents;

3. whether a prospective adopter is suitable for a particular child, also known as 'matching'.

(Brammer, 2010, p332)

Additionally, the Adoption and Children Act 2002 (Section 12) established the requirement of adoption agencies to have in place an external form of appeal, an independent review mechanism (IRM), which provides a procedure for an independent review of an adopter's assessment and circumstances to assess suitability (Brammer, 2010; Lord and Cullen, 2006). If the prospective adopters are not approved for adoption by the panel, they have the choice whether to make further representations to the adoption agency or to apply to the IRM for a review (DfES, 2004b; IRM, 2005).

Special guardianship orders

In addition to the above, some adoption agencies are also responsible for assessing persons connected to a child who are applying for Special Guardianship Orders. These orders are another means of creating security and permanency for a child. The special guardian is awarded parental responsibility for the child. The child's parent(s) continue(s) to have parental responsibility also. However, the special guardian can make day-to-day decisions without parental involvement. These applications relate to both children who are looked after by the local authority as well as those living in the community whose families are not necessarily known to social services. Although most special guardians are already known to the child, and are often relatives, many of the issues that relate to adoption are present in these relationships.

RESEARCH SUMMARY

David Howe (1998) offers a comprehensive examination of patterns in terms of outcomes achieved through adoptions, using data from government sources and a number of research studies undertaken in the USA and UK. He also comments on what was known at the time about adoptions of older children from care.

The Department of Health publication (1999b) Adoption Now: Messages from Research offered a summary of adoption research prior to the Prime Minister's Review (PIU, 2000) and the Adoption and Children Act 2002. These documents summarised the research as stating:

- *adoption is an effective option for some looked after children;*

- *early placement is crucial in avoiding disruption;*

- *the most difficult children to place, in terms of finding adopters, are older children, boys, sibling groups and black and ethnic minority children;*

- *older children and those with special needs can successfully be adopted with the right preparation and support;*

- *adoption is not the answer for all looked after children unlikely to return home – some do not wish to be adopted, and some require such intensive support that adoption is never going to be an option.*

(PIU, 2000, p18)

Rushton's (2003) scoping review of adoption research literature for looked after children who have been adopted provides an overview of research undertaken in the adoption field over the past 40 years. Rushton's review is succinct and offers a summary of literature available in many key areas of the adoption process, including:

- *recruitment, assessment, matching, preparation and placement of children;*

- *adoption outcomes;*

- *common behavioural, relationship and educational problems experienced by adopted children;*

- *late adoptions;*

- *contact with birth family post-adoption;*

- *post-adoption support.*

Sellick, Thoburn and Philpot (2004) identify a number of key messages from research for adoption placements in their What Works *volume. These include the following:*

- *Successful adoptive parenting of children placed as infants relies on: the parents' ability to accept the child's dual identity; the emotional significance which the birth family will always have for the child; and the adoptive parents' view of themselves as new parents.*

- *For older children, age at placement is key. Beyond the age of six months, vulnerability to emotional problems stemming from difficulties with attachment, separation and loss increase with age at placement.*

- *On average, one in five placements from care with adoptive parents or permanent foster carers not previously known to the child breaks down within five years of placement. However, this figure may not be helpful as so much depends on the age of the child and other characteristics at the time of placement.*

- *Children who have been institutionalised, who have behavioural or other emotional difficulties, or who have been abused or neglected face a greater likelihood of their placement breaking down.*

- *Having continued contact with members of the birth family is also found in some studies to be associated with a reduced risk of breakdown but appears to make no difference in others.*

(Sellick, Thoburn and Philpot, 2004, p108–109)

Rushton and Monck's literature review (2009) describes what makes a difference with regard to the skills and abilities of adopters to successfully parent adopted children.

Practice debates

Within adoption work, there are many debates about what constitutes 'good practice' within any given area. For the purposes of this chapter, we have chosen to present information on two areas: adoption by lesbians and gay men and trans-racial placements. In each of these areas, we will present a summary of the known research.

Lesbian and gay adoption

There is now a growing body of research evidence available that examines children growing up in lesbian families where one parent is the birth parent, with more limited research specifically about children with gay fathers. See Tasker and Golombok (1991, 1997); Tasker (1999); and Patterson (2005) for systematic reviews looking at outcomes for children growing up in lesbian households; and Patterson (2004); Barrett and Tasker (2001, 2002); and Tasker (2005) for studies involving children growing up with gay fathers. What the literature tells us is that the sexual orientation of the parent makes little if any difference to the outcomes for children. Golombok argues that *it is what happens within families, not the way families are composed, that seems to matter most* (Golombok, 2000, p101). However, while this research has been fundamentally important in shifting negative attitudes and prejudices toward public perceptions of lesbian and gay families, most of the current research evidence is reductionist in nature; that is, the research looks for problems and negative differences between samples of children of lesbian parents and heterosexual parents (albeit single women), and whether the outcomes for the children are 'as good as' those raised within heterosexual families (which they are), rather than developing a more complex understanding of the ways in which non-heterosexual family structures work.

There is, however, a lack of research about outcomes for children in public care placed with lesbian and gay adopters in the UK. This is partly due to problems with accessing such families after adoption has occurred, given the still relatively small numbers of lesbians and gay men who adopt children. It is only in the last three years that the DCSF has begun collecting data about the number of adoptions involving lesbian and gay adopters (see Table 7.2).

Additionally, the available information from the Adoption Register, concerning numbers of lesbian and gay adopters waiting to be placed with children and the time they have to wait, suggests that in terms of families on the register waiting to be matched with children, heterosexual two-parent families waited the least amount of time, lesbian two-parent carers came next, and single carers waited the longest to be matched with a child, often after other potential families had said no to the child. There are not enough approved gay men currently to know how social workers are matching children with gay families (Stott, 2009). There may also be differences in terms of the type of children lesbians and gay men are matched with as compared with their heterosexual counterparts.

Stott (2009) commented that of the 51 couples referred in 2006–07, 42 have had placements (18 female and 24 male couples); four have withdrawn (one female and three male couples); and five couples are still available (two female and three male couples).

Table 7.2 Looked after children who were adopted during the years ending 31 March by number of adopters, legal status of adopters and by gender of adopters[1]
Years ending 31 March 2007 to 2009
Coverage: England

	Numbers			Percentages		
	2007	2008	2009	2007	2008	2009
All looked after children who were adopted during the year ending 31 March	3,300	3,200	3,300	*100*	*100*	*100*
Number of adopters	3,300	3,200	3,300	*100*	*100*	*100*
1 person	290	270	270	*9*	*9*	*8*
2 person	3,000	2,900	3,000	*91*	*91*	*92*
Legal status and gender of adopters	3,300	3,200	3,300	*100*	*100*	*100*
Single adopter	290	270	270	*9*	*9*	*8*
Single male adopter	20	10	10	*1*	*0*	*0*
Single female adopter	280	280	280	*8*	*8*	*8*
Same sex couple not in civil partnership	70	50	50	*2*	*2*	*1*
Adopting couple are both male	20	20	20	*0*	*1*	*1*
Adopting couple are both female	60	30	30	*2*	*1*	*1*
Different sex unmarried couple	150	140	190	*4*	*5*	*6*
Civil partnership couple	20	30	80	*1*	*1*	*2*
Adopting couple are both male	10	—	40	*0*	—	*1*
Adopting couple are both female	10	20	40	*0*	*1*	*1*
Married couple	2,800	2,700	2,700	*84*	*84*	*82*

Source: SSDA 903

1. Historical data may differ from older publications. This is mainly due to the implementation of amendments and corrections sent by some local authorities after the publication date of previous materials.

(DCSF, 2009d)

Stott (2009) also presented a small amount of data about lesbian and gay couple adopters compared to other adopters, including single adopters (see Table 7.4). Interpreting this data enables some cautionary comments to be made about the patterns present between the sample of 51 lesbian and gay couple adopters referred to the register in 2006–07 and all other adopters coming forward. It would appear that there is a broader ethnic mix within the lesbian and gay adopters in this sample than within the general adopter category, although it is not clear what the different ethnicities represented are, and how they relate to the children who are waiting to be adopted. Because the adoption register is not reflective of all adoption activity across England, this is only reflective of families who have not immediately been matched with a child. A proportion of black and mixed-ethnicity families will not appear on the register as the local authorities have frequently identified children for them at the time of their approval. It would also appear that the lesbian and gay adopters were more open to considering older children in sibling groups. While these differences may not be significant in terms of the eventual match that is made between the adopters and child(ren), this information highlights the need for more research to be undertaken to examine these differences, to see whether they are significant.

Table 7.3 Adopters referrals to the National Adoption Register from 2004–05 to 2007–08

Year	Adopters referred	Same-sex couples referred	Percentage of same-sex couples referred
2004–05	1,131	23	2
2005–06	1,250	42	3.4
2006–07	1,333	51 (21 female and 30 male couples)	4.2
2007–08	1,098	47	4.3

(Stott, 2009)

Table 7.4 Adopters' characteristics of 2006–07 referrals to the National Adoption Register

	Other couples (including single carers)	Same-sex couples
Ethnicity other than white	18%	29%
Consider sibling group	43%	57%
Consider a child age five or over	52%	76%
Approved by a voluntary adoption agency	30%	11%

(Stott, 2009)

In terms of research specifically concerned with lesbian and gay adopters, Hicks and McDermott (1999) recount the experiences of 17 adopters and foster carers in the UK who had looked after children placed with them. However, they did not give an account of the outcomes for the children as this was not the aim of the study. Additionally, there are a small number of studies (for example Hicks, 1996, 1997, 1998; Cocker, 2011) that examine the assessment experiences of lesbian adopters. There is more literature available from the USA concerning the outcomes for children adopted and fostered by lesbians and gay men (Erich, 2005; Erich *et al.*, 2009). The results of the existing research broadly concur with the findings of Golombok's work (2000). There are two known examples of practice guidance (Mallon and Betts, 2005; Hicks and Greaves, 2007) that comment on the issues for the assessing social worker when undertaking home study reports with lesbians and gay prospective applicants. There is, however, some debate about whether the production of such practice guides and frameworks detailing best practice when working with lesbians and gay men and their families, or specialist books for lesbian or gay prospective adoption applicants (Hill, 2009) are useful (see Hicks, 2008), or whether they are in themselves reductionist because of the normative position they unconsciously or consciously adopt. Cocker and Hafford-Letchfield comment:

> There are occasions when certain types of assessments do need to cover different areas, because some experiences are particular to the lives of lesbians and gay men, such as coming out or homophobia. The question is whether existing frameworks should be flexible enough to adapt to people's individuality, and incorporate differences in a reflexive manner rather than as an 'add on' or not address them at all.

(Cocker and Hafford-Letchfield, 2010, p2002)

The legislative change in this area of practice has been considerable (see Brown and Kershaw, 2008; Brown, 2008; Fish, 2007). The Adoption and Children Act 2002 and the Equality Act (Sexual Orientation) Regulations 2007 are fundamental in this regard, as they offer lesbian and gay couples who are approved as prospective adopters the opportunity to jointly adopt children. The 2007 legislation ensures that lesbians and gay men have the same opportunity of assessment at any local authority or independent adoption agency as any other applicant. Cocker and Brown (2010) suggest that this has had an effect on adoption agencies needing to rethink their recruitment strategies. Word of mouth is already known to be a powerful aid to recruitment (Fostering Network, 2006), therefore it stands to reason that lesbian and gay adopters' positive experiences of agencies assessments will have a snowballing effect on those agencies being approached by other lesbians and gay men interested in adoption.

Trans-racial adoption

The term 'trans-racial' is a contested one, as is much of the language used to describe children in care who are not white. Current practice is to use the term 'minority ethnic children' to encompass all children who are not white, and this includes mixed-ethnicity children, where one parent is white. This is an acknowledged problem with terminology that extends beyond social care. For example, it was only in 2001 that the national census established a category of 'mixed ethnicity'. In addition, some research studies that are highly regarded, such as the prevalence study examining mental disorder within the looked after population of children in England undertaken by Meltzer *et al.* (2003) used basic definitions of ethnicity labels such as 'white', 'black' and 'other' (this included south Asian, Chinese and mixed-heritage children) which then makes finer examination of data according to distinct ethnic groups difficult.

In general, children from minority ethnic backgrounds are over-represented within the care system, but the experiences of all black and minority ethnic children are not the same. There are some areas where minority ethnic children are under-represented within the care system (those Asian children who are in care have more specialist needs in terms of disability), and other areas where they are over-represented (children with mixed ethnicity) and this has been a long-standing pattern within the English welfare system. Overall, the numbers of children in care are slowly creeping up. This is because some children are staying in care longer – more children of mixed heritage stay in care longer, as do white children (Thoburn *et al.*, 2005).

For those children from minority ethnic groups who are adopted, there is an important contribution to the debate to be made through research knowledge, but there is still a long way to go and a need to identify what we know and what we don't know in a systematic way. Thoburn, Chand and Procter's book (2005) is a very good start to this, commenting on the research that has been undertaken and the social context within which this was taking place. For example, Gill and Jackson (1983) recount the work of the British Adoption Project, which set out to counteract the pervading view of the 1960s that 'black children were unadoptable'. Although practice has changed considerably since the 1960s, this study sets an important 'benchmark' for practice. Rowe *et al.* (1989) is the only large-scale source of data on outcomes for minority ethnic children placed for short-term care in the full range of placements.

Strong opinions are held and expressed by individuals and institutions about the 'rightness' or 'wrongness' of trans-racial adoption. Selwyn and Wijedasa (2009) provide a useful summary of the debates around trans-racial or 'same race' placements and the issues for the placement of looked after minority ethnic children.

> *The placement of minority ethnic children has been dominated for the last forty years by competing arguments about the benefits and disadvantages of 'trans-racial' placement. The debate is often polarised with one camp (Gilroy, 1990; Macey, 1995; Hayes, 2003) arguing that placing children according to 'race' is a form of apartheid, not supported by the research evidence and deeply divisive. The opposite camp (Maxime, 1993; Small, 2000) argues that research has been Eurocentric and children's mental health needs are best met in an ethnically matched placement to allow the development of a 'Black' identity. Both camps accuse each other of racism and this has limited the willingness of others to become involved and engage with the issues.*

(Selwyn and Wijedasa, 2009, p363)

Rushton (2003) discusses the literature that examines outcomes for children who are trans-racially placed, and comments that current professional opinion does not support this kind of placement being made, therefore there are difficulties in undertaking current longitudinal studies to examine outcomes for these children. Rather he suggests that research is more likely to adopt a retrospective approach to assessing a trans-racially adopted adult's current adjustment and identity (2003, p11).

Frazer and Selwyn (2005) also identify some of the practice issues for finding suitable and timely placements for children of black, Asian and black mixed parentage in England, including the damaging consequences of delay. They argue that there is now broad agreement by researchers *that young people require placements that promote their self-esteem and a sense of identity and that wherever possible this should be a 'same race' placement'* (Frazer and Selwyn, 2005, p136). They reference Rushton and Minnis's (2000) study which concluded that children should have a 'same race' placement wherever possible but if no family is identified then a trans-racial placement should be considered.

However, Frazer and Selwyn focus their recommendations on local authority recruitment and retention policies and processes so as to ensure that wider groups of suitable adopters are targeted and recruited, and that ethnicity should be part of the planning around appropriate campaign strategies: *People from minority ethnic groups are undoubtedly motivated to adopt . . . little is known, however, about the reasons why this interest doesn't translate into more applications and approvals* (Frazer and Selwyn, 2005, pp136–137). They also highlight many other difficulties in this debate, including the matching of mixed-parentage children waiting for adoption with the *wishes and expectations* (2005, p46) of suitable prospective adopters whose details are on the Adoption Register: *given that most black, Asian and mixed-parentage families available to the register voice a preference for and are approved for, children under three years* (2005, p146).

Wood (2009) comments:

> *There is a danger that among these uncertainties, the individuality of the child will be lost as his or her identity needs become viewed narrowly. Social workers may seek to simplify and classify the identities of mixed-ethnicity children in the adoption process through pressures they feel to find 'matched' placements.*

> (2009, p431)

Wood examines how theories of identity have contributed to the debates that now occur within this particular area of practice, commenting on how *values, ideology and the history of anti-oppressive practice* all have their part to play (2009, p434). She identifies six different approaches that she believes have influenced practice in this area:

- the 'one-drop' rule;
- black solidarity;
- 'political correctness';
- precise matching;
- mixed with mixed;
- religious matching.

According to Brammer (2010, p321) current case law presents an inconsistent picture as to the significance of ethnicity in placement. Regarding placement choice, Brammer argues that the duties for social workers in choosing an adoption placement are the same as the Children Act 1989 (Section 22: 5c) in terms of *due consideration shall be given to religious persuasion, racial origin and cultural and linguistic background*. The welfare checklist in the Adoption and Children Act 2002 is also significant. The important distinction to make here is the use of the word 'must' not 'shall' in the 2002 legislation, thus there is no element of discretion in terms of this being a requirement of practice, but how this is understood, interpreted and applied is decided on a case-by-case basis. Wood (2009) argues that it is when simplistic definitions of mixed ethnicity are used that the complexity of ethnic identity is not understood.

> *An over-emphasis on matching for mixed-ethnicity children risks 'writing off' many children, for whom there will never be an exact or even close match, as having torn,*

problematic identities. These negative labels can have real dangers for the way these children will see themselves. Raising issues of ethnic identity and identity construction is intended to inspire further debate that will go beyond any simplistic notions of 'same race' vs 'trans-racial' adoption arguments.

(Wood, 2009, p438)

It is important that social workers have a comprehensive knowledge about children's identity and their need to feel that they belong in their new family. If children are placed trans-culturally or trans-racially, the social worker should ensure that the carers are able to provide an environment for the children whereby they can experience aspects of their culture, but this should be fully integrated into their lives. This is relevant for all children, including black children who may not share the cultural heritage of the family they are placed with. For example, a Nigerian child adopted by a Ghanaian family will have a different cultural heritage and different cultural traditions that should be celebrated and incorporated into the child's life. Families should be able to deal with issues of racism and be able to have discussions about identity (Rashid, 2000).

REFLECTION POINT

- *What is your view on either of these practice areas? On what evidence are you basing your view?*

- *Have you read any of the studies or articles listed above, or any other studies on these topics that have informed your opinion? If so, what are they?*

Comment

Both of the areas discussed above relate to areas of difference and diversity within practice. The current practice context is complex and complicated because people's lives are complex and complicated. Practitioners can and do make a difference – we have seen this in the British Adoption Project (Gill and Jackson, 1983), or the effort made by practitioners to recruit black and minority ethnic foster carers in the 1980s that is still reaping benefits now. Researchers can also make a difference. The work of Susan Golombok in particular (Golombok *et al.*, 1983; Golombok, 2000) has made a considerable contribution to our knowledge concerning the effects of lesbian families parenting children. The important message is that debate and dialogue can avoid polarised positions being taken when assessing what service provision is appropriate for our children in public care in relation to adoption.

Chapter summary

This chapter has provided an overview of the adoption process in England for children in state care who are adopted and for prospective adopters. In addition, the chapter has highlighted a number of practice areas related to diversity and has asked practitioners to consider how issues of difference, equality and diversity are debated within the adoption field.

Archer, C and Burnell, A (eds) (2003) *Trauma, attachment and family permanence: Fear can stop you loving.* London: Jessica Kingsley.

This volume explores some of the emotional issues associated in caring for adopted children who have experienced trauma in their lives prior to adoption.

Fahlberg, V (1994) *A child's journey through placement.* London: BAAF.

This book outlines the theoretical knowledge base and skills necessary for understanding working with and planning for looked after children and their families. It provides many practical ideas and is essential reading for any practitioner undertaking work in this area.

Lord, J (2008) *The adoption process in England: A guide for children's social workers.* London: BAAF.

This book outlines the adoption process in more detail than this chapter allows and is used by social workers.

Neil, B and Howe, D (2004) *Contact in adoption and permanent foster care: Research, theory and practice.* London: BAAF.

This book discusses the complexities of contact for children moving into adoptive families.

Rushton, A and Monck, E (2009) *Enhancing adoptive parenting: A test of effectiveness.* London: BAAF.

The literature review is particularly good.

Schofield, G and Beek, M (2006) *Attachment handbook for foster care and adoption.* London: BAAF.

This book shows the importance for child and family social workers of understanding attachment theory.

Schofield, G and Simmonds, J (eds) (2008) *The child placement handbook: Research, policy and practice.* London: BAAF

This is an edited text that covers a variety of areas concerning the placement experiences of looked after children. The various chapters are authored by an impressive array of well known academics and researchers. This book is an essential investment for those working with looked after children.

Verrier, NN (2000) *The primal wound: Understanding the adopted child.* Baltimore: Gateway Press.

This book is written by an adopter and uses psycho-dynamic and attachment theories to understand the experiences of adopted children.

Adoption Research Initiative: **www.adoptionresearchinitiative.org.uk**

Adoption UK: **www.adoptionuk.org.uk**

After Adoption: **www.afteradoption.org.uk**

British Agencies for Adoption and Fostering: **www.baaf.org.uk**

Family Futures: **www.familyfutures.co.uk**

Family Law: **www.familylawweek.co.uk**

New Family Social: **www.newfamilysocial.co.uk**

Norcap: **www.norcap.org.uk**

Post Adoption Centre: **www.postadoptioncentre.org.uk**

Chapter 8

Practice education: enabling others' learning within a children and families context

Paul Dugmore

CHAPTER OBJECTIVES

If you are a registered social worker, this chapter will assist you to evidence post-registration training and learning. It relates to the national post-qualifying framework for social work education and training at the specialist level:

viii. *Teach, mentor and support social work or other students and /or colleagues and contribute to assessment against national occupational standards.*

ix. *Take responsibility for the effective use of supervision to identify and explore issues, develop and implement plans and improve own practice.*

It will also help you to meet the Children and Families standards for social work:

iii. *Co-ordinating services in a multi-agency service delivery context, including the knowledge and skills required to ensure professional networks are able to meet complex needs and where appropriate undertake lead professional roles.*

Introduction

This chapter is aimed at practitioners who are undertaking modules within the practice education strand of the PQ framework, or enabling others as part of the Specialist Award and who are involved in supervising and assessing qualifying social work students on assessed practice learning placements.

The role and function of practice learning and student supervision has, for many years, been considered fundamentally important to the development of qualifying social work students, with many attributing the success of their qualification to their practice learning placements (Davis, 1984, cited in Shardlow and Doel, 1996; Kadushin, 1992). The practice learning placement provides students with an opportunity to develop skills and knowledge in a specific area of social work practice, to integrate theory into their practice with service users and to ensure that their practice is firmly located in the overarching values underpinning the profession. This chapter focuses on the management of placements, supervision, enabling learning, and assessing students' practice.

The current context of practice learning

The issue of practice learning has been high on the agenda of both the social work profession and government over the last decade as the drive to recruit additional numbers to enter the profession has increased following the implementation of the degree in 2002 (DoH, 2002b). This increase in students, coupled with the rise in the number of assessed practice learning days from 120 to 200 introduced with the new degree qualification, placed an overwhelming demand on agencies to provide adequate practice learning opportunities (Practice Learning Taskforce, 2006). Over the last ten years a variety of strategies have been introduced by the Department of Health (DoH) Practice Learning Taskforce and the sector skills councils, Skills for Care and the Children's Workforce Development Council, including a practice learning performance indicator which measured how many practice learning opportunities local authority social services departments were providing. While the DoH requirements for the degree (DoH, 2002b) established that qualifying students must complete 200 days of assessed practice learning in contrasting placements involved in statutory social work, a drive for new types of placements in less conventional settings, such as in the private, voluntary and independent sectors and schools, led to an increase in practice learning opportunities being provided.

Within this context the change in social work education and training brought with it a review of the post-qualifying (PQ) framework (GSCC, 2005) which led to the introduction of a new PQ framework in 2007. Within this new framework, the old PQSW was replaced with a new Specialist Award and the old Practice Teaching Award introduced by the Central Council for Education and Training in Social Work (CCETSW) in 1989 was abolished, much to the concern of many practitioners and academics (Gilchrist, 2007). Instead, 'practice teaching', renamed 'practice education', would be taught at the Higher Specialist and Advanced Level Awards and a compulsory element of the Specialist Award would be 'enabling others', which all students studying at this level would be required to undertake. Thus, there are numerous ways in which social workers can study a form of practice education or enabling others, ranging from short five-day modules to full Master's programmes. Alongside the demise of the Practice Teaching Award, the term 'practice teacher' was replaced by 'practice assessor'. This chapter will not focus on the differences of these varied approaches or critique the benefits and drawbacks of each. Such detail on the PQ framework is available on the GSCC website (see **www.gscc.org.uk**) and both Bhatti-Sinclair (2009) and Higham and Sharp (2009) provide some critique of the imposed changes.

There has been enormous interest in and scrutiny of the social work profession in the last two years following the conviction of the killers of Peter Connelly (Baby P) in 2008 and the publicised failings of Haringey Council and its partner agencies to safeguard Peter. This led to the establishment by the Government of the Social Work Taskforce, which published the findings of its 'root and branch' review of the profession in November 2009, recommending significant change both to social work practice and education and training at qualifying and post-qualifying levels, particularly in relation to social work with children and families. This follows Laming's review of safeguarding (2009) in which he highlighted that, due to a lack of appropriate placements, it is possible to start work as a new children's social worker without any practical experience of child protection. His report recommended that the GSCC and the Government should work with higher educational institutions (HEIs) to reform current arrangements towards a system of *specialism in children's social work, including statutory children's social work placements after the first year* (Laming, 2009). The report of the House of Commons Children, Schools and Families Committee on the Training of Children and Families Social Workers published in July 2009 (Section 4, para 1.22) recommended that:

> *Requirements for placements should be amended to stipulate that all placements be supervised by qualified and experienced social workers who either hold or are working towards specific qualifications in practice teaching.*

(House of Commons Children, Schools and Families Committee, 2009)

Therefore, further change to practice learning and practice education is imminent. Alongside this, the GSCC has been reviewing the PQ framework and the 'enabling others' module and is considering implementing changes to this. At present, the GSCC guidance on practice education is laid out in *Guidance on Assessment of Practice in the Workplace* (GSCC/TOPSS England, 2002). This is a framework of statements grouped into three domains outlining the process and tasks involved in assessing the practice of others and the minimum expectations in the assessment process. These domains (which will be explored further below) relate to the management of the placement, the enabling of learning and assessing students. There is also a series of statements that relate to the value base of work-based assessment. This framework is currently subject to review and new national standards for practice education are being piloted at the time of writing (Social Work Taskforce Report, 2009). The term 'practice assessor' also appears to be replaced by that of 'practice educator'. Therefore 'practice educator' will be used in this chapter to describe social work practitioners who provide practice learning placements to social work qualifying students.

Students studying the social work degree currently spend half of their time on a practice learning placement and, according to the DoH, each student must:

- undertake a minimum of 200 days practice learning across the length of their course;

- spend time in at least two practice settings, working with at least two different groups of people who use services and carers, and including statutory tasks involving legal interventions.

(DoH, 2002b, p3)

Additionally, the regulatory criteria state that for qualifying students undertaking their final placement, a qualified and experienced social worker and professional educator must be involved (Skills for Care, 2009).

Given that the role of the practice educator is so important in gatekeeping the entry of a suitable, competent and skilled workforce into the profession (Furness and Gilligan, 2004), social work practitioners need to think carefully before they apply to undertake a programme of study that involves supervising and assessing a student. There are many reasons why practitioners decide to embark on a practice education course, such as career development and satisfying registration requirements (GSCC, 2002), wanting to give something back to the profession, improving their own practice (Shardlow *et al.*, 2002) or acknowledgement of the importance of practice learning to students' overall development as social workers.

ACTIVITY *8.1*

Before you agree to start a practice education course or offer a placement to a social work qualifying student, think about whether you are in a position to prepare and plan a supportive and challenging practice curriculum.

- *What arrangements do you need to put in place and what barriers might there be preventing you from doing so?*

- *How might these be overcome?*

Comment

You may have given consideration to your own stage of development as a social worker, the length of time that you have been qualified, as well as the time that you have been practising as a social worker in a children and families context. Do you feel confident enough in your own practice to share your experience, skills and knowledge with a student? Have you got the time to provide regular supervision for your student in addition to attending university and studying yourself? Are you in a stable team that will assist you in providing a placement for a student and making them feel welcomed and supported? Do you have the support of your line manager and team and will they assist you both in being released to attend university and in managing a student placement? Are there support mechanisms in your agency? If you work for a local authority or a large voluntary organisation, there will probably be a practice learning co-ordinator who has responsibility for arranging placements and supporting practice educators. All of these issues need to be given serious thought before you take on the role of practice educator and any potential issues addressed with your manager and agency.

Preparing for and managing a placement

Once you have agreed to offer a placement to a student, you will need to meet any potential student and determine whether you wish to proceed with the placement. This process is usually left to the practice educator to manage; however, your agency may have a particular format for the interview. You need to ensure that the student and placement are well matched. This can be hard to assess at this early stage so you may want to think about the questions that you would like to ask the student and what you wish to know about them so that you can both set out your expectations (Doel *et al.*, 1996). You need to bear in mind that students come from a variety of backgrounds and have varying levels of experience. They may be young, having recently left school with little or no experience of social work or experience with a particular client group; or, at the other end of the spectrum, they may be a mature student with many years experience of working in social work related fields. Either way, you must assess the student's ability to undertake the social work role in your area of practice with the appropriate level of support, supervision and guidance.

Before a practice learning placements starts, it is crucial that significant planning and preparation are undertaken to ensure that the student's arrival in the agency and team is a positive, structured and organised one. Parker *et al.* (2006) demonstrate the importance of appropriate and planned induction and the impact that this can have on a student's experience. In planning for a student's arrival, much can be done in advance, such as ensuring practical, domestic arrangements are in place, for example computer logins, desk, telephone and storage space. In preparing an induction programme it is important to identify what a student needs to know as well as how they will be introduced to the team. Ensuring the team knows that a student is starting and the dates, days and length of the placement is important in encouraging the team to take some ownership of the placement so you are not seen as completely responsible for the student's learning. Other members of the team can help with this process, for instance in arranging shadowing opportunities with other practitioners so that the student also gets to see different styles of practice. The induction should be an opportunity for the student to be introduced to the area of social work practice within the agency and the particular setting of the placement, with a clear focus on the values of the profession, the service users accessing the agency and an understanding of some of the issues faced by the people with whom they will be working. Referring to the *Common Induction Standards* (2006) published by the Children's Workforce Development Council may assist you as these outline the knowledge all those in the children's workforce should acquire within their first six months of employment. The induction period is also a valuable opportunity for you and the student to get to know each other and start building an open and honest relationship that considers how you both approach learning. It is worth bearing in mind that recent attention on children and families' social work will probably heighten already high anxiety levels of students undertaking placements in such teams and opportunities to talk about and reflect on this will be useful.

Setting the parameters for learning

A crucial part of any placement is the framework to support it and in most cases this is referred to as a learning agreement or placement contract. This needs to set out practical arrangements covering issues such as hours and dates of work as well as the learning opportunities provided for the student. If the student has already completed a placement, reading the reports from this placement and incorporating areas of development identified is important in order to link the progress of learning from one placement into the new placement. As the person responsible for the placement, you need to identify the range of learning opportunities that will be available to the student.

- *List the different types of available learning opportunities – you may want to do this by reference to the six key roles of the National Occupational Standards and break them down into knowledge and skills.*

- *Think widely in relation to all aspects of practice in which the student may have the opportunity for involvement.*

Comment

Your list may have included some of the following:

Knowledge

- Acquire knowledge of child development theories and apply this to practice.

- Develop a working knowledge of key legislation and guidance, e.g. the Children Act (1989, 2004), *Every Child Matters* (2003), the Framework for the Assessment of Children in Need and their Families (2000), the Youth Justice Board National Standards (2010).

- Understand different types of abuse, signs and symptoms and develop a working knowledge of Pan London Child Protection procedures.

Skills

- Develop communication skills in working with children from babies through to teenagers and their carers.

- Undertake a range of assessments – initial, core, parenting, risk assessments, Asset assessment tool in youth offending teams – and develop interview skills, observational skills, analytical skills.

- Opportunity to shadow social workers at child protection conferences, looked after children reviews, core group meetings, court hearings.

- Write reports for panel, attend panel, prepare pre-sentence reports and attend court.

- Preparing care plans, pathway plans, personal education plans, supervision plans.

- Write contemporaneous, accurate, evidence-based and succinct case records using IT systems.

- Work to deadlines and prioritise work accordingly.

- Work as part of a multi-agency team and attend professionals' meetings, joint home visits with health visitors, etc.

- Prepare for and participate in supervision that enables reflection and challenge.

This is by no means an exhaustive list and you will need to think carefully about identifying work that is appropriate for a student to undertake. A student is on placement to learn, not just to act as 'an extra pair of hands'. Your agency may have guidelines about the types of work students cannot be involved in, such as having responsibility for child protection cases or a high risk case of a young person offending. However, a good placement should provide opportunities for a student to shadow social workers undertaking child protection work where possible so that they can learn about this complex area of practice. From the available learning opportunities, your student should be able to identify their learning needs. This is often an area in which students may struggle as they do not yet understand the role they will be occupying and the learning they need to undertake. Your role as the practice educator is to help them identify the areas they need to develop and the areas they have transferable skills in (Doel and Shardlow, 2005; Beverley and Worsley, 2007).

Learning needs may be simple, such as the student knowing how to introduce him/herself to a service user and outline their role and purpose, or more complex, such as writing a report for a panel. For instance, your student may have limited experience of working with children and lack confidence in communicating with them or assessing their needs. In response, you may identify opportunities for a student to observe children playing in a children's centre, where they can observe how children generally interact and play relative to their age, as well as require a student to read around child development so they begin to build up a picture of the developmental stages a child goes through. You may give a student case studies or a film to watch to help develop their ability to assess signs and symptoms of abuse or neglect. Additionally, you may organise opportunities for a student to shadow experienced workers carrying out assessments. While the early part of the placement may be characterised by the student shadowing others to learn how to observe and analyse different situations, this will gradually shift as you begin to observe them taking the lead and practising their newly acquired knowledge and skills. While some students may find this onerous, there is much to be said for easing the student into the complex world of child and family social work so that they learn how to practice quality social work rather than rush into using the timescaled, prescribed, procedurally-based assessment tools without understanding what it is they are really looking for in undertaking such assessments. Thus, the needs of the children are lost sight of as the performance management of the case is focused on (Broadhurst *et al.*, 2009).

Cartney (2004) suggests that knowledge of a student's learning style can help practice educators to provide appropriate learning opportunities that encompass a diverse range of methods. Thus, requiring students to complete a learning style questionnaire such as Honey and Mumford's (1986) can be a useful way of facilitating a discussion about the student's preferred learning style as well as your own. This means that planned learning opportunities are geared towards the student, but also that, as the placement develops, you challenge them by introducing other styles of learning.

Once learning needs and opportunities have been identified you need to think about and plan the specific work you will allocate. This needs to take into account the placement the student is undertaking, their learning needs and preferred learning style, confidence level and your assessment of their current competence, knowledge and skill base. You should also think about what your expectations of a social work student in a children and families setting are and perhaps discuss this with your line manager and team so you can identify work at an appropriate level. For instance, in a referral and assessment team, arranging for the student to shadow you undertaking an initial assessment and then reading your assessment before allocating an initial assessment to the student would be appropriate at the start of the placement, before building up to a core assessment later on in the placement. Consideration needs to be given to the fact that current social work practice is heavily technical and proceduralised, which some claim has led to a rise in managerialism while reducing the need for professional discretion (Cooper and Lousada, 2005) and that creative practice may be stifled by bureaucratic, prescriptive management (Broadhurst *et al.*, 2009). If your manager does not support or facilitate reflective practice, the challenge for you to incorporate this into your practice with the student is greater.

Supervision

Research demonstrates that the practice learning experience is hugely affected by the quality of the relationship between the practice educator and student (Lefevre, 2005) and that integral to effective supervision is a *supportive relationship within a non-critical context* (Bennett and Saks, 2006, p669). While it is important for practice educators to be open and approachable from the outset of the placement, supervision is perhaps the most effective vehicle for facilitating such a relationship and creating an environment where the student feels safe to make mistakes, receive constructive feedback and share their own experiences of how the placement is progressing; a process that is more likely to lead to a positive experience. It is also the opportunity for you and the student to establish and maintain a professional relationship based on trust, openness and honesty. This requires both parties to acknowledge the power differences in the relationship, which will always include the power inherent in the assessor/assessed relationship and the fact that the practice educator ultimately makes a decision about whether the student passes or fails the placement.

Additionally, other structural differences may exist, such as age, race, gender, class and educational background, as well as personal characteristics and qualities. A candid discussion about all the potential power differentials is vitally important at the outset of the placement and also paves the way for a discussion about personal and professional values so that the student is able to think about their own value base and how this may impact on their work with service users from complex and varied backgrounds. It may also inform their understanding about oppression and its impact on the people who they will be providing services to. Similarly, in line with the values domain in the *Assessment of Practice in the Workplace* (GSCC/TOPSS England, 2002), practice educators need to develop their own self-awareness so they consider how their value base may affect their ability to support and assess students as fairly and as objectively as possible.

As a practice educator your role is to enable your student's learning and nowhere is this more important than in relation to issues of power and difference in ethical social work practice. While the terms 'anti-discriminatory' and 'anti-oppressive' practice have been used interchangeably and consistently in practice and in social work education in the last 20 years, these are not without their critics. Writers such as Humphries (2004) have suggested that the notion of anti-oppressive practice serves as a convenient 'gloss' that the profession uses to 'feel better' and that there is a need to go beyond individualistic models of power (Humphries, 2004, p105). She suggests that social work needs to be informed instead by engaging critically with debates within social sciences and, as Healy (2005) identifies, see power and difference as complex phenomena that are not resolved by simplistic and polarised dualities that, for instance, see people only as black or white, gay or heterosexual. As Brown and Cocker conclude:

> *We need to remind ourselves of the role of social work in countering [disadvantage for particular groups], and that countering disadvantage associated with diversity isn't about creating or expecting sameness, or returning to assimilationist practices of the past. Rather there are many ways to live in this world with dignity, honour and grace. The role of social work is not only to value the concept and politics of diversity, but to execute it in our work with others.*

(Brown and Cocker, 2011, p58)

ACTIVITY *8.3*

- *Think about the complexities involved in supervising and assessing your student and the power differentials that may come into play. Think widely, not just focusing on more obvious and visible factors.*

- *How can you use these to help make links with the values statements for work-based assessors in the GSCC guidance?*

- *Use this as a basis to have a discussion with your student about the reasons underlying the disadvantage and difficulties faced by the people receiving services with whom the student will be working.*

Comment

Your response to this activity will depend on your own experience as an individual and your own perceptions of people from any of the groups listed. It may be that you make assumptions about people from particular backgrounds or you may have little personal or professional knowledge of some areas of difference. How comfortable would you be in talking to a student about them? Perhaps you could role play or discuss this with a member of your team with whom you feel comfortable.

Supervision contracts provide a framework for both parties, outlining how the formal supervisory process will operate and the expectations and requirements of both student and practice educator. The social work programme at university will require supervision to be undertaken regularly, in most cases weekly. Regular supervision enables practice educators to have a very clear grasp of how the student is managing and progressing with the placement and serves a number of purposes:

- enabling the student's learning and development through supporting them and their practice;

- developing their knowledge of good practice and knowledge and theoretical base of what works in your practice context;

- facilitating the development and application of skills in practice;

- supporting students in identifying their value base and the application of a professional value base;

- supporting students in understanding the impact of oppression, discrimination, poverty and social exclusion;

- drawing on your professional knowledge, skills and practice; and

- providing a forum to inform, evaluate, assess, challenge and encourage the student.

(Adapted from Walker *et al.*, 2008, p102)

There are many models for supervision (Kadushin, 1992; Hawkins and Shohet, 2000) and your own experiences of supervision will undoubtedly come into play. Whichever model you adopt, it is important that you have a clear understanding of the importance and value of supervision if provided regularly and to a high quality. The model outlined by Morrison (2009) in the *Supervision Guide for Social Workers* produced for the Newly Qualified Social Workers Pilot Programme is called the '4 × 4 × 4 model' of supervision. This assimilates the four functions of supervision with the four stakeholders in supervision and the four elements of the supervision cycle. Morrison adapts Harries' (1987) functions of supervision: management, development, support and mediation. The four stakeholders: the supervisee, service user, supervisor (who represents the agency) and other partner agencies, may have differing, sometimes conflicting needs. Given that the four functions interrelate, Morrison argues that there needs to be a healthy balance of all, as an over-reliance on one function to the negation of the others will lead to problems. This is exemplified in the managerialist, performance-led culture that has predominated social work in the last few years that some (Munro, 2005; Fish *et al.*, 2008) suggest has, in part, resulted in tragic child protection cases, where the 'management accountability' part of supervision has overridden the other functions. Finally, Morrison outlines the four stages of the supervisory cycle: experience, reflection, analysis and planning, which supervisors should move through with supervisees to ensure a thorough approach is taken when looking at individual cases. This should confirm that an accurate understanding of the situation is arrived at following a problem-solving method and an appropriate evidence-based plan of action is put into place.

Such a model should facilitate a full exploration of the presenting factors in a case that has been allocated to the student. For instance, if the student is undertaking an assessment on a child or young person, this model will enable you to assist the student in thinking about and articulating what they have observed and what information they have gained in their assessment, and their own responses to these. Your role in asking open questions about the service user and the situation will help the student to 'tell the story'. The reflection process will encourage the two of you to process the feelings evoked by the interaction(s) and consider the values or assumptions that may lead from this, so that decisions are not made on the basis of presumed behaviour but evidence. It also encourages the student to grapple with the complex and multi-layered emotions that can arise from carrying out such emotive work. The fact that you will be supervising your student weekly enables you to really explore in detail the work the student is undertaking and the impact this is having on the service user and the student. The analysis part of the model enables the understanding of the situation to be placed within a context of formal knowledge; for instance, making sense of the variety of information gathered and drawing on research evidence, theory and practice wisdom to identify an appropriate course of action.

As the student is new to social work practice, this discussion is vital so together, through analysis of the case, you can ensure the intervention is appropriate, timely and based on a thorough assessment of the facts. Thus, it will determine the outcome of the assessment and the next steps to be taken.

It is recommended that you read and engage with this model and use the exercises and questions provided by Morrison (2009) to assist you in ensuring the supervision you are providing is fully effective. This is particularly important in supervising students who are at the start of their social work journey and for whom supervision will enable their progression and development into critical, analytical and reflective practitioners.

Enabling learning

In order to enable a social work student to develop as a competent practitioner, some awareness and understanding of adult learning theory is required. Theories of adult learning (Knowles, 1980) suggest some common principles about the ways in which adults learn:

- the learning environment is important and conducive to learning where the adult feels respected and valued with their own experiences and contribution;

- adults are able to define their own learning needs and should be involved in planning their learning;

- learning opportunities should be geared towards the application of knowledge to specific problems or situations;

- learning should be timely and focus on what the learner needs to know.

This fits in well with a Humanist approach in which Rogerian principles advocate that intervention is 'person-centred' and in which a working alliance or partnership is established. As mentioned previously, identifying a student's preferred learning style should enable you to establish whether they would prefer to be immersed in practice from the outset as an 'activist' or whether, as a 'reflector', they would suit a more progressive approach in which they have the opportunity to read, observe and reflect on aspects of practice before embarking on tasks themselves. Other theories of learning that you would benefit from looking at include Kolb's (1984) cycle of learning. This contains a useful model in which students' experiences are developed further through reflection and analysis (Morrison, 2009). Additionally, Schön's (1983) work on the process of reflection is useful (see Chapter 1).

Informed by theories of learning and listening to the experiences and preferences of your student, you now need to think about, and plan, how you are going to manage the aspect of teaching in your practice. The change of the term 'practice teacher' to 'practice assessor' seemed to suggest a move away from the importance of the teaching role to one of practice learning (Beverley and Worsley, 2007). However, given that practice learning makes up at least half of a social work student's education, and that this is one of the areas practice educators are assessed against on 'enabling others' and 'practice education' modules, teaching and enabling learners still need to be common features of the practice learning placement. While the student will be studying a range of modules at university, there is an expectation that their practice educator will help them to integrate their academic learning into their practice. The chasm that often exists between the worlds of practice and academia is well documented (Clapton *et al.*, 2006, 2007) and there remains work to be done to bring these two equally important contributors to social work education together.

ACTIVITY 8.4

Imagine that you are providing a placement to a final-year student who undertook their first placement in a voluntary organisation that provides services to older people. While the student is very comfortable with children, having two young ones of their own, they have no prior experience in statutory children's social work. As such, the student has many learning needs.

- *What kind of teaching strategies might you put in place to enable their learning in your area of practice?*

Comment

You may have thought of giving your student relevant documentation or guidance to read on aspects of practice which you can then discuss in supervision. However, this will not suit all students' learning styles and may only secure learning at a 'surface' rather than 'deep' level (Marton and Saljo, 1997). To counter this, setting particular reading and then creating space within supervision to talk about the reading and requiring the student to relate their learning to a particular case they are working with might develop their learning more effectively. You might have thought of more interactive methods in which your student can participate more fully, such as role play, which can be particularly useful in the teaching or transmission of skill acquisition. Race (2002) and Doel and Shardlow (2005) provide a range of methods, tools and techniques that teachers can employ that you may want to experiment with. Remember that you are also learning, and acknowledging this to your student can be empowering for them and may encourage a two-way process of learning.

A more formal teaching method is perhaps the practice tutorial (Doel *et al.*, 1996), which enables direct teaching to be planned and executed in relation to a particular learning need(s) that you or the student may have identified. Having identified a theme, such as 'the Assessment Framework' or child protection, you need to think what the objectives of the teaching session are so you can plan how to meet them and evaluate whether you have done so after the event. Preparing for the session is crucial and you need to think about the methods you intend to employ in the session. This might involve a short presentation that makes links between the subject chosen and the legislative and policy framework, issues of values and ethics, current research evidence and underpinning theory. You may require the student to make links with some of the work that they are undertaking with a particular child or family. The session may include exercises such as working through a set case study or a critical incident analysis on a piece of work they are involved in (Fook, 2002). You might also provide some essential guided reading for the student to take away and digest for a follow-up session. The session may end with a series of questions on the topic which you can ask the student in order to assess how much they have learnt. If there are other students placed in your team or service, it may be a good idea to deliver the practice tutorial to a number of students and for other practice educators to deliver other sessions to the students, thus sharing resources and expertise and exposing the students to different styles. It is a good idea to familiarise yourself with your student's academic curriculum so that you can make links with this and supplement the student's learning as well as enabling them to integrate their learning from university into their practice.

There are also many electronic resources available to assist you in facilitating learning, such as the Social Care Institute of Excellence's range of e-based activities, documents and Social Care TV (see **www.scie.org.uk**), which you can incorporate into your formal sessions or ask your student to go away and engage with. All social work students are required to undertake learning about research methods as part of their social work programme in order that they are able to use research evidence to inform their practice. Research suggests that many students struggle with this area of education and practice (Adam *et al.*, 2004; Cox and Jackson, 2003) and lack motivation to increase their knowledge (Knee, 2002). A similar picture appears with qualified social workers (McCrystal, 2000), who are unsure about how to translate research findings into their practice. Given this, as a practice educator, you could familiarise yourself with your student's academic curriculum and then, together with your student, identify research studies carried out in your area of practice and critically evaluate these findings and their application to practice. This will bring benefits to you as a PQ student because, as the rest of this book will testify, you will be required to embrace current research evidence and critically evaluate its contribution to social work knowledge.

Assessing your student

Perhaps the most daunting aspect of practice education is the assessment that is involved, as this requires the practice educator to make a professional judgement about whether the student should pass or fail the placement. The assessment framework, laid out in the *National Occupational Standards for Social Work* (NOS) (TOPSS, 2002), replaced the DipSW (Diploma in Social Work) core competencies and contains six key roles and 21 accompanying units, all of which must be evidenced to demonstrate that the student has reached acceptable levels of competence. This competence framework is not without its critics (Harris, 1996; Furness and Gilligan, 2004) as a student may meet all the requirements but uncertainty or uneasiness may remain about their fitness for practice. As with all types of assessment it is important that evidence is obtained from as wide a range of sources as possible to ensure triangulation (Shardlow and Doel, 1996). Thus, you need to ensure that the student is assessed undertaking a wide range of social work tasks relevant to their stage of professional development. However, while a clear competence framework has been implemented with the NOS, it is important to incorporate principles of adult learning theory and, as Cowburn *et al.* (2000) suggest, ensure there is open dialogue and negotiation with the student, rather than a rigid imposition of this framework. This also involves taking an anti-oppressive approach to the process of assessment and taking issues of difference into account, which you must be able to demonstrate in meeting the values requirements outlined by the GSCC in the *Guidance on Assessment of Practice in the Workplace* (GSCC/TOPSS England, 2002, p 9).

- *Think of all the different sources of evidence you will be able to draw on to assess your student's competence across all of the units outlined in the NOS within your area of practice.*

Comment

You may have identified some or all of the following:

- Direct observation of the student with a service user.

- Direct observation of the student engaging in other activities such as a core group meeting, team meeting or presenting at a panel.

- Discussions with the student in supervision.

- The student's case records, reports or other written work.

- Feedback from service users with whom the student has worked.

- Feedback from your team and other professionals.

- Informal discussion and interaction with the student.

- The student's self-assessments and reflective journal or logs.

Direct observation

Undertaking a direct observation of your student in a session with a service user is perhaps the most important source of evidence available to you, as the person charged with assessing suitability and competence to practice, and you should plan from the outset when and what you will be observing. The university programme will probably have a pro-forma report that you will need to complete and indicate how many observations will need to be completed. Preparation needs to be carried out so that both you and the student are clear about what you will be observing and the service user also needs to have agreed to the observation taking place. Observing your student is an important source of evidence as it will enable you to see how your student engages and communicates with some of the people they are working with. It will also provide you with an opportunity to give some feedback on what they have done well and areas that they can and should develop, which research shows provides a major role in the learning process (Evans, 1999). You should agree in advance with your student when and how you will give feedback and allow some time for reflection on both sides. Feedback needs to be given only with the intention of improving a student's competence and should be undertaken sensitively as your student may well feel exposed being observed, which may lead to defensiveness. Beverley and Worsley (2007) offer a useful mnemonic to assist in giving feedback – SCORE:

- **S**pecific;
- **C**lear;
- **O**wned;
- **R**egular;
- **E**ven-handed.

(Beverley and Worsley, 2007, p137)

It is important that you read sufficiently around the area to ensure understanding of the principles of assessment. Walker *et al.* (2008) provide a useful staged approach to the process of assessment that involves four key stages:

- planning for assessment – learning opportunities related to learning needs;
- collecting the evidence – as outlined above;
- weighing the evidence – is it clear, understandable, reliable, valid and agreed?;
- producing a report – containing evidence and your analysis, summary and recommendations.

(Walker *et al.*, 2008, p89)

Students on most social work programmes will also be required to produce their own report on their placement which demonstrates their learning against the competency framework of the NOS. Therefore, it is useful for both you and your student to jointly agree the range of evidence that best reflects their practice and progress during the placement, as well as agreeing what the outstanding learning needs and areas for development may be as they finish the placement and move on to their next placement or potentially qualify.

Working with marginal or failing students

The processes described above need to be adhered to for all students regardless of whether they are passing or at risk of failing. If your student's practice is falling short of expected, suitable competence in relation to any of the NOS units or the GSCC Codes of Practice (2002), it is equally important that you have clear and specific examples of evidence that demonstrate where, how and why the student is not meeting the requirements. You should also identify further opportunities and support to improve and develop their practice to the required level and this must be outlined clearly to them. As soon as any issues arise in the student's practice these should be brought to the attention of the student clearly, sensitively and in a way that ensures the student feels confident that they will be supported in addressing such issues. It is important to be specific rather than general when giving feedback so the student is able to understand what aspect of their practice is problematic or insufficient, such as timekeeping or case recording, for instance. Early identification and discussion can lead to potential resolution if the student was unaware of a procedural or practice-based issue. If there is no improvement once the issue of concern has been raised with the student, it is important that you do not leave things to unravel further. This may be the time to have a discussion with the student's tutor at university so that a three-way meeting can be arranged. Here the issues underlying your concern about the student's practice can be discussed fully and a detailed plan of how to address this over the coming weeks can be agreed and drawn up, with a review mechanism also being established.

If the issue concerns the student's conduct or suitability, these issues also need to be raised with the student immediately. Hopefully, you will have had a discussion with the student about expectations of the agency in relation to professional conduct and what this means in their role as a social work student in your team, service and organisation. Students are sent on practice learning placements to learn and some of them will require guidance and support in developing their professionalism. However, if emerging concerns continue, it is important that specific examples are identified to the student as unacceptable, with clear reasons why as well as suggested or expected alternative approaches.

Communication with the student's tutor is vital as the university and the placement agency need to take a joint approach to dealing with failing students. While you are required to make a recommendation to the university about whether the student passes or fails the placement, the university will have the final decision. It is important that you make yourself familiar with the process of managing a placement breakdown or a failing student as well as the procedure where the suitability of the student to practise is called into question. If any element of the student's practice has the potential to put a service user at risk or is in breach of the Code of Practice for Social Care Workers you will need to discuss this with your line manager and the university will need to be informed so the specific suitability procedures can be followed to manage this effectively and efficiently. For more detail on failing students, see Sharp and Danbury (1999).

Reflecting on your own practice

As a student yourself, you will be required to submit academic work related to your emerging role as a practice educator, which may be in the form of a portfolio. As Chapter 1 outlined, you will need to be able to articulate your development from a critically reflective standpoint. Thus, you will need to demonstrate how you have approached the role of practice educator, the values that have informed your practice, the theory that has underpinned it and the skills that you have developed over the duration of the placement you have managed. All of this will need to be with reference to the currently piloted national standards for practice education (Social Work Taskforce, 2009). Being self-aware and engaging in exercises that require you to demonstrate emotional intelligence will help you think about what you bring to the role and how you may be perceived by your student, and is essential if you are to work well with both service users and learners (Chilton, 2008). This requires some honest self-assessment, appraisal and evaluation that you can test out through seeking feedback from those involved in the practice learning placement, notably the student, your line manager, colleagues and university tutors. The purpose of engaging in these processes is not only to demonstrate that you have met the required competencies to teach and assess the practice of a social work student, but also to help you to continue to develop your own practice in undertaking this very important role. Part of this involves a commitment to updating your knowledge through reading and research. As the Social Work Reform Board carries out its work and makes recommendations or implementations to improve social work education and practice, the role of the practice educator, as a qualified, reflective and knowledgeable professional, may be more important than ever.

Chapter summary

This chapter has considered the current context for practice learning in social work education. It has explored the motivations of agreeing to provide a practice learning placement and the main roles and responsibilities associated with this: managing learning opportunities and the practice curriculum, teaching and enabling learning, supervision and assessment. The activities should help you to plan and prepare as you begin the journey of enabling the learning of social work students in a children and families context. Now that you have started reflecting on whether you are ready to support someone at the start of their social work education, further suggested reading is identified to explore these aspects of practice learning more thoroughly.

FURTHER READING

Doel, M and Shardlow, S (2005) *Modern social work practice: Teaching and learning in practice settings.* Aldershot: Ashgate.

This book contains a range of exercises for practice educators to use with their students across a wide range of areas from inter-professional practice to working with difficult students.

Morrison, T (2009) *Supervision guide for social workers.* Leeds: Children's Workforce Development Council.

This guide fully outlines the '4 x 4 x 4 model' introduced in this chapter and explores good practice in supervision with social work practitioners in a children and families setting.

Smith, A, McAskill, H, and Jack, K (2008) *Developing advanced skills in practice teaching.* Basingstoke: Palgrave.

Written by a range of healthcare professionals, this book provides an overview of practice education for those in health and social care settings, including a range of activities and resources.

Walker, J, Crawford, K and Parker, J (2008) *Practice education in social work: A handbook for practice teachers, assessors and educators.* Exeter: Learning Matters.

This book is specifically written for practice educators and contains chapters on assessment, supervision, learning and teaching, mapped against the PQ Standards for Practice Education.

Chapter 9

What's important for looked after children? The views of young people leaving care

Lucille Allain and Christine Cocker, with Orland Hinds, Erina Naluwaga and Anne Babondock

CHAPTER OBJECTIVES

If you are a registered social worker, this chapter will assist you to evidence post-registration training and learning. It relates to the national post-qualifying framework for social work education and training at the specialist level:

iv. *Draw on knowledge and understanding of service users and cares issues to actively contribute to strategies and practice which promote services user and carers rights and participation in line with the goals of choice, independence and empowerment.*

It will also help you to meet the Children and Families standards for social work:

i. *Working in partnership with children, young people, their families or carers including effective:*

- *communication;*
- *support;*
- *advocacy; and*
- *involvement of children and young people in decision-making.*

ii(f). *The needs of children and young people accommodated, looked after and leaving care (including a knowledge and understanding of how to use the services that exist to meet those needs and the nature of the specific responsibilities of corporate parents, such as those associated with responsibilities for development and educational attainment).*

Introduction

This chapter focuses on children's rights and participation and is co-authored with three young people who have left care and who contribute to social work teaching at Middlesex University and deliver training workshops for social work and social care staff in a local authority. The voices of care leavers and their experiences of being in care are central to this chapter. Their views are presented throughout in the form of direct quotes taken from questionnaires that they completed. Their responses show that having a reliable, honest, thoughtful, respectful and understanding social worker is key. As one young person said, a good social worker is: *'Someone who is eager to make a difference and help the young person, who does not make false promises; for example, saying they will call back and not doing so'*.

Staff workshop

In this chapter, links are made between feedback from the young people and from local authority social work staff obtained during a one-day staff conference, where the authors were involved in delivering a workshop focused on the needs of young people in care. Following a presentation from the young people, a round-table discussion involving approximately 100 social work staff took place, with each table focusing on one of the following questions, which had emerged as themes from responses to the young people's questionnaires completed earlier in the workshop:

i.   What are the ways in which we show respect to children and young people?

ii. How do we prepare children and young people for independence?

iii. How can children and young people be helped to feel more at ease in contributing their views?

ACTIVITY 9.1

- *Before you read on about the results of the workshop that was run with young care leavers and social work staff, have a go at answering these questions yourself.*

Comment

In our analysis and discussion of the views of young people, you will notice a number of similarities between their views about how best to meet the care and support needs of looked after children and those of the staff we consulted with. There is an emphasis on the importance of professionals developing supportive and nurturing relationships, being honest about care planning and being creative about how children and young people can be meaningfully involved in shaping their own future and that of other children and young people through participation and training events.

In seeking to develop your social work skills and knowledge you will encounter new policies and procedures and legislative changes which you will be required to integrate into your practice. However, what should remain constant is your commitment to social work values as detailed within the *National Occupational Standards* (TOPSS, 2002) and the General Social Care Council's Codes of Practice (GSCC, 2010). In addition, if you are engaged in post-qualifying study, you must demonstrate that the values outlined in Requirement 5 of the *Specialist Standards and Requirements for Post-Qualifying Social Work Education and Training: Children and Young People, their Families and Carers* (GSCC, 2005b) are evidenced in your practice.

Children's rights and participation

A key global charter for children is the United Nations Convention on the Rights of the Child which was ratified by the UK Government in 1991. Although it was not incorporated into UK legislation, it is important as it sets a standard or benchmark in terms of children's rights, thus enabling countries to measure and judge their own provision for children, even if they are not signatories. Also, for countries who are signatories, their childcare systems and legislation are examined every five years by the United Nations and feedback is given about what may need to be changed (Johns, 2009, p44). Brammer (2010, p178) states that to: *find legal recognition of the concept of children's rights . . . UK case law and legislation needs to be considered*. In an examination of the Children Act 1989, Brammer (2010) emphasises that although within the Children Act 1989 *there is no specific provision . . . that promotes 'children's rights'* (p179), there is clear evidence of the influence of this concept. This is linked to the Court needing to ascertain *the wishes and feelings of the child* (Section 1(3) (a)) and the child's welfare being of paramount importance when decisions are made by Courts. A central tenet of the Act is that *an appropriate level of respect is given to the child as an individual who is entitled to separate consideration in his or her own right* (Brayne and Carr, 2008, p185). The developments in relation to children having rights in law go *beyond protection and provision . . to [having] a voice in decision-making provoked controversy* (Williams, 2008, p28). For example, in Sir William Utting's Report (1997) into long-standing concerns about the abuse of children in public care, he states that discussions about children's rights were not always welcomed as there was a belief that it undermined parental authority. Despite the critics of the development of children's rights, the debates about children being 'active agents' and not passive bystanders (Prout, 2002) have impacted on society's views about the meaning of 'adulthood' and 'childhood'. The discourse about children having rights is now widely accepted. As argued by Qvortrup (1994): *children are human beings, not only 'human becomings', they have not only needs . . . also interests that may or may not be compatible with interests of other social groups or categories . . .'* (p18).

Given the development and acceptance of children's rights, the participation and involvement of children in decisions that affect them has been incorporated into many aspects of UK policy and practice. Alderson (1999) examines this in relation to children's involvement in schools and more broadly across a range of contexts (Alderson, 2000). Hart's (1992) model, the 'Ladder of Participation', has been used to explore levels of participation of service users and carers in social work education (Allain *et al.*, 2006) and more specifically in relation to children (Shier, 2001). Listening and responding to the views of children and young people has been a political priority and has been at the heart of recent child and family welfare government policy initiatives. These include: Sure Start, the Children's Fund,

Every Child Matters (DfES, 2003) and more recent developments in relation to looked after children with the Green Paper, *Care Matters: Transforming the Lives of Children and Young People in Care* (DfES, 2006a) followed by the White Paper, *Care Matters: Time for Change* (DfES, 2007a) which resulted in the enactment of new legislation, the Children and Young Persons Act 2008. As discussed by Cocker and Allain (2008): *from a policy perspective, we are at a point of significant change, as this current government is interested in looked after children's everyday experiences* (p193). As academics, practitioners and service user educators, we are interested in what looked after children think is important for them in terms of the services that they receive from social workers. The remainder of this chapter will outline some of the key issues raised by care leavers, which give vital messages about what is important in relation to the sort of social work service looked after children want to receive.

Questions posed to young people leaving care

In order to capture the views of young people who have experienced care, we asked the three young people who co-authored this chapter five general questions applicable to most children in care. However, we discussed the limitations of this approach with the young people. The first limitation was acknowledging that the views expressed were from three young people only. Secondly, asking general questions does not address the specific needs of all children. Finally, this approach does not fully account for the differing experiences of care that children and young people may have, based on whether they are looked after briefly or for a longer period (the issues of the fluidity and diversity within the looked after children population is explored within *Care Matters*, DfES, 2007a). However, we wanted to seek the views of the three young people about their experiences and views of being in care. We agreed we would then look for themes appearing in the responses and use these themes to stimulate discussion amongst social workers in the workshop, with reference to the burgeoning literature available on this topic. In developing the questions, we also referred to key themes from *Care Matters: Time for Change* (DfES, 2007a), from *Care Matters: Ministerial Stocktake Report* (DCSF, 2009g) and from advocacy and support groups including: Voice for the Child in Care, the Who Cares? Trust and the Care Leavers Association. For example, one of the key areas that children and young people have expressed concern about in *Care Matters: Time for Change* (DfES, 2007a) was having frequent changes of social worker. The children who were consulted as part of the *Care Matters* consultation (DfES, 2007a), and the three young people who co-authored this chapter, repeatedly said they wanted stability; both in terms of their day-to-day carers and their social worker. This theme stresses the importance of social workers taking time to build and maintain relationships with looked after children, some of whom may have experienced multiple carers, placements and social workers, which can lead to children losing trust in the adults around them. Therefore a child or young person may be wary about getting to know a new social worker and sharing their hopes and fears. Being clear about what commitment you can offer is therefore very important as the relationship-based practice model (Ruch, 2005) has at its heart the use of self in the professional helping relationship. This entails you getting to know the child or young person and using your own experiences to work with them directly and also working with their carers.

The views of young people leaving care

The first question we asked was: From a young person's point of view, what makes a good social worker? The young people thought that a good social worker would be thoughtful and decisive even when their manager was not present: *'They need to be able to think for themselves and also sometimes when their manager is not there they need to able to make a reasonable decision that would not keep the young person hanging on.'* The young people wanted their social worker to be genuine, which might mean *'going that extra mile'*.

There was also a focus on the importance of showing respect and understanding towards the young person and their foster parents. Young people wanted social workers to try to listen more and to accept that:

> . . . although they may not fully understand a young person's life experiences and/or how they feel, they can still understand that most of the time all a young person needs is someone to just sit and listen to them and understand what they are saying to them at that moment, as opposed to coming in and trying to act like they understand their whole life by just reading their file for ten minutes.

There was a wish for social workers to try to see things from the looked after child's viewpoint and to *'think about how they would feel'*. The young people said that some social workers really do try to do this, but not all.

The second question was: How can young people be helped to feel more at ease in their statutory review so that they can say what they honestly think?

The young people wanted their social worker to ensure only people who absolutely had to be at the review were invited.

> There is nothing worse than sitting at a review with a room full of people that the young person doesn't feel comfortable around. It would be good practice and respectful if the young person was asked beforehand who they would like there and who they would prefer not be there. This could make a huge difference to their attitude towards and outcome of the review.

Young people said that the role of the Chair or Independent Reviewing Officer was really important and that the Chair should take a few minutes alone with the young person before and after the review to speak with them. *'Doing this would give the young person the chance to think about whether there was anything they would like to say away from either their foster carer or social worker.'* The young people said that there could be issues that they did not feel comfortable about discussing in an open meeting because they felt a bit scared or embarrassed. To reassure young people, professionals could explain: *'that they [the young person] should say how they feel so that people can try helping improve their issues or problems'*.

The third question asked was: How can social workers help young people to achieve in school and college socially and academically?

Young people discussed the importance of talking to the child or young person about school or college and offering realistic choices about what they could study and where they could study, in accordance with the age of the looked after child. They wanted social workers and carers to offer to help children with school work and wanted help with preparing for exams. This included attending parents' evenings at school and taking an interest in homework and other school-based activities and projects. If a child had to move to a new placement in a different area, they suggested helping them to find new activities, for example *'local youth centres and activities in their area for socialising and making new friends'*. They also said that it was really important to help young people leaving care with applying to college or university: *'. . . it can be difficult to make lots of decisions all at the same time when you are leaving care and leaving school and you don't know what to study or what you are going to be'*.

The fourth question we asked also links to choices and opportunities for children and young people: How can young people in care be more involved in choices that affect their future, for example moving to a new placement or changing schools?

There was a focus on discussion and support with the aim of: *'helping young people feel responsible and able to make decisions for themselves'*. There was a real emphasis on not just telling young people what was happening but asking and listening to their ideas and responses about what they might want to happen in their lives:

> *. . . if you do ask a young person, make sure you listen as there is nothing worse than thinking that your opinion means something when it doesn't. Of course, young people may not always get what they want, but if they, for example, have to move into shared housing or independent living, ask them 'Is there anywhere you would not like to live or is there any way social services can make you feel more at ease/comfortable in your new place?' These small things help the young person to mentally start to take control of their own future; it encourages them to think about what they want their future to be, directly or indirectly.*

Finally, we asked: How can social workers work with foster carers to help them do the best job they can?

There was an emphasis on foster carers being the people in the professional network who really know the child best: *'they take care of the young person 24/7'*. The young people thought that some social workers did not always seem to recognise this and that social workers could on occasions undermine the foster carer. It was also felt that foster carers should have more autonomy in relation to decisions about the young person: *'As a social worker, you may feel that a young person is not ready to do something, however the person (foster carer) that sees them day in, day out and sees their potential and growth may feel that this young person can do this particular task.'*

Social workers sometimes took a while to respond to young people, due to their many responsibilities, and this was frustrating*: 'social workers sometimes take ages to get back to you'*. The young people thought there should be more joint training between foster carers and looked after children social workers so that they could understand each other more. Young people also wanted social workers to take time to explain to foster carers that some looked after children might have had really difficult experiences that may make it difficult for them to settle into a family. They wanted foster carers to be advised to: *'try and have patience and make them feel as welcome as possible. I think the main thing to* *do is to talk to the young person and don't say something will happen unless you're 100 per cent sure, as if it comes to this thing not happening the young person will feel even worse and be less trusting'.*

ACTIVITY 9.2

Reflect on one training event that you have attended which was focused on the needs of looked after children and which involved young people who had been looked after.

1. What did you learn from it that was different to other training you have attended?

2. How were the young people prepared and supported to undertake this training?

3. If you have not previously attended a training event delivered (fully or in part) by young people who have experienced care, why do you think this is?

Comment

If you have attended training delivered by young people who have experienced care, it may have made you think differently about aspects of your practice or how you can develop your work further. The idea of practice evolving and developing through interactions between individuals with different experiences is discussed by Wenger (1998). He discusses learning in practice as *evolving forms of mutual engagement, discovering how to engage, what helps and what hinders, developing mutual relationships, defining identities and who is who* (p95). Thinking about 'who is who' might have been important in relation to the training you attended that was delivered by young people as they were in a position of power and authority in relation to leading an event. If you have not been part of a training event delivered by young people, reflect on how you might want to develop this in your organisation. This will involve time commitment, funding and sharing power with young people who are service users.

Workshop with staff

The authors of the chapter were involved in delivering a workshop to social work staff from a London Council. This workshop focused on the young people feeding back their experiences of being in care, including what was positive and what needed to change. As part of this process, over 100 staff were asked to participate in round-table discussions, with each table focusing on one question.

The first five tables focused on the question: What are the ways in which we show respect to children and young people? The responses were ranked in terms of frequency of comment as listed below. It shows that of primary importance was being honest, spending time, listening and consulting, remembering to acknowledge when something has not gone well and listening to the young person's story:

1. Be honest.

2. Consideration to giving quality time to young people.

3. Listen and consult but don't dictate the agenda during pathway planning and in reviews.

4. Remember that workers are not always right. Acknowledge and apologise to children and young people when we get things wrong.

5. Listening is really important, especially to the young person's story.

The second five tables focused on: How do we prepare children and young people for independence? Recognising the differing needs of care leavers was identified as significant, as was independence being a staged process that takes time. The important role of foster carers was also discussed. Ensuring professionals have high expectations for young people and are also there to help when things go wrong is important so that young people can feel they have a second chance when they make mistakes:

1. Care leavers have different needs; they are not a homogeneous group.

2. Becoming independent is a process not an event.

3. Foster carers can give young people age-appropriate tasks to help them learn independence skills.

4. Life skills are important for raising the expectations of young people and can also be empowering.

5. Acknowledge that we all learn from our mistakes – help young people to realise they can still go forward even if something goes wrong.

The third five tables discussed: How can children and young people be helped to feel more at ease in contributing their views? The importance of building relationships was the most frequent response, alongside the development of key skills for working with children and young people individually and in groups. Professionals should be informing young people about how information shared in the review would be used and should be honest with young people about this:

1. Building relationships to facilitate views being shared.

2. Open body language and good communication skills.

3. Being creative to facilitate participation and include empowering and fun activities.

4. Need to be clear about how information will be used.

5. Be honest about how decisions are taken and what will happen.

What does the literature say about the views of looked after children and young people?

As stated in the introduction, there is an emphasis on honesty, patience and listening as a route to empowering children and young people. Young people's responses underline the power social workers hold and their importance in the lives of looked after children. This was also a finding in a study undertaken by Munro (2001) where social workers are described as potentially being *a very strong ally* (p131). Similarly, a study undertaken by McLeod (2010) indicated that young people in care viewed a good social worker as *like a 'friend'* and an equal (2010, p772), thus concurring with the consensus within the literature that *positive and stable relationships with their social workers promote good outcomes for children and young people in the care system* (2010, p773).

The idea of social workers being a powerful advocate and part of a young person's journey to independence when they are an unaccompanied asylum-seeking young person is explored by Kohli (2006, 2007). He describes the importance of social workers having *an emotional commitment* (2006, p4) to the young person and that through this approach trust is more likely to develop. He identifies three domains which give an important framework to understanding how to work with unaccompanied young people, although the domains he identifies can be applied to social work practice with all looked after children. The domain of 'cohesion' requires a focus on resettlement and creating a sense of order. The second domain of 'connection' requires consideration of how to help the young person negotiate new networks and family systems so that they can make sense of who they are. The third domain is 'coherence' where the young person needs support to help them bring together their past, present and future (Kohli, 2007, p154). Many of these ideas are also directly relevant to looked after children who are not unaccompanied asylum seekers.

In terms of understanding looked after children's role in decision making that takes into account the looked after child's relationship with their social worker, but also moves beyond this to broader participation issues, Cashmore (2002) conducted a review of the research literature on participation of children in care in decision-making. Cashmore found that although children in care want to have a say in decisions that are made about them, they do not think they are given enough opportunities for this to occur meaningfully. Cashmore concluded: *Genuine and effective participation depends on several conditions: opportunity and choice in ways to participate, access to relevant information, the availability of a trusted advocate, proper resourcing, and supportive policy and legislation* (2002, p837). Many of these themes are identified and expanded on within the literature (for example Buchanan, 1995; Sinclair, 1998; Thomas and O'Kane, 2002; Wright *et al.*, 2006; Leeson, 2007; McLeod, 2007; SCIE, 2007; Gunn, 2008; Holland, 2009; Percy-Smith and Thomas, 2009).

Gunn (2008) highlights the power dynamics present within children and young people's participation in social care environments and concludes that *the mechanisms used to facilitate participation and the culture of the organisations where participation takes place are important factors* (2008, p253). Gunn uses Levin's power typology (1997) to explore how groups exercise different types of power, namely:

> *Power to do – literally what an individual is actually able to do; to make a decision alone;*
>
> *Power over – the power of an individual or group over another individual or group to direct their actions or behaviour;*
>
> *Power to achieve – the power to realise one's will and determine that a policy will incorporate at least some of the characteristics desired by the power holder.*

(Gunn, 2008, p255)

As well as introducing a corporate 'pledge' from individual local authorities to the looked after children for whom they are responsible, the White Paper *Care Matters* (DfES, 2007a) outlined the development of Children In Care Councils (CICCs) in each local authority in England and Wales. While we await the outcomes from various studies examining the processes undertaken by councils in establishing these CICCs, including which young people and how young people have been consulted and involved in the process, it may well be that many of the experiences and themes that young people have already had and raised in previous consultation processes will remain pertinent. Carr (2007) believes that *formal consultation mechanisms and established decision making fora have not been adequate for the participation task* (2007, p271). Whether or not CICCs are able to provide the necessary difference in mechanism for participation (Gunn, 2008) to move the dialogue and process beyond tokenism for the young people taking part, or whether they are another vehicle providing more of the same, there will be a range of different models utilised across the CICCs within England and Wales, and some of these will be innovative and progressive. As Carr rightly highlights, there are many agendas underpinning these developments:

> *Some critics argue that user involvement is too easily exploited as a 'technology of legitimation'. Thus it sustains management and government authority by giving the appearance of democratising public services without allowing policy shifts in 'undesirable' directions.*

> (Carr, 2007, p271)

This is particularly significant in a social care environment facing considerable budget reductions.

ACTIVITY 9.3

Have a look at some of the websites that have information about Children In Care Councils. See if you can glean the following information from a particular site that you find:

- *Who is involved in the CICC? Which children and young people, social workers, senior managers and counsellors are represented on the council?*

- *What is the budget set aside for the work of the CICC?*

- *How is the business from the CICC fed back into the work of the Council? Who decides on the priorities? Who chairs the CICC? What real power and influence does the CICC have?*

- *How does the work of the CICC complement other participation initiatives that the local authority may have set up?*

How do social workers view their role?

We have discussed above how the relationship between a social worker and a young person can be helpful to the young person in working through individual problems and difficulties that he or she may face in his or her life. At its best, this will involve children and young people actively participating in decision making about their lives. However, at a broader policy level, Gunn (2008) found that many social workers felt marginalised from this process because they weren't perceived as powerful stakeholders. They were able to identify concerns:

> . . . *on the efficacy of the approaches employed, particularly the managers' selection of compliant young people to participate. They seem to feel even more powerless than young people. While being positive about participation, their concerns about it being tokenistic indicate that they view the structures in which participation operates to be weighed in favour of more powerful stakeholders, and therefore did not believe that the activities that they and the young people were involved in would lead to real change.*

(Gunn, 2008, pp259–60)

While McLeod (2007) discusses some of the dynamics at play between social worker and young person, including within individual relationships, Shemmings (2000) explores social workers' viewpoints about the age at which children and young people should be consulted and involved in decisions, as well as the specific type of environment appropriate for children and young people to be present at in order to contribute to these processes. Shemmings' research concentrates on attendance at child protection conferences by children and young people and the views of their social workers but again many of the findings are transferable.

REFLECTION POINT

This chapter has been written in a participatory style, with the young people we work with at Middlesex University centrally involved in producing the chapter.

- *How can you as a social worker model this approach and work collaboratively with young people in care in participation events and in care planning?*

- *Spend some time thinking about and planning how you are going to improve this part of your practice with children and young people over the next three months.*

Chapter summary

This chapter has explored children's rights and participation and how children and young people who are looked after can be supported to make decisions about their future. The voices of care leavers and their experiences of being in care are central to the discussion and show that what is important is having a reliable, honest, thoughtful, respectful and understanding social worker. We have argued that what children and young people who are looked after value, above all else, is having a special adult who will listen to them and offer appropriate guidance and support. This does not mean that there will always be full agreement between a young person and the adults who are caring for them but it will entail a process of negotiation, of listening and of helping to support a child though the care system, whatever the plan for them is. We hope that the messages the young people have given in this chapter will help you to develop your practice in this area.

Cocker, C and Allain, L (2008) *Social work with looked after children.* Exeter: Learning Matters.

This is a general text that looks at the needs of looked after children.

Percy-Smith, B and Thomas, N (eds) (2009) *A handbook of children and young people's participation: Perspectives from theory and practice.* London: Routledge.

This is an edited textbook that gives helpful approaches to participation with children and young people.

Warren, J (2007) *Service user and carer participation in social work.* Exeter: Learning Matters.

This gives an overview of various theories about service user and carer participation.

www.dcsf.gov.uk/everychildmatters/safeguardingandsocialcare/childrenincare/childrenincare/ An English Government site.

www.voypic.org/ A site for young people in care in Northern Ireland.

www.ltscotland.org.uk/lookedafterchildren/index.asp A Scottish Government site.

www.g2k.org.uk/ Lambeth Council's website for looked after children.

www.childreninwales.org.uk/1364.html A Welsh voluntary sector organisation site.

www.anationalvoice.org/ A site for young people in care by young people in care.

www.thewhocarestrust.org.uk/ A voluntary sector organisation whose sole focus is representing the interests of children and young people in care.

Conclusion

Qualified child and family social workers need to constantly keep abreast of new developments in their work with children, young people and their families and continually update their skills and knowledge about what constitutes best practice in any given area. This book has provided a solid foundation for child and family social workers interested in updating their knowledge about current policy, research and practice developments. We have focused on providing information about consolidating practice, practice teaching and assessing qualifying students, and we have highlighted effective communication skills with looked after children, best practice in fostering and adoption work, safeguarding and child protection.

So what was our motivation in writing this book? In our experience PQ students want to hear about current research, not only about standards and requirements to satisfy the managerialist agenda within social work. For example, social workers enjoy hearing about current developments in attachment theory, relationship-based social work and skills in doing direct work. Also, they want to know how to help students to learn and how to work with families where there are issues of fear, aggression and concealment. This is the book we have tried to write.

Staying on top of your game

Without doubt, working as a social worker in children and families is a demanding job. There are no easy answers, no magic formulas or pre-packaged solutions available for the range of problems social workers see on a daily basis in their work. The skills required of social workers are considerable and extensive. Continuing professional development is a necessary part of ensuring that social workers are cognisant of the knowledge base underpinning effective social work practice in any given area. While regular reading of trade publications is useful, it does not provide social workers with a formal educative framework and environment (whether real or virtual) in which to think critically and abstractly about the theories and research evidence that are influential in social work. Increasing research literacy amongst social workers is important if we are to continue to strive toward using research evidence effectively within practice and understand what this means, rather than just repeat the sound bite 'evidence-based practice' in the hope that this will be enough. In addition to the PQ training that many employers offer social workers, the profession needs more social workers to undertake Master's and Doctoral-level education and to be supported by their employers in this endeavour. This expertise can then increase the research-mindedness and literacy of the profession within practice and in academia, and hopefully go some distance towards removing the silos that can exist between universities and social work practice agencies.

There are examples of social work academics researching real-life problems for practice. The work of Donald Forrester and the Tilda Goldberg Centre at the University of Bedfordshire (see **www.beds.ac.uk/goldbergcentre**) predominantly researches parental substance misuse, which is linked to the huge rise over the last ten years in complex child protection cases where one or both parents has substance abuse problems. If we are talking about marrying research and practice issues, then this research centre provides a good model for how this can occur in practice once sufficient research funding has been identified. But there are many other research institutes that also successfully achieve this, for example: the Hadley Centre at Bristol University (see **www.bristol.ac.uk/sps/research/centres/hadley/**), which specialises in research in fostering and adoption; the Centre for Child and Family Research at Loughborough University (see **www.lboro.ac.uk/research/ccfr/index.htm**); and other research centres at the University of York and the University of East Anglia.

We are passionately committed to being involved in shaping change and being part of the solution in shifting public perceptions of social work. We are proud of our profession and the role taken by social workers in leading the way in responding to some of the most complex and distressing contemporary social problems, while continuing to uphold social work values and ethics. We believe in a partnership model between local authorities and universities where best practice is shared and where there are reciprocal arrangements between teaching and practice. This is an approach that we have developed at Middlesex University and we think it works well. It is also a model espoused by the Social Work Taskforce. We continue to be excited about being social workers and hope we have conveyed this to you throughout this book.

Bibliography

Adam, N, Zosky, DL and Unrau, YA (2004) Improving the research climate in social work curricula: clarifying learning expectations across BSW and MSW research courses. *Journal of Teaching in Social Work*, 24(3/4): 1–18.

Agass, R (2005) The containing function of supervision in working with abuse, in Bower, M (ed) *Psychoanalytic theory for social work practice: Thinking under fire*. London: Routledge.

Ahmad, A, Betts, B and Cowan, L (2008) Using interactive media in direct practice, in Luckock, B and Lefevre, M (eds) *Direct work: Social work with children and young people in care*. London: BAAF.

Alderson, P (1999) Human rights and democracy in schools: Do they mean more than 'picking up litter and not killing whales'? *International Journal of Children's Rights*, 7(2): 185–205.

Alderson, P (2000) *Young children's rights: Exploring beliefs, principles and practice*. London: Jessica Kingsley.

Allain, L, Brown, HC, Danso, C, Dillon, J, Finnegan, P, Gadhoke, S, Shamash, M and Whittaker, F (2006) User and carer involvement in social work education – A university case study: Manipulation or citizen control? *Social Work Education*, 25(4): 403–413.

Archer, C and Burnell, A (eds) (2003) *Trauma, attachment and family permanence: Fear can stop you loving*. London: Jessica Kingsley.

Atkins-Burnett, S and Allen-Meares, P (2000) Infants and toddlers with disabilities: Relationship-based approaches. *Social Work*, 45(4): 371–379.

Bandura, A (1977) *Social learning theory*. New York: General Learning Press.

Bannister, A (2001) Entering the child's world: Communicating with children to assess their needs, in Horwath, J (ed) *The child's world: Assessing children in need*. London: Jessica Kingsley.

Barrett, H and Tasker, F (2001) Growing up with a gay parent: Views of 101 gay fathers on their sons' and daughters' experiences. *Educational and Child Psychology*, (18): 62–77.

Barrett, H and Tasker, F (2002) Gay fathers and their children: What we know and what we need to know. *Lesbian and Gay Psychology Review*, (3): 3–10.

Bartlett, FC (1932) *Remembering: A study in experimental and social psychology*. Cambridge: Cambridge University Press.

Beecham, J and Sinclair, I (2007) *Costs and outcomes in children's social care: Messages from research*. London: Jessica Kingsley.

Bell, M (2002) Promoting children's rights through the use of relationship. *Child and Family Social Work*, (7): 1–11.

Benner, P (2001) *From novice to expert: Excellence and power in clinical nursing practice*. New Jersey: Prentice Hall.

Bennett, S and Saks, LV (2006) A conceptual application of attachment theory and research to the social work student-field instructor supervisory relationship. *Journal of Social Work Education*, 42(3): 669–682.

Beverley, A and Worsley, A (2007) *Learning and teaching in social work practice*. Basingstoke: Palgrave.

Bhatti-Sinclair, K (2009) Practice education and 'enabling others', in Ruch, G (ed) *Post-qualifying childcare social work*. London: Sage.

Bion, W (1962) *Learning from experience*. London: Heinemann.

Borthwick, S and Lord, J (2007) *Effective fostering panels*. London: BAAF.

Bourton, A and McCausland, J (2001) A service for children and a service for the courts: The contribution of guardians *ad litem* in public law proceedings. *Adoption and Fostering*, 25(3): 59–66.

Bower, M (ed) (2005) *Psychoanalytic theory for social work practice: Thinking under fire*. London: Routledge.

Brammer, A (2010) *Social work law (3rd edition)*. Harlow: Pearson Longman.

Brayne, H and Carr, H (2008) *Law for social workers (10th edition)*. Oxford: Oxford University Press.

Brayne, H and Carr, H (2010) *Law for social workers (11th edition)*. Oxford: Oxford University Press.

The Bridge Consultancy (1997) *Bridge report for Cambridgeshire County Council Social Services Department on professional judgements and accountability in relation to work with the Neave family*. Cambridge: Cambridgeshire County Council.

Briggs, S (2009) Risks and opportunities in adolescence: Understanding adolescent mental health difficulties. *Journal of Social Work Practice*, 23(1): 49–64.

Broadhurst, K, Wastell, D, White, S, Hall, C, Peckover, S, Thompson, K, Pithouse, A and Davey, D (2009) Performing 'initial assessment': Identifying the latent conditions for error at the front-door of local authority children's services. *British Journal of Social Work*, 40(2): 352–370.

Bronfenbrenner, U (1979) *The ecology of human development*. Cambridge, MA: Harvard University Press.

Brown, HC (2008) Social work and sexuality, working with lesbians and gay men: What remains the same and what is different? *Practice: Social Work in Action*, 20(4): 265–275.

Brown, HC and Cocker, C (2008) Lesbian and gay fostering and adoption: Out of the closet into the mainstream? *Adoption and Fostering*, 32(4): 19–30.

Brown, HC and Cocker, C (2011) *Social work with lesbians and gay men*. London: Sage.

Brown, HC and Kershaw, S (2008) The legal context for social work with lesbians and gay men in the UK: Updating the educational context. *Social Work Education*, 27(2): 122–130.

Buchanan, A (1995) Young people's views on being looked after in out-of-home care under the Children Act 1989. *Children and Youth Services Review*, 17(5/6): 681–696.

Buchanan, A (2007) Including the socially excluded: The impact of government policy on vulnerable families and children in need. *British Journal of Social Work*, (37): 187–207.

Burnell, A and Vaughan, J (2008) Remembering never to forget and forgetting never to remember: Rethinking life story work, in Luckock, B and Lefevre, M (eds) *Direct work: Social work with children and young people in care*. London: BAAF.

Burnham, A and Balls, E (2009) Government response to the Social Work Taskforce: Letter to Moira Gibb, Chair, Social Work Taskforce, 1.12.09, in Gibb, M (2009) *Building a safe, confident future: The final report of the Social Work Taskforce*. Nottingham: DCSF Publications. Available at: **http://publications. dcsf.gov.uk/eOrderingDownload/SWTF-GovResponse.pdf**

Caple, FS, Salcido, RM and Cecco, P (1995) Engaging effectively with culturally diverse families and children. *Social Work in Education*, 17(3): 159–70.

Carr, S (2007) Participation, power, conflict and change: Theorizing dynamics of service user participation in the social care system of England and Wales. *Critical Social Policy*, 27(2): 266–276.

Cartney, P (2004) How academic knowledge can support practice learning: A case study of learning styles. *Journal of Practice Teaching*, 5(2): 51–72.

Cashmore, J (2002) Promoting the participation of children and young people in care. *Child Abuse and Neglect*, (26): 837–847.

Child Poverty Action Group (2009) *Ending child poverty: A manifesto for success.* London: CPAG.

Children in Scotland (2009) *Key principles for effective participation.* Available at: **www. childreninscotland.org.uk**

Children's Workforce Development Council (2006) *Common induction standards.* Leeds: CWDC.

Children's Workforce Development Council (2007a) *Ordinary people doing extraordinary things: The training, support and development standards for foster care.* London: CWDC.

Children's Workforce Development Council (2007b) *Ordinary people doing extraordinary things: Your induction and workbook to foster care.* London: CWDC.

Children's Workforce Development Council (2009) *The Team Around the Child (TAC) and the lead professional: A guide for managers.* Leeds: CWDC.

Chilton, S (2008) Personal preparation, in Smith, A, McAskill, H and Jack, K (eds) *Developing advanced skills in practice teaching.* Basingstoke: Palgrave.

Clapton, G, Cree, VE, Allan, M, Edwards, R, Forbes, R, Irwin, M, Paterson, W and Perry, R (2006) Grasping the nettle: Integrating learning and practice revisited and re-imagined. *Social Work Education*, 25(6): 645–656.

Clapton, G, Cree, VE, Allan, M, Edwards, R, Forbes, R, Irwin, M, MacGregor, C, Paterson, W, Brodie, I and Perry, R (2007) Thinking outside the box: A new approach to integration of learning for practice. *Social Work Education*, 27(3): 334–340.

Clark, A and Statham, J (2005) Listening to young children: Experts in their own lives. *Adoption and Fostering*, 29(1): 45–56.

Clarke, M and Stewart, J (1997) *Handling the wicked issues: A challenge for government Discussion Paper.* Birmingham: Institute of Local Government Studies/University of Birmingham.

Cleaver, H, Unell, I and Aldgate, A (2010) *Children's needs – parenting capacity: The impact of parental mental illness, learning disability, problem alcohol and drug use, and domestic violence on children's safety and development (2nd edition).* London: TSO.

Cocker, C (2011) Sexuality before ability? The assessment of lesbians as adopters, in Hafford-Letchfield, T and Dunk, P (eds) *Sexual identities and sexuality in social work: Research and reflections from women in the field.* London: Ashgate.

Cocker, C and Allain, L (2008) *Social work with looked after children.* Exeter: Learning Matters.

Cocker, C and Brown, HC (2010) Sex, sexuality and relationships: Developing confidence and discernment when assessing lesbian and gay prospective adopters. *Adoption and Fostering*, 34(1): 20–32.

Cocker, C and Hafford-Letchfield, T (2010) Critical commentary: Out and proud? Social work's relationship with lesbian and gay equality. *British Journal of Social Work*, 40(6). Available at: **www.bjsw.oxfordjournals.org**

Cole, B, England, J and Rugg, J (2000) Spaced out? Young people on social housing estates: Social exclusion and multi-agency work. *Journal of Youth Studies*, (1): 21–33.

Commission for Social Care Inspection (2005) *Making every child matter: Messages from inspections of children's social services.* London: Commission for Social Care Inspection.

Cooper, A (2005) Surface and depth in the Victoria Climbié Inquiry Report. *Child and Family Social Work*, (10): 1–9.

Cooper, A and Dartington, T (2004) The vanishing organisation: Organisational containment in a networked world, in Huffington, C, Armstrong, D, Halton, W, Hoyle, L and Pooley, J (eds) *Working below the surface: The emotional life of contemporary organisations*. London: Karnac.

Cooper, A, Hetherington, R and Katz, I (2003) *The risk factor: Making the child protection system work*. London: Demos.

Cooper, A and Lousada, J (2005) *Borderline welfare: Feeling and fear of feeling in modern welfare*. London: Karnac.

Cooper, J (2010) Contact point database will close on 6 August. *Community Care Magazine*, 22 July 2010.

Cottrell, S (2003) *The study skills handbook*. Basingstoke: Palgrave Macmillan.

Cox, P and Jackson, S (2003) Editorial. *Social Work Education*, 22(1): 3–5.

Cowburn, M, Nelson, P and Williams, J (2000) Assessment of social work students: Standpoint and strong objectivity. *Social Work Education*, 19(6): 627–637.

Crisp, BR, Green-Lister, P and Dutton, K (2004) *Integrated assessment*. Glasgow: Scottish Institute for Excellence in Social Work Education.

Daniel, G (2005) Thinking in and out of the frame: Applying systemic ideas to social work with children, in Bower, M (ed) *Psychoanalytic theory for social work practice: Thinking under fire*. London: Routledge.

Davis, M (1984) Training: What we think of it now. *Social Work Today*, 15(20): 12–17.

De Boer, C and Coady, N (2007) Good helping relationships in child welfare. *Child and Family Social Work*, (12): 32–42.

Dent, R and Cocker, C (2005) Serious Case Reviews: Lessons for practice in cases of child neglect, in Taylor, J and Daniel, B (eds) *Child neglect: Practice issues for health and social care*. London: Jessica Kingsley.

Department for Children, Schools and Families (2006a) *Integrated children's system: The common assessment framework and contact point – An overview*. London: HMSO. Available at: **www.dcsf.gov.u**k

Department for Children, Schools and Families (2006b) *Working together to safeguard children: A guide to inter-agency working to safeguard and promote the welfare of children*. London: TSO.

Department for Children, Schools and Families (2007) *The children's plan: Building brighter futures*. London: TSO.

Department for Children, Schools and Families (2008a) *Outcomes for children and young people: Every Child Matters*. Available at: **www.dcsf.gov.uk**

Department for Children, Schools and Families (2008b) *Youth crime action plan*. London: HMSO. Available at: **www.dcsf.gov.uk**

Department for Children, Schools and Families (2009a) *Family Intervention Projects negative costing tool*. London: HMSO. Available at: **www.dcsf.gov.uk**

Department for Children, Schools and Families (2009b) *Think Family tool kit*. London: HMSO. Available at: **www.dcsf.gov.uk**

Department for Children, Schools and Families (2009c) *Think Family tool kit: Guidance note 3*. London: HMSO. Available at: **www.dcsf.gov.uk**

Department for Children, Schools and Families (2009d) *Children looked after in England (including adoption and care leavers) year ending 31 March 2009*. London: DCSF.

Department for Children, Schools and Families (2009e) *Fostering national minimum standards: Formal con-sultation draft*. London: DCSF.

Department for Children, Schools and Families (2009f) *Statistical first release 2009: Children looked after in England (including adoption and care leavers) year ending 31 March 2009.* Available at: **www.dcsf.gov.uk**

Department for Children, Schools and Families (2009g) *Care Matters: Ministerial stocktake report 2009.* Nottingham: DCSF Publications.

Department for Children, Schools and Families (2009h) *Referrals, assessment and children and young people who are the subject of a child protection plan, England – year ending 31 March 2009.* Available at: **www.education.gov.uk**

Department for Children, Schools and Families (2010a) *Working together to safeguard children: A guide to inter-agency working to safeguard and promote the welfare of children.* London: TSO. Available at: **www.dcsf.gov.uk**

Department for Children, Schools and Families (2010b) *Parenting and family support: Guidance for local authorities in England and Wales.* London: HMSO.

Department for Children, Schools and Families (2010c) *Think Family tool kit – Improving support for families at risk: Guidance note 4.* London: HMSO. Available at: **www.dcsf.gov.uk**

Department for Children, Schools and Families (2010d) *Youth crime intervention model.* London: HMSO. Available at: **www.dcsf.gov.uk**

Department for Education and Skills (2003) *Every Child Matters: Change for children.* London: TSO.

Department for Education and Skills (2004a) *Every Child Matters: Next steps.* London, DfES.

Department for Education and Skills (2004b) *The independent review mechanism: Local authority Circular LAC(2004)14, 27 April 2004.* London, DFES. Available at: **www.dh.gov.uk**

Department for Education and Skills (2005a) *Common core of skills and knowledge for the children's workforce.* Nottingham: DfES Publications.

Department for Education and Skills (2005b) *Statutory guidance to the Adoption and Children Act 2002.* London: DfES.

Department for Education and Skills (2005c) *Training for foster carers.* London: Office of Public Management.

Department for Education and Skills (2006a) *Care Matters: Transforming the lives of children and young people in care.* London: HMSO.

Department for Education and Skills (2006b) *The common assessment framework for children and young people: Practitioners' guide.* London: TSO. Available at: **www.teachernet.gov.uk/publications**

Department for Education and Skills (2006c) *Working together to safeguard children: A guide to inter-agency working to safeguard and promote the welfare of children.* London: HMSO.

Department for Education and Skills (2006d) *Common assessment framework for children and young people.* London: TSO. Available at: **www.dcsf.gov.uk**

Department for Education and Skills (2007a) *Care Matters: Time for change.* Norwich: TSO.

Department for Education and Skills (2007b) *Time for change: Young people's guide to the Care Matters White Paper.* Nottingham: TSO.

Department for Education and Skills and Department of Health (2004a) *National service framework for children, young people and maternity services.* London: TSO.

Department for Education and Skills and Department of Health (2004b) *Children Act.* London: TSO.

Department of Health (1989) *An introduction to the Children Act 1989.* London: HMSO.

Department of Health (1991) *The Children Act 1989: Guidance and regulations Vol 3: Family placements.*

London: HMSO.

Department of Health (1995a) *Looking after children: Good parenting good outcomes training guide.* London: HMSO.

Department of Health (1995b) *Child protection: Messages from research.* London: HMSO.

Department of Health (1998a*) The Quality Protects programme: Transforming children's services LDC(98) 28.* London: HMSO.

Department of Health (1998b) *Modernising social services: Promoting independence, improving protection, raising standards.* London: HMSO.

Department of Health (1999a) *Working together to safeguard children: A guide to inter-agency working to safeguard and promote the welfare of children.* London: HMSO.

Department of Health (1999b) Ado*ption now: Messages from research.* London: HMSO.

Department of Health (2000a) *Adoption: A new approach.* London: HMSO.

Department of Health (2000b) *Framework of assessment for children in need and their families.* London: TSO.

Department of Health (2000c) *Learning the lessons.* London: TSO.

Department of Health (2001) *The Children Act now: Messages from research.* London: TSO.

Department of Health (2002a) *Fostering services national minimum standards: Fostering services regulations.* London: TSO.

Department of Health (2002b) *Requirements for social work training.* London: HMSO.

Department of Health (2002c) *Studies informing the framework for the assessment of children in need and their families.* London: TSO.

Department of Health (2003) *Adoption agencies national minimum standards.* London: HMSO.

Department of Health (2006) *Invitation to bid: DoH/DfES health-led parenting support demonstration sites.* Available at: **www.dh.gov.uk**

Department of Health and Social Security (1974) *Report of the Committee of Inquiry into the care and supervision provided in relation to Maria Colwell.* London: HMSO.

Department of Health and Social Security (1987) *A child in trust: Jasmine Beckford.* London: HMSO.

de Winter, M and Noom, M (2003) Someone who treats you as an ordinary human being . . . homeless youths examine the quality of professional care. *British Journal of Social Work*, 33(3): 325–337.

Dimigen, G, Del Priore, C, Butler, S, Evans, S, Ferguson, L and Swan, M (1999) Psychiatric disorder among children at time of entering local authority care: Questionnaire survey. *British Medical Journal*, (319): 675.

Doel, M, Nelson, P and Flynn, E (2008) Experiences of post-qualifying study in social work. *Social Work Education*, 27(5): 549–571.

Doel, M, Shardlow, S, Sawdon, C and Sawdon, D (1996) *Teaching social work practice.* Aldershot: Ashgate.

Doel, M and Shardlow, S (2005) *Modern social work practice: Teaching and learning in practice settings.* Aldershot: Ashgate.

Doherty-Sneddon, G and Kent, G (1996) Visual signals and the communication abilities of children. *Journal of Child Psychology and Psychiatry*, 37(8): 949–959.

Drake, B (1994) Relationship competencies in child welfare services. *Social Work*, (30): 349–361.

Dreyfus, HL and Dreyfus, SE (1986) *Mind over machine: The power of human intuition and expertise in the era of the computer.* Oxford: Blackwell.

Dumbrill, GC (2006) Parental experience of child protection: A qualitative study. *Child Abuse and Neglect*, (30): 27–37.

Duncan-Smith, I (2006) *Chamberlain Lecture.* Available at: **www.centreforsocialjustice.org.uk**

Dunhill, A (2009) What is communication? The process of transferring information, in Dunhill, A, Elliott, B and Shaw, A (eds) *Effective communication and engagement with children and young people, their families and carers.* Exeter: Learning Matters.

Dunning, J (2010) GSCC to be scrapped. *Community Care Magazine*, 26 July 2010. Available at: **www.communitycare.co.uk**

Edwards, CP, Gandini, L and Forman, GE (eds) (1993) *The hundred languages of children: The Reggio Emilia approach to early childhood education.* Greenwich, CT: Ablex.

Elder, L (2009) I think critically, therefore I am. *Times Higher Education*, 6 August 2009. Available at: **www.timeshighereducation.co.uk**

Eraut, M (1994) *Developing professional knowledge and competence.* London: Routledge Falmer.

Eraut, M (2004) Transfer of knowledge between education and workplace settings, in Rainbird, HA, Fuller, A and Munro, H (eds) *Workplace learning in context.* London: Routledge.

Eraut, M (2007) Learning from other people in the workplace. *Oxford Review of Education*, 33(4): 403–422.

Erich, S (2005) Gay and lesbian adoptive families: An exploratory study of family functioning, adoptive child's behaviour and familial support networks. *Journal of Family Social Work*, 9(1): 17–32.

Erich, S, Kanenberg, H, Case, K, Allen, T and Bogdanos, T (2009) An empirical analysis of factors affecting adolescent attachment in adoptive families with homosexual and straight parents. *Children and Youth Services Review*, 31(3): 398–404.

Evans, D (1999) *Practice learning in the caring professions.* Aldershot: Arena/Ashgate.

Fahlberg, V (1994) *A child's journey through placement.* London: BAAF.

Fahmy, E, Levitas, R, Gordon, D and Patsios, D (2009) *Understanding the risks of social exclusion across the life course: Working-age adults without dependent children.* London: Cabinet Office. Available at: **www.cabinetoffice.gov.uk**

Family Delivery Team (2008) *Practice development tool.* London: Department of Education.

Farmer, E and Moyers, S (2008) *Kinship care: Fostering effective family and friends placements.* London: Jessica Kingsley.

Farnfield, S (2008) A theoretical model for the comprehensive assessment of parenting. *British Journal of Social Work*, (38): 1076–1099.

Ferguson, H (2005) Working with violence: The emotions and the psycho-social dynamics of child protection: reflections on the Victoria Climbié case. *Social Work Education*, 24(7): 781–795.

Ferguson, H (2009) Performing child protection: Home visiting, movement and the struggle to reach the abused child. *Child and Family Social Work*, 14(4): 471–480.

Ferguson, I (2008) *Reclaiming social work, challenging neo-liberalism and promoting social justice.* London: Sage.

Fish, J (2007) Getting equal: The implications of new regulations to prohibit sexual orientation discrimination for health and social care. *Diversity in Health and Social Care*, (4): 221–228.

Fish, S, Munro, E and Bairstow, S (2008) *Learning together to safeguard children: Developing a multi-agency systems approach for case reviews, Report 9.* London: SCIE.

Fook, J (2002) *Social work: Critical theory and practice.* London: Sage.

Forrester, D, Goodman, K, Cocker, C, Binnie, C and Jensch, G (2009) What is the impact of public care on children's welfare? A review of research findings from England and Wales and their policy implications. *Journal of Social Policy*, (38): 439–456.

Forrester, D, Kershaw, S, Moss, H and Hughes, L (2008) Communication skills in child protection: How do social workers talk to parents? *Child and Family Social Work*, (13): 41–51.

Fostering Network (2003) *The skills to foster.* London: Fostering Network.

Fostering Network (2006) *Improving effectiveness in foster care recruitment.* London: Fostering Network.

Frazer, L and Selwyn, J (2005) Why are we waiting? The demography of adoption for children of black Asian and black mixed parentage in England. *Child and Family Social Work*, (10): 135–147.

Freed-Kernis, A (2008) We're all human beings, aren't we? Working with lesbian, gay, bisexual and transgender young people in care, in Luckock, B and Lefevre, M (eds) *Direct work: Social work with children and young people in care.* London: BAAF.

Freedland, J (2010) There's a good idea in Cameron's 'big society' screaming to get out. *The Guardian*, 21 July 2010. Available at: **www.guardian.co.uk**

Frost, N, Mills, S and Stein, M (1999) *Understanding residential childcare.* Aldershot: Ashgate.

Frost, N and Parton, N (2009) *Understanding children's social care: Politics, policy and practice.* London: Sage.

Furness, S and Gilligan, P (2004) Fit for purpose: Issues from practice placements, practice teaching and the assessment of students' practice. *Social Work Education*, 23(4): 465–479.

Fursland, E (2010) Facebook has changed adoption forever. *The Guardian*, 19 June 2010. Available at: **www.guardian.co.uk**

Gaber, I and Aldridge, J (eds) (1994) *In the best interests of the child: Culture, identity and trans-racial adoption.* London: Free Association Books.

Garboden, M (2010) Eileen Munro spells out child protection review brief. *Community Care Magazine*, 11 June 2010.

Garrett, PM (2003) *Rethinking social work with children and families: A critical discussion on the 'modernisation' of social care.* London: Routledge.

Garrett, PM (2005a) New Labour's new electronic telephone directory: The Children Act 2004 and plans for databases on all children in England and Wales. *Social Work and Social Sciences Review*, 12(1): 5–21.

Garrett, PM (2005b) Social work's 'electronic turn': Notes on the deployment of information and communication technologies in social work with children and families. *Critical Social Policy*, 25(4): 529–553.

Garrett, PM (2008) How to be modern: New Labour's neo-liberal modernity and the Change for Children programme. *British Journal of Social Work*, (38): 270–289.

Garrett, PM (2009a) *Transforming children's services? Social work, neo-liberalism and the 'modern' world.* Berkshire: Open University Press/McGraw Hill.

Garrett, PM (2009b) The case of 'Baby P': Opening up spaces for debate on the 'transformation' of children's services? *Critical Social Policy*, (29): 533–547.

General Social Care Council (2002) *Codes of practice for social care workers and employers.* London: GSCC.

General Social Care Council (2005a) *Post-qualifying framework for social work education and training.* London: GSCC.

General Social Care Council (2005b) *Specialist standards and requirements for post-qualifying social work education and training: Children and young people, their families and carers.* London: GSCC.

General Social Care Council (2009) *Raising standards: Social work education in England 2007–08.* London: GSCC.

General Social Care Council (2010) *Code of practice for social care workers and code of practice for employers of social care workers.* London: GSCC.

General Social Care Council and Training Organisation for Personal Social Services England (2002) *Guidance on assessment of practice in the workplace.* London: GSCC.

Gerhardt, S (2004) *Why love matters: How affection shapes a baby's brain.* Hove, East Sussex: Brunner-Routledge.

Germain, C and Gitterman, A (1995) Ecological perspectives, in Edward, R (ed) *Encyclopaedia of social work (19th edition).* Washington DC: National Association of Social Workers.

Gibb, M (2009) *Building a safe, confident future: The final report of the Social Work Taskforce.* Nottingham: DCSF Publications.

Giddens, A (1998) *The third way: The renewal of social democracy.* Cambridge: Polity Press.

Gilchrist, J (2007) The challenges of practice learning today, in Tovey, W (ed) *The post-qualifying handbook for social workers.* London: Jessica Kingsley.

Gill, O and Jackson, B (1983) *Adoption and race: Black, Asian and mixed-race children in white families.* London: BAAF.

Golding, N (2010) More support for disabled children a key priority. *Community Care Magazine*, 17 June 2010. Available at: **www.communitycare.co.uk**

Goldstein, BP (2002) Black children with a white parent – social work education. *Social Work Education*, 21(5): 551–563.

Golombok, S (2000) *Parenting: What really counts?* London: Routledge.

Golombok, S, Spencer, A and Rutter, M (1983) Children in lesbian and single parent households: Psychosexual and psychiatric appraisal. *Journal of Child Psychology and Psychiatry*, (24): 551–572.

Gordon, W (2000) The relational paradigm in contemporary psychoanalysis: Towards a psycho-dynamically informed social work perspective. *Social Service Review*, (74): 352–379.

Gove, M (2010) *Munro review of child protection: Better front-line services to protect children.* Letter to Professor Eileen Munro, dated 10 July 2010. London: Department for Education. Available at: **www.education.gov.uk/munroreview/downloads/MichaelGovetoEileenMunro100610.pdf**

Graham, M (2007) *Black issues in social work and social care.* Bristol: The Policy Press.

Gunn, R (2008) The power to shape decision? An exploration of young people's power in participation. *Health and Social Care in the Community*, 16(3): 253–261.

Hafford-Letchfield, T (2007) *Practising quality assurance in social care.* Exeter: Learning Matters.

Hall, C and Slembrouck, S (2009) Communication with parents in child welfare: Skills, language and interaction. *Child and Family Social Work*, 14(4): 461–470.

Hargie, O and Dickson, D (2004) *Skilled interpersonal communication (4th edition).* London: Routledge.

Harker, M, Dobel-Ober, D, Berridge, D and Sinclair, I (2004) *Taking care of education.* London: National Children's Bureau.

Harries, M (1987) *Discussion paper on social work supervision.* Australia: WA Branch of Australian Association of Social Workers.

Harris, A (1996) Learning from experience and reflection in social work education, in Gould, N and Taylor, I (eds) *Reflective learning for social work*. Aldershot: Arena.

Harris, P (ed) (2006) *In search of belonging: Reflections by trans-racially adopted people*. London: BAAF.

Hart, R (1992) *Participation from tokenism to citizenship: Innocenti Essays, no.4*. Florence: UNICEF.

Harvey, A (2010) Getting a grip on social work. *Journal of Social Work Practice*, 24(2): 139–153.

Hawkins, P and Shohet, R (2000) *Supervision in the helping professions: An individual, group and organizational approach (2nd edition)*. Buckingham: Open University Press.

Healy, K (2005) *Social work theories in context: Creating frameworks for practice*. Basingstoke: Palgrave.

Hicks, S (1996) The 'last resort'?: Lesbian and gay experiences of the social work assessment process in fostering and adoption. *Practice*, 8(2): 15–24.

Hicks, S (1997) Taking the risk? Assessing lesbian and gay carers, in Kemshall, H and Pritchard, J (eds) *Good practice in risk assessment and risk management 2: Protection, rights and responsibilities*. London: Jessica Kingsley.

Hicks, S (1998) *Familiar fears: The assessment of lesbian and gay fostering and adoption applicants*. Lancaster University: PhD thesis.

Hicks, S (2000) 'Good lesbian, bad lesbian': Regulating heterosexuality in fostering and adoption assessments. *Child and Family Social Work*, 5(2): 157–68.

Hicks, S (2008) Thinking through sexuality. *Journal of Social Work*, 8(1): 65–82.

Hicks, S with Greaves, D (2007) *Practice guidance on assessing gay and lesbian foster care and adoption applicants*. Manchester: Manchester City Council.

Hicks, S and McDermott, J (eds) (1999) *Lesbian and gay fostering and adoption: Extraordinary yet ordinary*. London: Jessica Kingsley.

Higham, P and Sharp, M (2009) Practice education, in Higham, P (ed) *Post-qualifying social work practice*. London: Sage.

Hill, N (2009) *The pink guide to adoption for lesbians and gay men*. London: BAAF.

Hingley-Jones, H and Allain, L (2008) Integrating services for disabled children and their families in two English local authorities. *Journal of Interprofessional Care*, 22(5): 534–544.

HMCS (2006) *A quick guide to the Adoption and Children Act 2002*. London: HMSO. Available at: **www.hmcourts-service.gov.uk**

HMSO (1991) *Working together under the Children Act 1989: A guide to arrangements for inter-agency co-operation for the protection of children from abuse*. London: HMSO.

Holland, S (2009) Listening to children in care: A review of methodological and theoretical approaches in understanding looked after children's perspectives. *Children and Society*, 23(3): 226–235.

Hollows A and Nelson, P (2006) Equity and pragmatism in judgement-making about the placement of sibling groups. *Child and Family Social Work*, (11): 307–315.

Honey, P and Mumford, A (1986) *The manual of learning styles*. Maidenhead: Ardingley House.

House of Commons Children, Schools and Families Committee (2009) *Training of children and families social workers*. London: HMSO. Available at: **www.publications.parliament.uk**

Howe, D (1992) *An Introduction to social work theory*. Aldershot: Arena.

Howe, D (1996) Surface and depth in social work practice, in Parton, N (ed) *Social theory, social change and social work*. London: Routledge.

Howe, D (1998) *Patterns of adoption.* Oxford: Blackwell.

Howe, D (2005) *Child abuse and neglect: Attachment, development and intervention.* Basingstoke: Palgrave Macmillan.

Howe, D (2008) *The emotionally intelligent social worker.* Basingstoke: Palgrave Macmillan.

Hudson, B (2005) Information sharing and children's services reform in England: Can legislation change practice? *Journal of Interprofessional Care*, 19(6): 537–546.

Humphries, B (2004) An unacceptable role for social work: Implementing immigration policy. *British Journal of Social Work*, 34(1): 93–107.

Hunt, S (2002) In favour of online counselling? *Australian Social Work*, 55(4): 260–267.

Independent Review Mechanism (2005) *Making adoption work better.* Leeds: IRM. Available at: **www.independentreviewmechanism.org.uk**

Ironside, L (2008) Difficulties with reflective thinking in direct work: the role of supervision and consultation, in Luckock, B and Lefevre, M (eds) *Direct work: Social work with children and young people in care.* London: BAAF.

Johns, R (2009) *Using the law in social work (4th edition).* Exeter: Learning Matters.

Jordan, B (2000) Conclusion: Tough love: Social work practice in UK society, in Stepney, P and Ford, D (eds) *Social work models, methods and theories: A framework for practice.* Dorset: Russell House Publishers.

Jordan, B (2006) *Social policy in the twenty-first century: New perspectives, big issues.* Cambridge: Polity.

Jordan, B (2007) *Social work and well-being.* Lyme Regis: Russell House.

Juhilla, K (2009) From care to fellowship and back: Interpretative repertoires used by the social welfare workers when describing their relationship with homeless women. *British Journal of Social Work*, (39): 128–143.

Kadushin, A (1992) *Supervision in social work (3rd edition).* New York: Columbia University Press.

Keen, S, Gray, I, Parker, J, Galpin, D and Brown, K (2009) *Newly-qualified social workers: A handbook for practice.* Exeter: Learning Matters.

Kempe, H, Silverman, F, Steele, B, Droegemueller, W and Silver, H (1962) The battered child syndrome. *Journal of the American Medical Association*, (181): 17–24.

Knee, R (2002) Can service learning enhance student understanding of social work research? *Journal of Teaching in Social Work*, 22(1/2): 213–225.

Knowles, MS (1980) *The modern practice of adult education: Andragogy versus pedagogy.* Englewood Cliffs, NJ: Prentice Hall/Cambridge.

Kohli, R (2006) The comfort of strangers: Social work practice with unaccompanied asylum-seeking children and young people in the UK. *Child and Family Social Work*, 11(1): 1–10.

Kohli, R (2007) *Social work with unaccompanied asylum-seeking children.* Basingstoke: Palgrave.

Kolb, D (1984) *Experiential learning.* Englewood Cliffs, NJ: Prentice Hall.

Knott, C and Scragg, T (2007) *Reflective practice in social work.* Exeter: Learning Matters.

Labour Manifesto (1997). Available at: **www.labour-party.org.uk/manifestos**

Laming, H (2003) *The Victoria Climbié Inquiry.* London: TSO.

Laming, H (2009) *The protection of children in England: A progress report.* London: TSO.

Lee, CD and Ayon, C (2004) Is the client-worker relationship associated with better outcomes in mandated child abuse cases? *Research on Social Work Practice*, (14): 351–357.

Leeson, C (2007) My life in care: Experiences of non-participation in decision-making processes. *Child and Family Social Work*, (12): 268–277.

Lefevre, M (2005) Facilitating practice learning and assessment. *Social Work Education*, 24(5): 565–583.

Lefevre, M (2008) Knowing, being and doing: Core qualities and skills for working with children and young people who are in care, in Luckock, B and Lefevre, M (eds) *Direct work: Social work with children and young people in care*. London: BAAF.

Lefevre, M (2010) *Communicating with children and young people: Making a difference*. Bristol: The Policy Press.

Le Grand, J (2007) *Consistent care matters: Exploring the potential of social work practices*. Nottingham: TSO.

Levin, P (1997) *Making social policy*. Buckingham: Open University Press.

Levitas, R, Pantazis, C, Fahmy, E, Gordon, D, Lloyd, E and Patsios, D (2007) *The multi-dimensional analysis of social exclusion*. London: Cabinet Office. Available at: **www.cabinetoffice.gov.uk**

Lindsey, C (2005) Some implications of the children's national service framework for social work practice with regards to child mental health. *Journal of Social Work Practice*, 19(3): 225–234.

Local Authority Social Services Act 1970. Available at: **www.opsi.gov.uk**

Local Government Association (2010) *Press release, 10 March 2010*. Available at: **www.lga.gov.uk**

London Borough of Brent (1985) *A child in trust: Report of the Panel of Inquiry investigating the circumstances surrounding the death of Jasmine Beckford*. London: London Borough of Brent.

London Borough of Greenwich (1987) *A child in mind: Protection in a responsible society; Report of the Commission of Inquiry into the circumstances surrounding the death of Kimberley Carlile*. London: London Borough of Greenwich.

London Borough of Lambeth (1987) *Whose child? The report of the Panel appointed to inquire into the death of Tyra Henry*. London: London Borough of Lambeth.

Lonne, R, Parton, N, Thomson, J and Harries, M (2009) *Reforming child protection*. Abingdon: Routledge.

Lord, J (2008) *The adoption process in England: A guide for children's social workers*. London: BAAF.

Lord, J and Cullen, D (2006) *Effective panels: Guidance on regulations, process and good practice in adoption and permanence panels*. London: BAAF.

Lovell, T (2000) Thinking feminism with and against Bourdieu, in Fowler, B (ed) *Reading Bourdieu on society and culture*. Oxford: Blackwell.

Luckock, B and Lefevre, M (eds) (2008) *Direct work: Social work with children and young people in care*. London: BAAF.

Luckock, B with Stevens, P and Young, J (2008) Living through the experience: The social worker as the trusted ally and champion of young people in care, in Luckock, B and Lefevre, M (eds) *Direct work: Social work with children and young people in care*. London: BAAF.

Macdonald, G (2001) *Effective interventions for child abuse and neglect: An evidence-based approach to planning and evaluating interventions*. Chichester: Wiley.

Macdonald, G and Sheldon, B (1997) Community care services for the mentally ill: Consumers' views. *International Journal of Social Psychiatry*, 43(1): 35–55.

McCrystal, P (2000) Developing the social work researcher through a practitioner research training programme. *Social Work Education*, 19(4): 359–373.

McLeod, A (2007) Whose agenda? Issues of power and relationship when listening to looked after young people. *Child and Family Social Work,* 12(3): 278–286.

McLeod, A (2008) *Listening to children: A practitioner's guide.* London: Jessica Kingsley.

McLeod, A (2010) 'A friend and an equal': Do young people in care seek the impossible from their social workers? *British Journal of Social Work,* 40(3): 772–788.

Mallon, G and Betts, B (2005) *Recruiting, assessing and supporting lesbian and gay carers and adopters.* London: BAAF.

Marsh, P and Doel, M (2005) *The task-centred book.* London: Routledge/Community Care.

Marsh, P and Fisher, M (2008) The development of problem-solving knowledge for social care practice. *British Journal of Social Work* 38, (5): 971–987.

Marton, F and Saljo, R (1997) Approaches to learning, in Marton, F, Hounsell, D and Entwistle, N (eds) *The experience of learning: Implications for teaching and studying in higher education (2nd edition).* Edinburgh: Scottish Academic Press.

Maslow, A (1954) *Motivation and personality.* New York: Harper and Row.

Mehmet, M (2005) *What the standards say about fostering.* Lyme Regis: Russell House Publishing.

Meltzer, H, Corbin, T, Gatward, R, Goodman, R and Ford, T (2003) *The mental health of young people looked after by local authorities in England.* London: TSO.

Mezirow, J and Associates (1990) *Fostering critical reflection in adulthood: A guide to transformative and emancipatory learning.* San Francisco: Jossey-Bass.

Minnis, H, Devine, C and Pelosi, T (1999) Foster carers speak about training. *Adoption and Fostering,* 23(2): 42–47.

Minnis, H, Pelosi, AJ, Knapp, M and Dunn, J (2001) Mental health and foster carer training. *Archives of Disease in Childhood,* (84): 302–306.

Moon, J (1999) *Reflection in learning and professional development: Theory and practice.* London: Kogan Page.

Moon, J (2004) *A handbook of reflective and experiential learning: Theory and practice.* London: Routledge Falmer.

Moon, J (2006) *Learning journals: A handbook for reflective practice and professional development.* London: Routledge Falmer.

Moran, P, Ghate, D and van der Merwe, A (2004) *What works in parenting support? A review of the international evidence.* London: Home Office/Department for Education and Skills.

Morgan, R (2006) *About social workers: A children's views report.* Newcastle-upon-Tyne: Commission for Social Care Inspection.

Morris, K (2008) *Social work and multi-agency working: Making a difference.* Bristol: Policy Press.

Morrison, T (2009) *Supervision guide for social workers.* Leeds: Children's Workforce Development Council.

Munro, E (1996) Avoidable and unavoidable mistakes in child protection work. *British Journal of Social Work,* (26): 793–808.

Munro, E (2001) Empowering looked after children. *Child and Family Social Work,* 6(2): 129–137.

Munro, E (2002) *Effective child protection.* London: Sage.

Munro, E (2005) A systems approach to investigating child abuse deaths. *British Journal of Social Work,* (26): 793–808.

Munro, E (2008) *Effective child protection (2nd edition).* London: Sage.

Munro, E (2010) Learning to reduce risk in child protection. *British Journal of Social Work*, 40(4): 1135–1151.

National Centre for Social Research (2009) *Understanding the risks of social exclusion across the life course: Families with children.* Available at: **www.cabinetoffice.gov.uk**

National Centre for Social Research (2010) *Anti-social Behaviour Family Intervention Projects: Monitoring and evaluation.* Available at: **www.dcsf.gov.uk**

National Foster Care Association UK Joint Working Party on Foster Care (1999a) *The UK national standards for foster care.* London: National Foster Care Association.

National Foster Care Association UK Joint Working Party on Foster Care (1999b) *Code of practice on the recruitment, assessment, approval, training, management and support for foster carers.* London: National Foster Care Association.

National Implementation Team (2008) *Multi-dimensional Treatment Foster Care in England (MTFCE) annual project report.* London: DCSF.

Neil, B and Howe, D (2004) *Contact in adoption and permanent foster care: Research, theory and practice.* London: BAAF.

Ogilvie, K, Kirton, D and Beecham, J (2006) Foster carer training: Resources, payment and support. *Adoption and Fostering*, 30(3): 6–16.

Pallett, C, Scott, S, Blackeby, K, Yule, W and Weissman, R (2002) Fostering changes: A cognitive-behavioural approach to help foster carers manage children. *Adoption and Fostering*, 26(1): 39–48.

Pallett, C, Blackeby, K, Yule, W, Weissman, R and Scott, S (2005) *Fostering changes: How to improve relationships and manage difficult behaviour: A training programme for foster carers.* London: BAAF.

Parker, J, Doel, M and Whitfield, J (2006) Does practice learning assist the recruitment and retention of staff? *Research, Policy and Planning*, 24(3): 179–96.

Parr, S (2009) Family Intervention Projects: A site of social work practice. *British Journal of Social Work* (39): 1256–1273.

Parrott, B, MacIver, A and Thoburn, J (2007) *Independent inquiry into the circumstances of child sexual abuse by two foster carers in Wakefield.* Wakefield: Wakefield County Council.

Parton, N (1985) *The politics of child abuse.* Basingstoke: Macmillan.

Parton, N (2000) Some thoughts on the relationship between theory and practice in and for social work. *British Journal of Social Work*, (30): 449–463.

Parton, N (2006a) *Safeguarding childhood: Early intervention and surveillance in a late modern society.* Basingstoke: Palgrave Macmillan.

Parton, N (2006b) Every Child Matters: The shift to prevention whilst strengthening protection in children's services in England. *Children and Youth Services Review*, 28(8): 976–992.

Parton, N (2009) From Seebohm to Think Family: Reflections on 40 years of policy change of statutory children's social work in England. *Child and Family Social Work*, (14): 68–78.

Parton, N and O'Bryne, P (2000) *Constructive social work: Towards a new practice.* Basingstoke: Palgrave Macmillan.

Patterson, CJ (2004) Gay fathers, in Lamb, ME (ed) *The role of the father in child development (4th edition).* New York: John Wiley.

Patterson, CJ (2005) *Lesbian and gay parenting.* Washington DC: American Psychological Association.

Payne, M (2005) *Modern social work theory (3rd edition).* Basingstoke: Palgrave Macmillan.

Performance and Innovation Unit (2000) *The Prime Minister's review of adoption.* London: HMSO.

Percy-Smith, B and Thomas, N (eds) *(2009) A handbook of children and young people's participation: Perspectives from theory and practice.* London: Routledge.

Pemberton, C (2010) Disadvantaged children likely victims of Academies Bill. *Community Care Magazine*, 19 July 2010.

Pithouse, A, Young, C and Butler, I (2002) Training foster carers in challenging behaviour: A case study in disappointment. *Child and Family Social Work*, 7(3): 203–214.

Platt, D (2006) Investigation or initial assessment of child concerns? The impact of the refocusing initiative on social work practice. *British Journal of Social Work*, (36): 67–281.

Polanyi, M (1967) *The tacit dimension.* London: Routledge.

Powell, F (2001) *The politics of social work.* London: Sage.

Practice Learning Taskforce (2006) *Effective practice learning in local authorities (1): Strategies for improvement.* Leeds: Practice Learning Taskforce.

Preston-Shoot, M and Agass, D (1990) *Making sense of social work: Psychodynamics, systems and practice.* Basingstoke: Macmillan.

Price, JM, Chamberlain, P, Landsverk, J and Reid, J (2009) KEEP foster-parent training intervention: Model description and effectiveness. *Child and Family Social Work*, (14): 233–242.

Prout, A (2002) Researching children as social actors: An introduction to the children 5–16 programme. *Children and Society*, (3): 67–76.

Quality Assurance Agency (2008) *Framework for higher education qualifications.* Available at: **www.qaa.ac.uk**

Quinney, A (2006) *Collaborative social work practice.* Exeter: Learning Matters.

Qvortrup, J (1994) Childhood matters: An introduction, in Qvortrup, J, Bardy, M, Sgritt, G and Wintersberger, H (eds) *Childhood matters: Social theory, practice and politics.* Aldershot: Avebury.

Race, P (2000) *The lecturer's toolkit.* London: Kogan Page.

Rashid, SP (2000) The strengths of black families: Appropriate placements for all. *Adoption and Fostering*, 24(1): 15–22.

Reder, P and Duncan, S (1999) *Lost innocents: A follow- up study of fatal child abuse.* London: Routledge.

Reder, P and Duncan, S (2003) Understanding communication in child protection networks. *Child Abuse Review*, (12): 82–100.

Reder, P and Duncan, S (2004) *From Colwell to Climbié: Inquiring into fatal child abuse,* in Stanley, N and Manthorpe, J (eds) *The age of the inquiry.* London: Brunner Routledge.

Reder, P, Duncan, S and Gray, M (1993) *Beyond blame: Child abuse tragedies revisited.* London: Routledge.

Reid, W and Shyne, A (1969) *Brief and extended casework.* New York: Columbia University Press.

Respect Taskforce (2006) *The Respect action plan.* Available at: **www.homeoffice.gov.uk**

Richardson, S and Asthana, S (2006) Inter-agency information sharing in health and social care services: The role of professional culture. *British Journal of Social Work*, (36): 657–669.

Roberts, R, Scott, S and Jones, H (2005) Treatment foster care in England, in Wheal, A (ed) *The RHP companion to foster care.* Lyme Regis: Russell House Publishing.

Rogers, C (1967) *On becoming a person.* London: Constable and Company.

Romaine, M with Turley, T and Tuckey, N (2007) *Preparing children for permanence: A guide to undertaking direct work for social workers, foster carers and adoptive parents*. London: BAAF.

Rowe, J, Hundleby, M and Garnett, L (1989) *Childcare now: A survey of placement patterns*. London: BAAF.

Ruch, G (2005) Relationship-based practice and reflective practice: Holistic approaches to contemporary childcare social work. *Child and Family Social Work*, (10): 111–123.

Ruch, G (2007a) Reflective practice in contemporary childcare social work: The role of containment. *British Journal of Social Work*, (37): 659–680.

Ruch, G (2007b) Thoughtful practice: Childcare social work and the role of case discussion. *Child and Family Social Work*, (12): 370–379.

Ruch, G, Turney, D and Ward, A (eds) (2010) *Relationship-based social work: Getting to the heart of practice*. London: Jessica Kingsley.

Rushton, A (2003) *The adoption of looked after children: A scoping review of research*. London: SCIE/The Policy Press.

Rushton, A and Minnis, H (2000) Research review: Trans-racial placements. A commentary on a new adult outcome study. *Adoption and Fostering*, 24(1): 53–58.

Rushton, A and Monck, E (2009) *Enhancing adoptive parenting: A test of effectiveness*. London: BAAF.

Rustin, M (2005) Conceptual analysis of the critical moments in Victoria Climbié's life. *Child and Family Social Work*, (10): 11–19.

Saleeby, D (2009) *The strengths perspective in social work practice*. Boston: Mosby.

Saltzberger-Wittenberg, I (1970) *Psycho-analytic insights and relationships: A Kleinian approach*. London: Routledge and Keegan Paul.

Sayer, T (2008) *Critical practice in working with children*. Basingstoke: Palgrave.

Schofield, G and Beek, M (2006) *Attachment handbook for foster care and adoption*. London: BAAF.

Schofield, G and Simmonds, J (eds) (2008) *The child placement handbook: Research, policy and practice*. London: BAAF.

Schön, D (1983) *The reflective practitioner: How professionals think in action*. Aldershot: Ashgate.

Schön, D (1987) *Educating the reflective practitioner: Towards a new design for teaching and learning in the professions*. San Francisco: Jossey-Bass.

Schön, D (1991) *The reflective practitioner: How professionals think in action (2nd edition)*. Aldershot: Avebury.

Schore, AN (2001) The effects of early relational trauma on right brain development, affect regulation, and infant mental health. *Infant Mental Health Journal*, (22): 201–269.

Schwandt, T (1997) *Qualitative inquiry: A dictionary of terms*. Thousand Oaks: Sage.

Secretary of State for Social Services (1988) *Report of the inquiry into child abuse in Cleveland, Cm413*. London: HMSO.

Seebohm, F (1968) *Report of the Committee on Local Authority and Allied Social Services, Cmdn 3703*. London: HMSO.

Sellick, C, Thoburn, J and Philpot, T (2004) *What works in adoption and foster care?* Barkingside: Barnardo's.

Selwyn, J and Wijedasa, D (2009) The placement of looked after minority ethnic children, in Schofield, G and Simmonds, J (eds) *The child placement handbook: Research, policy and practice*. London: BAAF.

Sennett, R (2003) *Respect: The formation of character in an age of inequality.* London: Allen Lane.

Shardlow, S and Doel, M (1996) *Practice learning and teaching.* Basingstoke: Macmillan Press.

Shardlow, SM, Nixon, S and Rogers, J (2002) The motivation of practice teachers: Decisions relating to involvement in practice learning provision. *Learning in Health and Social Care,* 1(2): 67–74.

Sharp, M and Danbury, H (1999) *The management of failing DipSW students: Activities and exercises to prepare practice teachers for work with failing students.* Aldershot: Ashgate.

Shemmings, D (2000) Professionals' attitudes to children's participation in decision-making: Dichotomous accounts and doctrinal contests. *Child and Family Social Work,* (5): 235–243.

Sheppard, M, Newstead, S, Di Caccavo, A and Ryan, K (2000) Reflexivity and the development of process knowledge in social work: A classification and empirical study. *British Journal of Social Work,* (30): 465–488.

Shier, H (2001) Pathways to participation: Openings, opportunities and obligations: A new model for enhancing children's participation in decision making in line with Article 12.1 of the United Nations Convention on the Rights of the Child. *Children and Society,* (15): 107–117.

Simmonds, J (2009) Adoption: Developmental perspectives within an ethical, legal and policy framework, in Schofield, G and Simmonds, J (eds) *The child placement handbook: Research, policy and practice.* London: BAAF.

Sinclair, I (2005) *Fostering now: Messages from research.* London: Jessica Kingsley.

Sinclair, I, Baker, C, Lee, J and Gibbs, I (2007) *The pursuit of permanence.* London: Jessica Kingsley.

Sinclair, R (1998) Involving children in planning their care. *Child and Family Social Work* 3(2): 137–142.

Sinclair, R and Bullock, R (2002) *Learning from past experience: A review of Serious Case Reviews.* London: Department of Health.

Skills for Care (2009) *Quality assurance for practice learning: Quality assurance benchmark statement and guidance on the monitoring of social work practice learning opportunities (QAPL).* Leeds: Skills for Care.

Slade, J (2006) *Safer caring (2nd edition).* London: Fostering Network.

Smith, A, McAskill, H, and Jack, K (2008) *Developing advanced skills in practice teaching.* Basingstoke: Palgrave.

Smith, M, Nursten, J and McMahon, L (2004) Social workers' responses to experiences of fear. *Journal of Social Work Practice,* (34): 541–559.

Social Care Institute for Excellence (2007) Involving children and young people in decision-making. *Community Care,* 13 September 2007.

Social Care Institute for Excellence (2009a) *Learning together to safeguard children: Developing a multi-agency systems approach* SCIE Guide 24. London, SCIE. Available at: **www.scie.org.uk**

Social Care Institute for Excellence (2009b) *Think child, think parent, think family: A guide to parental mental health and child welfare* SCIE practice guide 30. London, SCIE. Available at: **www.scie.org.uk**

Social Exclusion Unit (2003) *A better education for children in care.* London: Office for the Deputy Prime Minister.

Social Exclusion Task Force (2007) *Reaching out: Think Family analysis and themes from the Families at Risk review.* London: SCIE. Available at: **www.cabinetoffice.gov.uk**

Social Exclusion Task Force (2008a) *Think Family: Improving the life chances for families at risk.* London: SCIE. Available at: **www.cabinetoffice.gov.uk**

Social Exclusion Task Force (2008b) *Think Family video.* London: HMSO. Available at: **www. cabinetoffice.gov.uk**

Social Work Taskforce (2009) *Building a safe, confident future: The final report of the Social Work Taskforce.* London: Department for Children, Schools and Families.

Stalker, K and Connors, C (2003) Communicating with disabled children. *Adoption and Fostering,* 27(1): 26–35.

Stein, M. (2006) Missing years of abuse in children's homes. *Child and Family Social Work,* 11(1): 11–21.

Stott, A (2009) Adoption register overview: Experience of the adoption register regarding lesbian and gay adopters. *Sharing Evidence, Overcoming Resistance – Celebrating the Role of Lesbian and Gay Carers.* London: BAAF Conference, 11 May 2009.

Sudbery, J (2002) Key features of therapeutic social work: The use of relationship. *Journal of Social Work Practice,* 16(2): 149–161.

Talbot, C and Wheal, A (2005) Education and training for foster carers and social workers, in Wheal, A (ed) *The RHP companion to foster care.* Lyme Regis: Russell House Publishing.

Tanner, K (1999) Observation: A counter culture offensive. Observation's contribution to the development of reflective social work practice. *The International Journal of Infant Observation,* 2(2): 12–32.

Tasker, F (1999) Children in lesbian-led families: A review. *Clinical Child Psychology and Psychiatry,* 4(2): 153–166.

Tasker, F (2005) Lesbian mothers, gay fathers and their children: A review. *Journal of Developmental and Behavioural Pediatrics,* (26): 224–240.

Tasker, F and Golombok, S (1991) Children raised by lesbian mothers: The empirical evidence. *Family Law,* 184–7.

Tasker, F and Golombok, S (1997) *Growing up in a lesbian family: Effects on child development.* New York: Guilford Press.

Thoburn, J, Chand, A and Procter, J (2005) *Child welfare services for minority ethnic families: The research reviewed.* London: Jessica Kingsley.

Thoburn, J, Lewis, A and Shemmings, D (1995) *Paternalism or partnership: Family involvement in the child protection process.* London: HMSO.

Thomas, N and O'Kane, C (2000) Discovering what children think: Connections between research and practice. *British Journal of Social Work,* 30(6): 819–35.

Thomas, N and O'Kane, C (2002) Experiences of decision-making in middle childhood: The example of children 'looked after' by local authorities. *Childhood,* 6(3): 369–387.

Thompson, N (2010) *Theorising social work practice.* Basingstoke: Palgrave Macmillan.

Thompson, N (2nd edition in press, due 2011) *Effective communication: A handbook for the people professions.* Basingstoke: Palgrave Macmillan.

Training Organisation for the Personal Social Services (2002) *The national occupational standards for social work.* Leeds: TOPSS.

Trevillion, S *(1999) Networking and community partnership (2nd edition).* Hampshire: Ashgate Publications.

Trevithick, P (2003) Effective relationship-based practice: A theoretical exploration. *Journal of Social Work Practice,* 17(2): 163–176.

Trevithick, P (2005) *Social work skills: A practice handbook (2nd edition).* Berks: Open University Press.

Triangle (2009) *Three-way street: Putting children at the centre of three-way communication.* Hove: Triangle.

Triseliotis, J, Borland, M and Hill, M (2000) *Delivering foster* care. London: BAAF.

Turnell, A and Edwards, S (1997) Aspiring to partnership: The signs of safety approach to child protection. *Child Abuse Review*, (6): 179–190.

Utting, W (1991) *Children in the public care.* London: HMSO.

Utting, W (1997) *People like us: The report of the safeguards for children living away from home.* London: Department of Health.

Verrier, NN (2000) *The primal wound: Understanding the adopted child.* Baltimore: Gateway Press.

Walker, R (ed) (1999) *Ending child poverty: Popular welfare for the 21st Century?* Bristol: The Policy Press.

Walker, J, Crawford, K and Parker, J (2008) *Practice education in social work: A handbook for practice teachers, assessors and educators.* Exeter: Learning Matters.

Warman, A, Pallett, C and Scott, S (2006) Learning from each other: Process and outcomes in the Fostering Changes training programme. *Adoption and Fostering*, 30(3): 17–28.

Warren, J (2007) *Service user and carer participation in social work.* Exeter: Learning Matters.

Warwick, I, Chase, E, Aggleton, P, with Sanders, S (2006) *Homophobia, sexual orientation and schools: A review and implications for action.* Nottingham: DfES.

Waterhouse, R (2000) *Lost in care: Summary of report.* London: TSO.

Wenger, E (1998) *Communities of practice-learning, meaning and identity.* Cambridge: Cambridge University Press.

White, S (2008) Drop the deadline. *The Guardian*, 19 November 2008.

White, S, Broadhurst, K, Wastell, D, Peckover, S, Hall, C, and Pithouse, A (2009) Whither practice-near research in the modernization programme? Policy blunders in children's services. *Journal of Social Work Practice*, 23(4): 401–411.

Williams, J (2008) *Child law for social work.* London: Sage.

Willis, R and Holland, S (2009) Life story work: Reflections on the experience by looked after young people. *Adoption and Fostering*, 33(4), 44–52.

Wilson, K, Sinclair, I, Taylor, C, Pithouse, A and Sellick, C (2004) *Fostering success: An exploration of the research literature in foster care.* London: SCIE.

Winefield, HR and Barlow, JA (1995) Child and worker satisfaction in a child protection agency. *Child Abuse and Neglect*, (19): 897–905.

Winter, K (2009) Relationships matter: The problems and prospects for social workers' relationships with young children in care. *Child and Family Social Work*, (14): 450–460.

Wolstenholme, D, Boylan, J and Roberts, D (2008) *SCIE Research Briefing 27: Factors that assist early identification of children in need in integrated or inter-agency settings.* Available at: **www.scie.org.uk**

Wood, M (2009) Mixed ethnicity, identity and adoption: Research, policy and practice. *Child and Family Social Work*, 14(4): 431–439.

Wright, P, Turner, C, Clay, D and Mills, H (2006) *The participation of children and young people in developing social care: Preparation and practice guide 06.* London: Social Care Institute for Excellence.

Yatchmenoff, DK (2005) Measuring client engagement from the client's perspective in non-voluntary child protective services. *Research on Social Work Practice*, (15): 84–96.

Index

Page numbers in **bold** refer to figures and tables.